ASBOG
Exam Secrets
Study Guide

DEAR FUTURE EXAM SUCCESS STORY

First of all, **THANK YOU** for purchasing Mometrix study materials!

Second, congratulations! You are one of the few determined test-takers who are committed to doing whatever it takes to excel on your exam. **You have come to the right place.** We developed these study materials with one goal in mind: to deliver you the information you need in a format that's concise and easy to use.

In addition to optimizing your guide for the content of the test, we've outlined our recommended steps for breaking down the preparation process into small, attainable goals so you can make sure you stay on track.

We've also analyzed the entire test-taking process, identifying the most common pitfalls and showing how you can overcome them and be ready for any curveball the test throws you.

Standardized testing is one of the biggest obstacles on your road to success, which only increases the importance of doing well in the high-pressure, high-stakes environment of test day. Your results on this test could have a significant impact on your future, and this guide provides the information and practical advice to help you achieve your full potential on test day.

Your success is our success

We would love to hear from you! If you would like to share the story of your exam success or if you have any questions or comments in regard to our products, please contact us at **800-673-8175** or **support@mometrix.com**.

Thanks again for your business and we wish you continued success!

Sincerely,
The Mometrix Test Preparation Team

Need more help? Check out our flashcards at:
http://MometrixFlashcards.com/ASBOG

TABLE OF CONTENTS

Introduction

Thank you for purchasing this resource! You have made the choice to prepare yourself for a test that could have a huge impact on your future, and this guide is designed to help you be fully ready for test day. Obviously, it's important to have a solid understanding of the test material, but you also need to be prepared for the unique environment and stressors of the test, so that you can perform to the best of your abilities.

For this purpose, the first section that appears in this guide is the **Secret Keys**. We've devoted countless hours to meticulously researching what works and what doesn't, and we've boiled down our findings to the five most impactful steps you can take to improve your performance on the test. We start at the beginning with study planning and move through the preparation process, all the way to the testing strategies that will help you get the most out of what you know when you're finally sitting in front of the test.

We recommend that you start preparing for your test as far in advance as possible. However, if you've bought this guide as a last-minute study resource and only have a few days before your test, we recommend that you skip over the first two Secret Keys since they address a long-term study plan.

If you struggle with **test anxiety**, we strongly encourage you to check out our recommendations for how you can overcome it. Test anxiety is a formidable foe, but it can be beaten, and we want to make sure you have the tools you need to defeat it.

1

Secret Key #1 – Plan Big, Study Small

There's a lot riding on your performance. If you want to ace this test, you're going to need to keep your skills sharp and the material fresh in your mind. You need a plan that lets you review everything you need to know while still fitting in your schedule. We'll break this strategy down into three categories.

Information Organization

Start with the information you already have: the official test outline. From this, you can make a complete list of all the concepts you need to cover before the test. Organize these concepts into groups that can be studied together, and create a list of any related vocabulary you need to learn so you can brush up on any difficult terms. You'll want to keep this vocabulary list handy once you actually start studying since you may need to add to it along the way.

Time Management

Once you have your set of study concepts, decide how to spread them out over the time you have left before the test. Break your study plan into small, clear goals so you have a manageable task for each day and know exactly what you're doing. Then just focus on one small step at a time. When you manage your time this way, you don't need to spend hours at a time studying. Studying a small block of content for a short period each day helps you retain information better and avoid stressing over how much you have left to do. You can relax knowing that you have a plan to cover everything in time. In order for this strategy to be effective though, you have to start studying early and stick to your schedule. Avoid the exhaustion and futility that comes from last-minute cramming!

Study Environment

The environment you study in has a big impact on your learning. Studying in a coffee shop, while probably more enjoyable, is not likely to be as fruitful as studying in a quiet room. It's important to keep distractions to a minimum. You're only planning to study for a short block of time, so make the most of it. Don't pause to check your phone or get up to find a snack. It's also important to **avoid multitasking**. Research has consistently shown that multitasking will make your studying dramatically less effective. Your study area should also be comfortable and well-lit so you don't have the distraction of straining your eyes or sitting on an uncomfortable chair.

 The time of day you study is also important. You want to be rested and alert. Don't wait until just before bedtime. Study when you'll be most likely to comprehend and remember. Even better, if you know what time of day your test will be, set that time aside for study. That way your brain will be used to working on that subject at that specific time and you'll have a better chance of recalling information.

Finally, it can be helpful to team up with others who are studying for the same test. Your actual studying should be done in as isolated an environment as possible, but the work of organizing the information and setting up the study plan can be divided up. In between study sessions, you can discuss with your teammates the concepts that you're all studying and quiz each other on the details. Just be sure that your teammates are as serious about the test as you are. If you find that your study time is being replaced with social time, you might need to find a new team.

Secret Key #2 – Make Your Studying Count

You're devoting a lot of time and effort to preparing for this test, so you want to be absolutely certain it will pay off. This means doing more than just reading the content and hoping you can remember it on test day. It's important to make every minute of study count. There are two main areas you can focus on to make your studying count.

Retention

It doesn't matter how much time you study if you can't remember the material. You need to make sure you are retaining the concepts. To check your retention of the information you're learning, try recalling it at later times with minimal prompting. Try carrying around flashcards and glance at one or two from time to time or ask a friend who's also studying for the test to quiz you.

To enhance your retention, look for ways to put the information into practice so that you can apply it rather than simply recalling it. If you're using the information in practical ways, it will be much easier to remember. Similarly, it helps to solidify a concept in your mind if you're not only reading it to yourself but also explaining it to someone else. Ask a friend to let you teach them about a concept you're a little shaky on (or speak aloud to an imaginary audience if necessary). As you try to summarize, define, give examples, and answer your friend's questions, you'll understand the concepts better and they will stay with you longer. Finally, step back for a big picture view and ask yourself how each piece of information fits with the whole subject. When you link the different concepts together and see them working together as a whole, it's easier to remember the individual components.

Finally, practice showing your work on any multi-step problems, even if you're just studying. Writing out each step you take to solve a problem will help solidify the process in your mind, and you'll be more likely to remember it during the test.

Modality

Modality simply refers to the means or method by which you study. Choosing a study modality that fits your own individual learning style is crucial. No two people learn best in exactly the same way, so it's important to know your strengths and use them to your advantage.

For example, if you learn best by visualization, focus on visualizing a concept in your mind and draw an image or a diagram. Try color-coding your notes, illustrating them, or creating symbols that will trigger your mind to recall a learned concept. If you learn best by hearing or discussing information, find a study partner who learns the same way or read aloud to yourself. Think about how to put the information in your own words. Imagine that you are giving a lecture on the topic and record yourself so you can listen to it later.

For any learning style, flashcards can be helpful. Organize the information so you can take advantage of spare moments to review. Underline key words or phrases. Use different colors for different categories. Mnemonic devices (such as creating a short list in which every item starts with the same letter) can also help with retention. Find what works best for you and use it to store the information in your mind most effectively and easily.

3

Secret Key #3 – Practice the Right Way

Your success on test day depends not only on how many hours you put into preparing, but also on whether you prepared the right way. It's good to check along the way to see if your studying is paying off. One of the most effective ways to do this is by taking practice tests to evaluate your progress. Practice tests are useful because they show exactly where you need to improve. Every time you take a practice test, pay special attention to these three groups of questions:

- The questions you got wrong
- The questions you had to guess on, even if you guessed right
- The questions you found difficult or slow to work through

This will show you exactly what your weak areas are, and where you need to devote more study time. Ask yourself why each of these questions gave you trouble. Was it because you didn't understand the material? Was it because you didn't remember the vocabulary? Do you need more repetitions on this type of question to build speed and confidence? Dig into those questions and figure out how you can strengthen your weak areas as you go back to review the material.

 Additionally, many practice tests have a section explaining the answer choices. It can be tempting to read the explanation and think that you now have a good understanding of the concept. However, an explanation likely only covers part of the question's broader context. Even if the explanation makes perfect sense, **go back and investigate** every concept related to the question until you're positive you have a thorough understanding.

As you go along, keep in mind that the practice test is just that: practice. Memorizing these questions and answers will not be very helpful on the actual test because it is unlikely to have any of the same exact questions. If you only know the right answers to the sample questions, you won't be prepared for the real thing. **Study the concepts** until you understand them fully, and then you'll be able to answer any question that shows up on the test.

It's important to wait on the practice tests until you're ready. If you take a test on your first day of study, you may be overwhelmed by the amount of material covered and how much you need to learn. Work up to it gradually.

On test day, you'll need to be prepared for answering questions, managing your time, and using the test-taking strategies you've learned. It's a lot to balance, like a mental marathon that will have a big impact on your future. Like training for a marathon, you'll need to start slowly and work your way up. When test day arrives, you'll be ready.

Start with the strategies you've read in the first two Secret Keys—plan your course and study in the way that works best for you. If you have time, consider using multiple study resources to get different approaches to the same concepts. It can be helpful to see difficult concepts from more than one angle. Then find a good source for practice tests. Many times, the test website will suggest potential study resources or provide sample tests.

Copyright © Mometrix Media. You have been licensed one copy of this document for personal use only. Any other reproduction or redistribution is strictly prohibited. All rights reserved. This content is provided for test preparation purposes only and does not imply an endorsement by Mometrix of any particular political, scientific, or religious point of view.

Practice Test Strategy

If you're able to find at least three practice tests, we recommend this strategy:

UNTIMED AND OPEN-BOOK PRACTICE

Take the first test with no time constraints and with your notes and study guide handy. Take your time and focus on applying the strategies you've learned.

TIMED AND OPEN-BOOK PRACTICE

Take the second practice test open-book as well, but set a timer and practice pacing yourself to finish in time.

TIMED AND CLOSED-BOOK PRACTICE

Take any other practice tests as if it were test day. Set a timer and put away your study materials. Sit at a table or desk in a quiet room, imagine yourself at the testing center, and answer questions as quickly and accurately as possible.

Keep repeating timed and closed-book tests on a regular basis until you run out of practice tests or it's time for the actual test. Your mind will be ready for the schedule and stress of test day, and you'll be able to focus on recalling the material you've learned.

Secret Key #4 – Pace Yourself

Once you're fully prepared for the material on the test, your biggest challenge on test day will be managing your time. Just knowing that the clock is ticking can make you panic even if you have plenty of time left. Work on pacing yourself so you can build confidence against the time constraints of the exam. Pacing is a difficult skill to master, especially in a high-pressure environment, so **practice is vital**.

Set time expectations for your pace based on how much time is available. For example, if a section has 60 questions and the time limit is 30 minutes, you know you have to average 30 seconds or less per question in order to answer them all. Although 30 seconds is the hard limit, set 25 seconds per question as your goal, so you reserve extra time to spend on harder questions. When you budget extra time for the harder questions, you no longer have any reason to stress when those questions take longer to answer.

Don't let this time expectation distract you from working through the test at a calm, steady pace, but keep it in mind so you don't spend too much time on any one question. Recognize that taking extra time on one question you don't understand may keep you from answering two that you do understand later in the test. If your time limit for a question is up and you're still not sure of the answer, mark it and move on, and come back to it later if the time and the test format allow. If the testing format doesn't allow you to return to earlier questions, just make an educated guess; then put it out of your mind and move on.

On the easier questions, be careful not to rush. It may seem wise to hurry through them so you have more time for the challenging ones, but it's not worth missing one if you know the concept and just didn't take the time to read the question fully. Work efficiently but make sure you understand the question and have looked at all of the answer choices, since more than one may seem right at first.

Even if you're paying attention to the time, you may find yourself a little behind at some point. You should speed up to get back on track, but do so wisely. Don't panic; just take a few seconds less on each question until you're caught up. Don't guess without thinking, but do look through the answer choices and eliminate any you know are wrong. If you can get down to two choices, it is often worthwhile to guess from those. Once you've chosen an answer, move on and don't dwell on any that you skipped or had to hurry through. If a question was taking too long, chances are it was one of the harder ones, so you weren't as likely to get it right anyway.

On the other hand, if you find yourself getting ahead of schedule, it may be beneficial to slow down a little. The more quickly you work, the more likely you are to make a careless mistake that will affect your score. You've budgeted time for each question, so don't be afraid to spend that time. Practice an efficient but careful pace to get the most out of the time you have.

Secret Key #5 – Have a Plan for Guessing

When you're taking the test, you may find yourself stuck on a question. Some of the answer choices seem better than others, but you don't see the one answer choice that is obviously correct. What do you do?

The scenario described above is very common, yet most test takers have not effectively prepared for it. Developing and practicing a plan for guessing may be one of the single most effective uses of your time as you get ready for the exam.

In developing your plan for guessing, there are three questions to address:

- When should you start the guessing process?
- How should you narrow down the choices?
- Which answer should you choose?

When to Start the Guessing Process

Unless your plan for guessing is to select C every time (which, despite its merits, is not what we recommend), you need to leave yourself enough time to apply your answer elimination strategies. Since you have a limited amount of time for each question, that means that if you're going to give yourself the best shot at guessing correctly, you have to decide quickly whether or not you will guess.

Of course, the best-case scenario is that you don't have to guess at all, so first, see if you can answer the question based on your knowledge of the subject and basic reasoning skills. Focus on the key words in the question and try to jog your memory of related topics. Give yourself a chance to bring the knowledge to mind, but once you realize that you don't have (or you can't access) the knowledge you need to answer the question, it's time to start the guessing process.

It's almost always better to start the guessing process too early than too late. It only takes a few seconds to remember something and answer the question from knowledge. Carefully eliminating wrong answer choices takes longer. Plus, going through the process of eliminating answer choices can actually help jog your memory.

Summary: Start the guessing process as soon as you decide that you can't answer the question based on your knowledge.

7

How to Narrow Down the Choices

The next chapter in this book (**Test-Taking Strategies**) includes a wide range of strategies for how to approach questions and how to look for answer choices to eliminate. You will definitely want to read those carefully, practice them, and figure out which ones work best for you. Here though, we're going to address a mindset rather than a particular strategy.

Your odds of guessing an answer correctly depend on how many options you are choosing from.

Number of options left	5	4	3	2	1
Odds of guessing correctly	20%	25%	33%	50%	100%

You can see from this chart just how valuable it is to be able to eliminate incorrect answers and make an educated guess, but there are two things that many test takers do that cause them to miss out on the benefits of guessing:

- Accidentally eliminating the correct answer
- Selecting an answer based on an impression

We'll look at the first one here, and the second one in the next section.

To avoid accidentally eliminating the correct answer, we recommend a thought exercise called **the $5 challenge**. In this challenge, you only eliminate an answer choice from contention if you are willing to bet $5 on it being wrong. Why $5? Five dollars is a small but not insignificant amount of money. It's an amount you could afford to lose but wouldn't want to throw away. And while losing

$5 once might not hurt too much, doing it twenty times will set you back $100. In the same way, each small decision you make—eliminating a choice here, guessing on a question there—won't by itself impact your score very much, but when you put them all together, they can make a big difference. By holding each answer choice elimination decision to a higher standard, you can reduce the risk of accidentally eliminating the correct answer.

The $5 challenge can also be applied in a positive sense: If you are willing to bet $5 that an answer choice *is* correct, go ahead and mark it as correct.

Summary: Only eliminate an answer choice if you are willing to bet $5 that it is wrong.

8

Which Answer to Choose

You're taking the test. You've run into a hard question and decided you'll have to guess. You've eliminated all the answer choices you're willing to bet $5 on. Now you have to pick an answer. Why do we even need to talk about this? Why can't you just pick whichever one you feel like when the time comes?

The answer to these questions is that if you don't come into the test with a plan, you'll rely on your impression to select an answer choice, and if you do that, you risk falling into a trap. The test writers know that everyone who takes their test will be guessing on some of the questions, so they intentionally write wrong answer choices to seem plausible. You still have to pick an answer though, and if the wrong answer choices are designed to look right, how can you ever be sure that you're not falling for their trap? The best solution we've found to this dilemma is to take the decision out of your hands entirely. Here is the process we recommend:

Once you've eliminated any choices that you are confident (willing to bet $5) are wrong, select the first remaining choice as your answer.

Whether you choose to select the first remaining choice, the second, or the last, the important thing is that you use some preselected standard. Using this approach guarantees that you will not be enticed into selecting an answer choice that looks right, because you are not basing your decision on how the answer choices look.

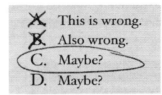

This is not meant to make you question your knowledge. Instead, it is to help you recognize the difference between your knowledge and your impressions. There's a huge difference between thinking an answer is right because of what you know, and thinking an answer is right because it looks or sounds like it should be right.

Summary: To ensure that your selection is appropriately random, make a predetermined selection from among all answer choices you have not eliminated.

Test-Taking Strategies

This section contains a list of test-taking strategies that you may find helpful as you work through the test. By taking what you know and applying logical thought, you can maximize your chances of answering any question correctly!

It is very important to realize that every question is different and every person is different: no single strategy will work on every question, and no single strategy will work for every person. That's why we've included all of them here, so you can try them out and determine which ones work best for different types of questions and which ones work best for you.

Question Strategies

☑ READ CAREFULLY

Read the question and the answer choices carefully. Don't miss the question because you misread the terms. You have plenty of time to read each question thoroughly and make sure you understand what is being asked. Yet a happy medium must be attained, so don't waste too much time. You must read carefully and efficiently.

☑ CONTEXTUAL CLUES

Look for contextual clues. If the question includes a word you are not familiar with, look at the immediate context for some indication of what the word might mean. Contextual clues can often give you all the information you need to decipher the meaning of an unfamiliar word. Even if you can't determine the meaning, you may be able to narrow down the possibilities enough to make a solid guess at the answer to the question.

☑ PREFIXES

If you're having trouble with a word in the question or answer choices, try dissecting it. Take advantage of every clue that the word might include. Prefixes can be a huge help. Usually, they allow you to determine a basic meaning. *Pre-* means before, *post-* means after, *pro-* is positive, *de-* is negative. From prefixes, you can get an idea of the general meaning of the word and try to put it into context.

☑ HEDGE WORDS

Watch out for critical hedge words, such as *likely, may, can, sometimes, often, almost, mostly, usually, generally, rarely*, and *sometimes*. Question writers insert these hedge phrases to cover every possibility. Often an answer choice will be wrong simply because it leaves no room for exception. Be on guard for answer choices that have definitive words such as *exactly* and *always*.

☑ SWITCHBACK WORDS

Stay alert for *switchbacks*. These are the words and phrases frequently used to alert you to shifts in thought. The most common switchback words are *but, although*, and *however*. Others include *nevertheless, on the other hand, even though, while, in spite of, despite*, and *regardless of*. Switchback words are important to catch because they can change the direction of the question or an answer choice.

⊘ FACE VALUE

When in doubt, use common sense. Accept the situation in the problem at face value. Don't read too much into it. These problems will not require you to make wild assumptions. If you have to go beyond creativity and warp time or space in order to have an answer choice fit the question, then you should move on and consider the other answer choices. These are normal problems rooted in reality. The applicable relationship or explanation may not be readily apparent, but it is there for you to figure out. Use your common sense to interpret anything that isn't clear.

Answer Choice Strategies

⊘ ANSWER SELECTION

The most thorough way to pick an answer choice is to identify and eliminate wrong answers until only one is left, then confirm it is the correct answer. Sometimes an answer choice may immediately seem right, but be careful. The test writers will usually put more than one reasonable answer choice on each question, so take a second to read all of them and make sure that the other choices are not equally obvious. As long as you have time left, it is better to read every answer choice than to pick the first one that looks right without checking the others.

⊘ ANSWER CHOICE FAMILIES

An answer choice family consists of two (in rare cases, three) answer choices that are very similar in construction and cannot all be true at the same time. If you see two answer choices that are direct opposites or parallels, one of them is usually the correct answer. For instance, if one answer choice says that quantity x increases and another either says that quantity x decreases (opposite) or says that quantity y increases (parallel), then those answer choices would fall into the same family. An answer choice that doesn't match the construction of the answer choice family is more likely to be incorrect. Most questions will not have answer choice families, but when they do appear, you should be prepared to recognize them.

⊘ ELIMINATE ANSWERS

Eliminate answer choices as soon as you realize they are wrong, but make sure you consider all possibilities. If you are eliminating answer choices and realize that the last one you are left with is also wrong, don't panic. Start over and consider each choice again. There may be something you missed the first time that you will realize on the second pass.

⊘ AVOID FACT TRAPS

Don't be distracted by an answer choice that is factually true but doesn't answer the question. You are looking for the choice that answers the question. Stay focused on what the question is asking for so you don't accidentally pick an answer that is true but incorrect. Always go back to the question and make sure the answer choice you've selected actually answers the question and is not merely a true statement.

⊘ EXTREME STATEMENTS

In general, you should avoid answers that put forth extreme actions as standard practice or proclaim controversial ideas as established fact. An answer choice that states the "process should be used in certain situations, if…" is much more likely to be correct than one that states the "process should be discontinued completely." The first is a calm rational statement and doesn't even make a definitive, uncompromising stance, using a hedge word *if* to provide wiggle room, whereas the second choice is far more extreme.

⊘ BENCHMARK

As you read through the answer choices and you come across one that seems to answer the question well, mentally select that answer choice. This is not your final answer, but it's the one that will help you evaluate the other answer choices. The one that you selected is your benchmark or standard for judging each of the other answer choices. Every other answer choice must be compared to your benchmark. That choice is correct until proven otherwise by another answer choice beating it. If you find a better answer, then that one becomes your new benchmark. Once you've decided that no other choice answers the question as well as your benchmark, you have your final answer.

⊘ PREDICT THE ANSWER

Before you even start looking at the answer choices, it is often best to try to predict the answer. When you come up with the answer on your own, it is easier to avoid distractions and traps because you will know exactly what to look for. The right answer choice is unlikely to be word-for-word what you came up with, but it should be a close match. Even if you are confident that you have the right answer, you should still take the time to read each option before moving on.

General Strategies

⊘ TOUGH QUESTIONS

If you are stumped on a problem or it appears too hard or too difficult, don't waste time. Move on! Remember though, if you can quickly check for obviously incorrect answer choices, your chances of guessing correctly are greatly improved. Before you completely give up, at least try to knock out a couple of possible answers. Eliminate what you can and then guess at the remaining answer choices before moving on.

⊘ CHECK YOUR WORK

Since you will probably not know every term listed and the answer to every question, it is important that you get credit for the ones that you do know. Don't miss any questions through careless mistakes. If at all possible, try to take a second to look back over your answer selection and make sure you've selected the correct answer choice and haven't made a costly careless mistake (such as marking an answer choice that you didn't mean to mark). This quick double check should more than pay for itself in caught mistakes for the time it costs.

⊘ PACE YOURSELF

It's easy to be overwhelmed when you're looking at a page full of questions; your mind is confused and full of random thoughts, and the clock is ticking down faster than you would like. Calm down and maintain the pace that you have set for yourself. Especially as you get down to the last few minutes of the test, don't let the small numbers on the clock make you panic. As long as you are on track by monitoring your pace, you are guaranteed to have time for each question.

⊘ DON'T RUSH

It is very easy to make errors when you are in a hurry. Maintaining a fast pace in answering questions is pointless if it makes you miss questions that you would have gotten right otherwise. Test writers like to include distracting information and wrong answers that seem right. Taking a little extra time to avoid careless mistakes can make all the difference in your test score. Find a pace that allows you to be confident in the answers that you select.

⊘ KEEP MOVING

Panicking will not help you pass the test, so do your best to stay calm and keep moving. Taking deep breaths and going through the answer elimination steps you practiced can help to break through a stress barrier and keep your pace.

Final Notes

The combination of a solid foundation of content knowledge and the confidence that comes from practicing your plan for applying that knowledge is the key to maximizing your performance on test day. As your foundation of content knowledge is built up and strengthened, you'll find that the strategies included in this chapter become more and more effective in helping you quickly sift through the distractions and traps of the test to isolate the correct answer.

Now that you're preparing to move forward into the test content chapters of this book, be sure to keep your goal in mind. As you read, think about how you will be able to apply this information on the test. If you've already seen sample questions for the test and you have an idea of the question format and style, try to come up with questions of your own that you can answer based on what you're reading. This will give you valuable practice applying your knowledge in the same ways you can expect to on test day.

Good luck and good studying!

General and Field Geology

LAW OF SUPERPOSITION AND THE LAW OF INITIAL HORIZONTALITY

According to the law of superposition, one of the earliest postulations in geology, older layers of rock and sediment always lie beneath younger layers. The law of initial horizontality, meanwhile, describes the fact that geologic layers were originally deposited in horizontal layers. Although both these laws attempt to explain the original placement of sedimentary or extrusive igneous rock, initial horizontality does not imply any age relationship between beds or suggest their origins. The law of superposition, although generally true in the field, does not allow for the existence of intrusive sills, sediment dykes, or other instances of younger rocks occurring within older rocks. This law has been clarified and placed in quotation marks in modern geology by the discovery of many exceptions from many different geologic environments. The law of original horizontality is still a basic premise of geology. Certain variations to absolute horizontal sedimentation, such as flysch sequences and steep gradient alluvial fans, have been discovered but this basic law is still in force.

Law of superposition

Younger layers of rock sit atop older layers.

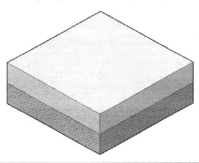

Law of initial horizontality

Layers of sedimentary rock are initially deposited flat.

A. initial orientation

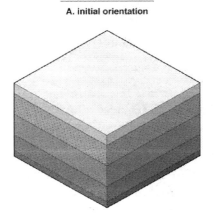

B. Orientation after tilting (folding)

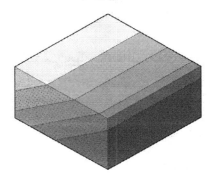

15

IDENTIFYING THE STRATIGRAPHIC SUCCESSION OF GEOLOGIC UNITS DURING ANALYSIS OF A GEOLOGIC MAP

During the analysis of the geologic map, there are a few different ways that the stratigraphic succession of geologic units can be identified. The first and best way is by consulting the stratigraphic key that accompanies every geologic map. The key is a graphic representation of the rock units on the map, their names and ages, and their relative stratigraphic positions. If no key is available, the topographic lines on the map must be used to ascertain how stratigraphic units crop out on the surface. For example, units on the map that occur concentrically around the bases of hills etc., are generally older and deeper than inner ring units farther up a hill. Many geologic maps contain symbols that indicate the attitude of bedding that can be used to determine stratigraphic relationships. There are also generally agreed standards for selected colors of known classification and ages of rocks on many geologic maps allowing the user to see stratigraphic relationships in a glance.

GEOLOGICAL AGE-DATING TECHNIQUES

Oftentimes geologists will use paleontology and evolutionary theory to date geological units. This type of age dating is referred to as relative age dating because the age of the material in question is assigned a bracketed age instead of an absolute number. The fossil assemblage existing within a rock specimen can be used to determine an upper and lower possible age of the material based on the known or suspected histories of these animals and/or plants preserved as fossils. As many plant and animal species display a known progression of morphological development or transposition into sub-species through time, a relative age for the material which hosts their remains or impressions of their remains can be determined. Frequently, the relative age can be narrowed down by looking at a number of fossils within a sample and cross referencing with known material nearby that may have been radiometrically dated.

The thickness, composition, and sedimentation or emplacement patterns of a geologic unit can give clues to its age, as can stratigraphic position. Additionally, radiometrically dateable materials within a unit such as ash beds or meteorite impact events can occasionally provide an absolute date. Interbedded lava flows or intrusive sills within a rock sequence can help to unravel the history of the entire sequence if the index rocks have known dates or can be dated radiometrically. Sedimentation patterns can be analyzed to determine depositional environments which can aid in age determination. Chemical isotopes or fluid inclusions can be analyzed and used to determine the age of geologic materials or events. Weathering rates of geologic materials can be determined, in part, by chemical methods leading to age determination. Paleomagnetism is a method used for geologic dating, which utilizes a known fluctuation of the poles of the Earth's magnetic field over time and compares it to the remanent magnetization found in the magnetic mineralogy of a particular formation.

RADIOMETRIC DATING TECHNIQUES

Different radiometric methods for age-dating material are available according to the range of ages believed for the material to be tested. Radiometric dating utilizes known rates for the decay of unstable elements into stable daughter elements and the ratios of relative abundances of these isotopic species within a sample. Carbon-14 or radiocarbon dating is used to date organic material up to 60,000 years old. Potassium-argon isotope dating is used to date geologic materials greater than 100,000 years in age. Uranium-thorium dating is used to date carbonate materials that are younger than about 500,000 years. Rubidium-strontium isotope dating is a whole rock dating technique used for igneous materials over 10 million years old. Uranium-lead isotopes are used to date geologic materials between 1 million and 4.5 billion years old. Radiometric age dating is typically referred to as absolute age dating because a specific age or range of ages is obtained.

16

DIVISION OF GEOLOGIC TIME INTO EONS, ERAS, PERIODS, AND EPOCHS

Geologic time is divided into eons; these are subdivided into eras, which in turn are subdivided into periods, which are further subdivided into epochs. The supereon before the appearance of the first macro-life, is known as the Precambrian supereon. The Precambrian is divided into the Hadean, Archean and Proterozoic eons. The following eon, the Phanerozoic, is divided into the Paleozoic, Mesozoic and Cenozoic eras. The Paleozoic era saw the subsequent appearance of invertebrates, fish, and amphibians. The subsequent Mesozoic era saw the appearance of reptiles, while the most recent era, the Cenozoic witnessed the appearance first of mammals and man. The Paleozoic era is divided into, in order of occurrence, the Cambrian, Ordovician, Silurian, Devonian, Carboniferous, and Permian periods. The Carboniferous period is further divided into the Pennsylvanian and Mississippian epochs. The Mesozoic era is divided into the Triassic, Jurassic, and Cretaceous periods. The Cenozoic era is divided into the Tertiary and Quaternary periods. The Tertiary period is divided into the Paleocene, Eocene, Oligocene, Miocene, and Pliocene epochs, while the Quaternary period is divided into the Holocene and Pleistocene epochs.

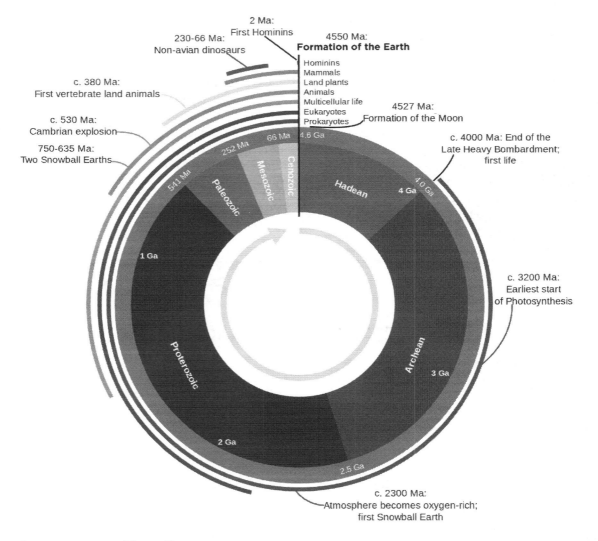

TYPE LOCALITY AND TYPE SECTION

Geologists use the expressions type locality and type section to describe the specific location, and the specific rock outcropping, respectively, that a new mineral or geologic formation was first

17

described. A type locality is the place where a mineral or geologic feature is first found, described, and best represented. It is not uncommon for a newly discovered mineral to be named after this location, although minerals can also be named for the person who first described them or for their chemical compositions. A geologic formation, or genetically related group of sedimentary rocks, on the other hand, is assigned a name based on the specific location or area where the formation is best exposed or best represented. This is the type section. It is most often named for a town or cultural feature near to where the formation occurs. The type section more refers to a stratigraphic group of rocks that are the most typical of a depositional environment. The type locality and the type section are representative of the best example of a mineral or geologic feature.

FAULTS

A fault is a fracture or a fracture zone in crustal rocks along which there has been displacement of the two sides relative to one another parallel to the fracture. The displacement may be a few inches or many miles long. The dip of a fault (the angle of the fault relative to horizontal) can be between 90 degrees (vertical) and 0 degrees (flat-lying). The opposing sides of a fault are referred to by the terms footwall and hanging wall; The lower surface is the footwall and the higher surface is the hanging wall. In vertical faults there is no distinguishable footwall or hanging wall since both surfaces are vertical.

Normal faults, reverse faults, and strike-slip faults typically range from 45° to 90° of dip. Fault orientation and relative movement are described in terms of the two surfaces involved, the footwall, and the upper hanging wall. In a normal fault, the hanging wall will move downward in relation to the footwall. Normal faults characterize extensional tectonic environments in many instances. A reverse fault is opposite from a normal fault in that the upper hanging wall is displaced upward past the footwall. Reverse faults suggest compressional tectonic regimes. In a strike-slip fault the movement is parallel to the strike of the fault plane with no relative up or down displacement of headwall or footwall. From an elevated vantage point, a normal or reverse fault will have appeared to have moved up or down, whereas the strike-slip fault will appear to move from side to side.

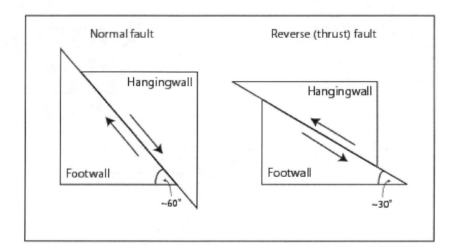

A growth fault is similar to a normal fault, except that it occurs simultaneously with the deposition of sedimentary rock. This kind of fault is typical in areas characterized by on-going sedimentation such as in river deltas or any other region in which the sediments are subsiding at a fast pace. Detachment faults are low angle regional normal faults typically with displacement in the tens of

Copyright © Mometrix Media. You have been licensed one copy of this document for personal use only. Any other reproduction or redistribution is strictly prohibited. All rights reserved. This content is provided for test preparation purposes only and does not imply an endorsement by Mometrix of any particular political, scientific, or religious point of view.

kilometer range. These large faults are found in areas of extensional tectonism and usually juxtapose unmetamorphosed headwall rocks against mildly to highly metamorphosed footwall rocks. A listric fault has a curved shape with the angle of the curve greatest near the surface. An oblique-slip fault is one with both strike-slip and dip-slip components. The footwall and hanging wall do not move exclusively along the fault's strike or dip, but instead move in a diagonal direction. A thrust fault is essentially a low angle reverse fault in which the plane of the fault is between zero and 45°.

There are a number of different kinds of fault displacement. Both vertical and horizontal components of displacement may be active simultaneously. Horizontal movement along a fault is referred to as heave, whereas vertical movement is called throw. A number of specific measurements are made to determine displacement in faults. Net slip is the measure of the distance between two points that were adjacent before the first movement in a fault. A vector between these points indicates the distance and direction of fault displacement. Strike separation is measured across the strike of the fault, and is defined as the horizontal distance between each side of the fault. Offset, finally, is the component of displacement measured perpendicular to the strike of the disrupted side of the fault.

The first step in interpreting faults on a geologic map is reading the map key. The key will include descriptions of all map symbol notation and explanations. On geologic maps, faults are often shown as much thicker lines than those used to show geologic contacts. Offset on faults can be shown by a bar and ball on downthrown side of the fault or by placing a "D" and a "U" on the downthrown and upthrown sides, respectively. Thrust faults will typically be notated with teeth on the upper plate. In the absence of map symbols, outcrop patterns can be useful in determining fault orientation and dip. Also, very useful is the rule of V's wherein the outcrop pattern of faults in relation to the topography can be used to determine fault characteristics. Additionally, cross sections often display a vertical representation of sub-surface structure and are frequently laid out to show the attitude or style of major faulting. Plotting surface and subsurface data on an equal area stereo net is also very useful in interpreting faults.

The Rule of V's can be utilized to analyze fault orientation on a geologic map that does not include topography. Valleys will always be at the lowest topographic point because rivers and streams flow downhill. Faults which cross a valley will trace a V-shape outcrop pattern depending on the dip angle of the fault. The general rules are the wider the V-shaped outcrop pattern, the steeper the dip of the fault crossing a valley, and that the V-shaped outcrop pattern always points in the direction of dip. If the V-shaped outcrop of a fault points downstream, the dip of the fault is downstream and greater than the gradient of the valley. If the V is wide and points upstream, it indicates that the dip of the fault is upstream and steep. The outcrop pattern produced by a fault with vertical dip will be straight line across the valley. Whether the fault is normal or reverse cannot be determined by the Rule of V's. This information must be obtained from map notation or by analysis of geologic units in contact across a fault. Low angle faults such as thrust faults or detachments will produce much tighter V-shaped outcrop patterns across drainages.

A

Beds dip upstream

V points upstream; blunter than contours

B

Horizontal beds

V points upstream; parallel to contours

C

Beds dip gently downstream

V points upstream; sharper than contours

D

Beds dip steeply downstream

V points downstream

E

Beds vertical

No V shape

20

Geomorphic features on a geologic map can indicate the general location of a fault. Large scale faults with significant displacements are recognizable on maps as these faults bring rocks of different units or formations into contact across their traces. Large-scale fault movement produces deformation or folding in both hanging wall and footwall rocks recognizable as drag folds and breccia zones. Fault or shear zones can form positive topography if they become silicified, rendering them more resistant to erosion than bounding rocks. Other map features that can indicate faulting include: scarplets, offset ridges, aligned springs, offset streams, and sag ponds. Lithological or mineralogical changes caused by faulting may be included on a geologic map. Rock debris and clay gouge material may be present indicating the fault trace. Broken and recemented breccias may indicate faulting. The actual plane of fault movement can often be observed and displacement direction measured in slickensides, an oriented crystalline mineralic coating on faces.

Faults on geologic maps can be identified by using stratigraphic or geomorphic fault indicators. Stratigraphic fault indicators tend to be more reliable, since geomorphic fault indicators may be caused by rock movements that are not related to faults. The most common stratigraphic fault indicators are structural discontinuities, neighboring noncontiguous sedimentary facies, and repeating or missing bedding. Large scale faults with significant displacements are recognizable on maps as these faults bring rocks of different units or formations into contact across their traces. Large-scale fault movement produces deformation or folding in both headwall and footwall rocks recognizable as drag folds. These features are recognizable as variations in the mode of normal stratigraphy. Although erosion can obscure faulting, stratigraphic clues such as repeated or inverted bedding, or missing portions of known sections, can indicate faulting. In areas of thrust faulting, thrust-bend-folding or stacked thrust sheets with repeated stratigraphic sections are indicators of regional faulting.

The following terms are used to discuss the geomorphic characteristics of a fault:

- fault scarp: an escarpment or break in normal erosional topography caused by a line of faulting. A linear ridge caused by the upthrown side of a fault.
- scarplet: a small fault scarp.
- slickensides: parallel grooves formed on the surface of a fault plane attributable to opposite movement of fault surfaces. Slickensides are striations or grooves on a fault surface.
- breccia: a coarse-grained, unsorted, clastic rock composed of highly angular broken rock fragments in a fine-grained matrix. Typically lithified by secondary minerals. Can occur within the fault zone.
- mylonite: a dense chert-like metamorphic rock with a streaky or banded structure formed by shear stress. Typically lacking in cleavage. Mylonite is produced by the extreme pulverization and shearing of rocks that have been involved in thrust faulting or intense dynamic metamorphism.

VERTICAL ORIENTATION OF A ROCK BED

The geologist can determine the vertical orientation of a rock bed at deposition or formation by the orientation of fluid flow and deposition structures, or by observation of flow structures and grading in a lava bed. Because these processes are dependent on gravity, rocks displaying these structures can usually be reoriented and can provide a great deal of information about prior vertical orientation. Graded bedding in which large particles give way to particles with decreasing size in individual beds are a common sedimentary feature recognizable and helpful in strata re-orientation. Lava flows contain very indicative internal structures such as alternating dense flow rock with vesicular flow top rocks that can be recognized and used to re-orient lava flows.

Packages of successive lava flows display an alternating pattern of dense and vesicular lava that can aide in reorientation.

Sedimentary rocks and packages of sedimentary rocks contain many structures that can be useful in re-orientating strata that have been disrupted from the original vertical position. Original depositional textures of individual beds, such as graded bedding, slump bedding, and lateral facies relationships can be recognized and used to re-orient strata. Post-depositional deformational characteristics such as bioturbation (worm and insect burrows), ripples and ripple markings, sole markings, and other erosional and water-flow phenomenon are very useful in orientation of strata to their original positions. Asymmetrical bedding and depositional features related to wind, such as cross bedding, can be useful in reorienting out-of-place stratigraphic sequences. Entire packages of strata can also be re-oriented by an understanding of stratigraphic sequences operating in an area.

UNCONFORMITY

An unconformity is an interruption in the normal sequence of the geologic record. An unconformity is frequently an erosion surface that is buried by younger sediments in a reactivated area. Frequently, it is not possible to determine exactly what amount of time an unconformity comprises, though an estimate can be made by determining the ages of the surrounding rocks. An unconformity can be millimeters in thickness yet represent a great amount of missing time. A sedimentary rock package can contain numerous unconformities such that the rock record is very incomplete. An unconformity typically indicates erosion, non-deposition, or regional uplift. Unconformities provide specific information about the geologic history of a region including tectonic events, sedimentation patterns, and basin histories.

There are four basic types of unconformity: nonconformity, disconformity, paraconformity, and angular unconformity. Unconformity that forms when granitic or metamorphic rocks are exposed to erosion and then covered by sedimentary rocks is called a nonconformity. If the older surface remains essentially horizontal during non-deposition, the plane formed between it and new sedimentation is called a disconformity. Visibly, a disconformity can look like continuous sedimentation. A paraconformity is an unconformity in which strata are parallel and the contact is a simple bedding plane. If the old erosion surface is more complex and has been subjected to tectonic episodes, an angular unconformity can develop as sediments are laid down over tilted

Copyright © Mometrix Media. You have been licensed one copy of this document for personal use only. Any other reproduction or redistribution is strictly prohibited. All rights reserved.
This content is provided for test preparation purposes only and does not imply an endorsement by Mometrix of any particular political, scientific, or religious point of view.

bedrock. This type of unconformity records not only missing time but changing geologic environments.

nonconformity

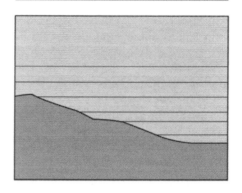

disconformity

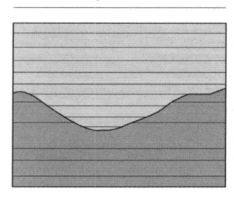

angular unconformity

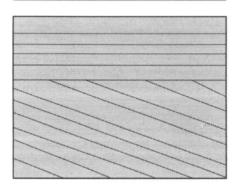

paraconformity

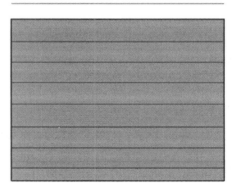

REPEATED OR MISSING ROCK UNITS IN A CROSS-SECTION

Rock units can either repeat or be missing in a particular cross-section due to bedding plane faulting, thrust faulting, or interruption by an unconformity. An unconformity in a sedimentary rock section is caused by periods of non-deposition caused by erosion due to exposure or uplift. Bedding plane faulting is often associated with regional low angle thrust or detachment structures. Thrust and detachment faults can break rock sections along bedding planes and transport these partial rock sections along with thrust plate movement. This can cause missing rock units where low angle faults or structures fractured along bedding planes. It is common in areas of thrust faulting for large sections or pieces of rock units to be stacked atop each other to produce a repeated section.

FOLDS

Folds on a geologic map may be recognized both by outcrop pattern and by special map notation symbols. Typically, these attributes occur together on a map and can both be used to understand geologic structure. Gentle folding in sedimentary rocks will only be recognizable by outcrop pattern if erosion has cut into the structure exposing deeper beds within a fold. Concentric or sub-

23

concentric outcrop patterns typically result. Bed thickness is also a factor in outcrop pattern in folded geology. Map symbols relating to folds consist of a line tracing the fold axis, frequently including an arrow indicating plunge direction and a number value for plunge angle. The fold axis line traces the zone of zero dip or dip rollover with dips increasing laterally away from the axis. Folds may be symmetrical or asymmetrical. Geologic maps contain other symbols such as dip direction and value of individual beds or units and overturned bedding symbols that can be used in conjunction with fold axis symbols and outcrop pattern to understand sub-surface structure.

A *synform* is a concave fold whose limbs close downward to the fold axis in strata for which the stratigraphic sequence is unknown. If the stratigraphic sequence is known and involved in the folding, and the core of the fold contains stratigraphically younger rocks, the feature is called a *syncline*. A convex fold whose limbs close upward to the fold axis in strata for which the stratigraphic sequence is unknown is called an *antiform*. If the stratigraphic sequence is known and the core of the fold contains older rocks, the structure is called an *anticline*. *Upwarps* are any areas of the Earth's crust that have been subjected to generic upward or convex deformation short of anticlinal formation. *Downwarps* are any regions of the earth's crust that are concave due to structural deformation.

On a geologic map a plunging fold will generally produce a U-shaped outcrop pattern. If the fold is symmetrical, the fold axis line will evenly bisect this U-shaped outcrop and will be offset if the fold is asymmetrical. Strike and dip (attitude) symbols on the limbs of the fold will also trace a U-shaped pattern on the map outcrop pattern. The plunge angle of the fold is determined by the value of dip for attitude symbols occurring closest to the fold axis line with strike azimuth most perpendicular to the azimuth of the fold axis line. Plunging folds are said to be closed folds due to the U-shaped outcrop pattern produced. A plunging anticline dips towards the closure in the U-shaped outcrop pattern, whereas a plunging syncline will dip away from the closure in the U-shaped outcrop pattern. The youngest components of a syncline will lie along the fold axis, whereas the oldest units of the anticline will lie along the fold axis.

INTERPRETING A MAP THAT DOES NOT INCLUDE TOPOGRAPHY

It is possible to use the Rule of V's to interpret a geologic map that does not include topography by examining the V-shaped outcrop pattern of geologic units that directly cross stream valleys. The general rule is the wider the V, the steeper the dip of the bed crossing a valley. If the V-shaped outcrop of a geologic unit points downstream, the dip of the bed must be greater than the gradient of the valley. If the V is wide, open, and points upstream, it indicates that the dip of the formation is upstream and steep. If the V is particularly narrow, the bed is probably close to horizontal or nearly flat-lying. Completely horizontal bedding will not produce V-shaped outcropping at all. The outcrop pattern produced by a unit with vertical bedding will be straight lines across the topography of the valley.

SAG PONDS AND ALIGNED SPRINGS

A sag pond is a small body of water that occupies a depression along the trace of an active fault. Uneven settling along the trace of the fault allows a small pond to collect through upwelling of groundwater along the fault. Surface runoff may contribute in part to sag pond formation. Sag ponds are most often found along active strike-slip fault zones. Aligned springs are occurrences of water at the surface along a fault trace related to normal and artesian groundwater occurring along the fault. When the fault shifts, groundwater that had previously been traveling through porous rock may be diverted up to the surface. Aligned springs are an effective ground indicator of faults that may be hidden or unknown.

OFFSET RIDGES AND OFFSET STREAMS

Both offset ridges and offset streams are geomorphic features suggestive of very young or recent faulting. Offset ridges are prevalent when faulting occurs in areas with incline bedding related to prior tectonic activity. Offset in hogback ridges is very indicative of faulting. Normal moderate- to steep-angle, dip-slip and reverse faulting will cause offset in hogback ridges when faults are perpendicular or mostly oblique to ridgelines. Offset ridges on a geologic map can be used to calculate fault displacement. Offset streams are suggestive of very recent faulting or recently reactivated faulting. This feature most often occurs in areas with young or recent strike-slip faulting when disrupted stream patterns have not been given sufficient time to regain equilibrium with the landscape.

MAP SCALES

Map scale will be indicated in one of two ways: either with a bar scale or a ratio. A bar scale is typically a graduated line placed near the bottom center of a map that displays distances on the actual map. Bar scales usually show miles and kilometers and allow the map user to directly measure distances on the map by observing the number of defined graduations (miles, kilometers, feet) between desired points on the map. A ratio scale is somewhat more difficult to use than a bar scale. The ratio used for map scales is always in the form of 1: X. In a ratio scale the numerals do not refer to any specific unit or length of measure. Accordingly, the map scale of 1:5,000 can be interpreted as "one unit on the map is equal to 5,000 units on the ground. Or, one inch on the map equals 5,000 inches on the ground. Some commonly used map scales have convenient conversion factors such as 1:50,000 is equivalent to 2 centimeters equals one kilometer, and 1:24,000 is equivalent to 1-inch equals 2000 feet. Maps may be prepared at any scale depending upon level of detail required.

Very small map scales are needed for large areas such as maps of continents or countries. Map scaling is such that map detail must be forfeited at the expense of coverage area. As the area of interest becomes smaller, such as in state maps, more detail can be presented. An example is a world map that is presented at a scale of 1:30,000,000 and a state map that is prepared at a scale of 1:500,000. Many geologic maps designed to portray the geology of an entire region are prepared at the commonly used scales of 1:250,000 or 1:100,000, allowing for geologic relationships across an entire area to be seen. As the need for local detail increases to serve societal needs, such as maps of counties or sub-regions, scales typically increase with 1:50,000 or 1:24,000 being common. A very commonly used scale for topographic maps is 1:24,000 as this scale balances required detail with coverage area. With experience, the map user can come to recognize map scale at a glance by learning the content that is typically included on different maps.

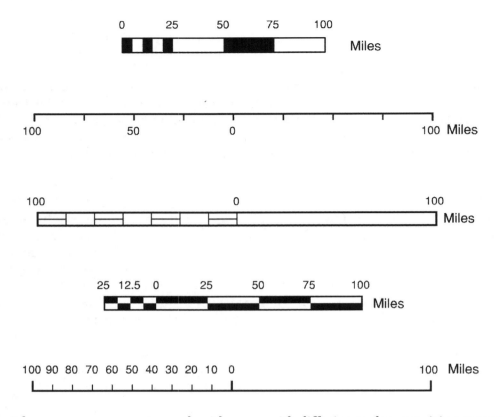

Frequently it becomes necessary to work with maps with differing scales, requiring conversion from one map scale to another. The most effective method for working with differing map scales is utilization of an engineering ruler with multiple scales. The map reader can also obtain packaged individual rulers that are prepared in commonly-used map scales. These rulers typically are graduated in miles, kilometers, feet, and meters, allowing the conversion between maps with different scales at a glance. If only one scale ruler is available, the quickest way to convert between map scales is to divide the new scale by the old scale and then multiply that conversion ratio by the number of feet an inch represents on the first scale. This will give the number of feet an inch represents on the second scale. Modern computerized mapping software is pre-programmed to automatically convert between map scales, removing the need for manual conversion in many instances.

The United States Geologic Survey releases maps at standardized scales for products with various types of uses. Very small-scale maps that depict the entire United States are often prepared at a scale of 1:3.5M or approximately 1-inch equals 55 miles. Advances in computer cartography have allowed for immense increases in detail at such map scales. An example is a popular USGS digital elevation model map of the contiguous United States at this scale. State maps are typically prepared at the scale 1:500,000 allowing for the depiction of moderate detail. These maps are typically large format wall maps. Maps designed for more regional detail are released at scales of 1:250,000 or 1:100,000. These scales are common for compilation geologic maps. Individual topographic quadrangle maps are issued at the scale 1:24,000. These quadrangle maps are also called 7.5-minute quadrangles and are at the effective scale for detailed topographical and geological maps. Detailed geology is often mapped at this 1:24,000, 7.5-minute quadrangle scale and subsequently compiled into regional 1:250,000 scale geologic maps.

INFORMATION PROVIDED BY VARIOUS SYMBOLS ON A MAP

Most geologic maps give a magnetic declination, which indicates the difference in degrees between true geographic north and magnetic north for the area covered in the map at the time the map was published. Magnetic declination changes over time. Most geologic maps are true geographic north oriented such that the presented north arrow on the map points to the top of the map indicating no need to rotate to achieve true geographic north orientation. This is not universally true as north may be presented at any orientation around a 360° circle. The map scale, usually presented both in bar and ration form, represents the distance on a map relative to the distance on the ground. Most maps will contain a key or legend, describing all the symbols and units used on the map. Also, topographic maps will indicate the basic geomorphic features of the region. The geologic map symbols are used to indicate fold, lithology, thickness, bedding, fault, cleavage, foliation, and information about joints. The map key for a given map usually only contains the symbols that appear on that map.

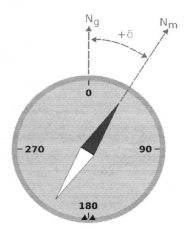

Bedding attitude, composed of the strike and dip of a particular bed, is indicated with a T-shaped symbol. The top crossbar is oriented on the strike of the bedding, with the tail of the "T" showing the direction of dip. Usually, a numeral accompanies the symbol to indicate degree of dip. If the bed is overturned, the tail of the "T" is curled back over the crossbar, with dip degree indicated. Approximate strike and dip our denoted by a dashed T. The strike of a vertical bed is denoted by a cross that is long on one side. Horizontal beds are indicated by a circled cross. An apparent dip is denoted by an arrow with a filled circle at the terminus. The strike and dip of a joint is denoted by a line with a square at one side. The line is oriented to reflect joint strike. The strike of a vertical joint is denoted by a line bisected by a filled rectangle. A horizontal joint is indicated by an X with a filled square at the center.

On geologic maps fault are indicated by solid, dashed, or dotted lines with various symbols used to indicate relative displacement. Exposed faults between rock units are shown as a solid line tracing fault across topography. Dashed lines indicate approximate or inferred location, and dotted lines depict faults that are covered by surficial deposits or concealed. Displacement of a high angle fault is indicated by a bar and ball on downthrown side. Fault dip, if know, is indicated as a numeral next to bar and ball. Thrust faults are shown as solid, dashed, or dotted lines and the upper plate is marked with black triangular teeth. Fold axes are traced with similar rules pertaining to faults: solid where exposed, dashed where inferred, and dotted where concealed. Smaller arrows are placed perpendicular to fold axis and radiate outward for an anticline and inward for a syncline. Fold depiction on a geologic map is facilitated by strike and dip symbols working together with the fold axis line. From these sets of symbols, a mental picture of structure emerges.

Foliation is a general term for a planar or sheeted arrangement of textural or structural features in any type of rock. It refers to the planar structure that is caused by flattening of the grains of a metamorphic rock. Cleavage is the property or tendency of a rock to split along aligned fractures or closely spaced planes. These foliation controlling textures are caused by deformation or metamorphism. Foliation and cleavage are indicated by a strike symbol, marked with a triangle that is oriented with dip angle noted. Horizontal foliation is denoted by a cross with a diamond at the center. Horizontal cleavage is indicated by a cross with bars at the end of each line. Cleavage generally does not include a value.

THREE-DIMENSIONAL CHARACTERISTICS OF LITHOLOGIC FEATURES THAT MAY BE FOUND ON A MAP

A geologic map displays geology occurring on the surface but also provides a three-dimensional picture of the quadrangle. This is accomplished through the use of structure symbols and cross sections. In a general sense, sedimentary rocks often have a consistent thickness throughout a quadrangle. However, this is by no means universally true. Many times, in cross sections and in structural analyses, thicknesses of sedimentary units are generalized. Igneous bodies will be described by outcrop patterns and sub-surface structure and dimensions. In many instances, outcrop pattern of igneous rocks will not represent total size or extent of such rocks and referring to cross sections becomes essential. The geologic map is a 2-dimensional depiction of surface geology with the 3-dimensional attributes of lithologic units represented by symbology.

CONTACT METAMORPHISM, REGIONAL METAMORPHISM, AND CATACLASTIC METAMORPHISM

Regional metamorphism, depending on map scale, would most likely extend beyond map borders and would hence define an individual lithologic unit for that map. If the outward extent of regional metamorphism is captured on a geologic map, lithologic changes between metamorphosed and un-metamorphosed rocks would need to be defined in the map key or accompanying report. As areas of contact metamorphism are usually localized around intrusive bodies, they are typically shown on a geologic map by a hachured pattern or area of shading. This can be addressed in the map report by describing mineralogic and textural changes to a lithologic formation affected by contact metamorphism in the hachured area. Cataclastic metamorphism is defined as rock deformation accomplished by fracture and rotation of mineral grains or aggregates without chemical reconstitution. This type of metamorphism is associated with faulting, shears zones, and impact sites. Cataclasism can also be shown on a geologic map with hachuring or shading, similar to depiction of contact metamorphism, unless effects extend regionally necessitating a separate lithologic unit.

FEATURES REPRESENTED BY A MAPPED OUTCROP PATTERN THAT CONSISTS OF CONCENTRIC CIRCLES

Concentric circles on a geologic map indicate structural deformation of sedimentary rocks by doming, sagging or diapirism. A convex erosional feature in horizontal strata would produce a concentric-ringed "shield" pattern in outcrop, as would a concave conical depression in the same horizontal strata. For a conical hill or mountain in horizontal strata, the innermost ring in the outcrop pattern would represent the youngest rock, whereas in a depression, the center rocks of the ring outcrop pattern are the older rocks. This relationship would be invalidated if intrusive bodies were involved. A salt dome or intrusive pluton or batholith can cause a concentric circled pattern in sedimentary rocks on a geologic map after exposure by erosion. A circular pattern on a geologic map could also be caused by a meteorite impact in horizontal strata.

OROGENIC EVENTS

OROGENIC EVENTS THAT FORMED FEATURES IN NORTH AMERICA

West and west-central North America is dominated in the north by the Canadian Shield, in the middle of the continent by the stable continental platform, and in the south by the coastal plain. The Canadian Shield consists of ancient crustal and oceanic rocks of Archean and early Proterozoic age representing at least 5 episodes of accretion and assembly. In the middle of the continent, deep Precambrian rocks of the continental core are mostly covered by thick sequences of Phanerozoic sedimentary rocks representing the stable continental platform. Tectonic activity is minor to nonexistent with occasional broad domes and basins. The coastal plain extends from southern Texas through the northern Gulf of Mexico and into the Mississippi embayment. It is a passive continental margin consisting of a deep wedge of clastic sedimentary rocks that was derived from the platform and bounding orogenic belts. The coastal plain formed mostly during the Jurassic and Cretaceous periods. The western portions of North America were formed by numerous orogenic events with associated deformation, faulting, and volcanic activity related to continental convergence.

OROGENIC EVENTS THAT FORMED FEATURES IN THE EASTERN UNITED STATES

The Appalachian Mountains of the eastern USA are the product of several orogenic events that culminated in the construction of the supercontinent Pangaea. During the early Paleozoic, the continent that would become North America straddled the equator. The Anti-Atlas Mountains of Morocco and the Appalachian Mountains were formed on the supercontinent of Pangaea and were subsequently separated by the opening of the Atlantic Ocean at 220 million years ago. The first mountain building episode, the Taconic Orogeny, occurred during the middle Ordovician period. Mountain building continued during the next 250 million years with the Caledonian, Acadian, Ouachita, Hercynian, and Allegheny orogenies contributing to produce a mountain belt as great as the Himalayan mountain range of today. Pangaea began to break apart in the early Mesozoic era as rifting produced the Atlantic Ocean. Since the separation of Pangaea, the eastern portion of North America has been a passive continental margin with erosion of the mountainous terrain and active formation of a coastal plain.

DETERMINING ROCK HARDNESS IN THE FIELD USING A POCKET KNIFE

The Mohs Hardness scale can be estimated in the field with a steel-bladed pocket knife. The Mohs scale indicates the relative hardness of minerals by observing their scratch resistance. Units of Mohs hardness are expressed with numbers ranging from 1 through 10. Each number indicates mineral hardness based on ability to scratch any other mineral with a lower-ranking number. A ranking from softest to hardest of common minerals in the Mohs scale is: talc (1) ranging upward in hardness through gypsum (2), calcite (3), fluorite (4), apatite (5), orthoclase (6), quartz (7), topaz

(8), corundum (9), to the hardest, diamond. A steel-bladed pocket knife has a hardness between 6 and 7 and will scratch feldspar but will not scratch quartz.

Mohs Scale of Hardness

Mineral	Scale Number	Common Objects
Talc	1	
Gypsum	2	
Calcite	3	Fingernail / Copper Penny
Fluorite	4	
Apatite	5	Steel Nail
Orthoclase	6	Glass Plate
Quartz	7	
Topaz	8	Streak Plate
Corundum	9	
Diamond	10	

GRAIN SIZE AND SHAPE

Aphanites are igneous rocks in which the individual mineral grains cannot be discerned with the naked eye. An aphanitic texture in igneous rocks indicates rapid cooling. This is commonly observed in extrusive rocks such as lavas or near-surface intrusive rocks such as sills and dikes. Phanerites are relatively large-grained intrusive rocks in which individual mineral grains can be discerned and described with the naked eye. Phaneritic texture in igneous rocks is caused when magma is trapped underground and allowed to cool slowly, facilitating larger mineral growth. Phaneritic texture characterized by large interlocking grains of different minerals is commonly seen in plutonic rocks such as granites. Porphyritic textures are observed in many plutonic rocks and contain both previously described textures: large megascopic phases and small microscopic mineral grains. Larger megascopic minerals are surrounded by a fine-grained groundmass in which minerals cannot be discerned with the naked eye (microscopic). Porphyritic textures occur in plutonic rocks when a magma is allowed to partially cool at a slow rate, generating some large mineral grains, and then rapidly cooled to produce the aphanitic groundmass.

Grain shape, or more accurately, mineral boundary interaction, in an igneous rock sample is described by the terms euhedral, subhedral, or anhedral. A euhedral mineral grain is completely bounded by its own rational faces indicating that the minerals growth during crystallization or recrystallization was not restrained or interfered with by adjacent grains. Full euhedral crystal specimens of minerals are prized by mineral collectors. A subhedral mineral grain is bounded partly by its own rational faces and partly by surfaces formed against preexisting grains as a result of either crystallization or recrystallization. Anhedral textures occur in igneous rocks when mineral grains are not bounded by their own crystal faces but have an imperfect form impressed on them by the adjacent minerals during crystallization.

GRADING AND SORTING

Grading and sorting refer to the distribution of grain sizes within a sedimentary rock. The relative distribution of particles sizes within a sedimentary rock indicates the depositional and post-depositional history of the sample. Graded bedding is a type of bedding in which layers display a progressive change in particle size from coarse at the base of the bed to fine at the top. It forms under conditions in which a prevailing current declined in energy or indicates rapid sedimentary events such as in a single short-lived turbidity current. Sorting is the process by which granular or fragmental with a particular characteristic such as similar size, shape, or specific gravity are selected from a larger mass. Sorting can indicate post-depositional redistribution of mineral grains or reveal spatial variations in a depositional system dependent upon distance from source.

WEATHERING

Weathering is defined as the destructive processes by which geologic materials exposed to atmospheric agents at or near the earth's surface are changed in color, texture, composition, firmness, or form. Weathering is the physical disintegration and chemical decomposition of rock to produce an in-situ mantle of alluvium and colluvium. Most weathering occurs at the surface, but it may take place at considerable depths, as in well-jointed rocks that permit easy penetration of atmospheric oxygen and circulating surface waters. Weathering is controlled by mineralogy, rock petrology, rock cementing agents, fracturing, and severity of external processes such as freeze-thaw cycles and precipitation levels. Wind is also a great agent of weathering. Weathering is classified as mild, medium, and severe, usually with sub-categories for each.

ROCK STRENGTH

Determination of rock strength in the field involves assessing its hardness, fracturing, porosity, and the degree to which it has been weathered. Field assessments of rock strength are generally subjective, as opposed to the very stringent and objective rock strength tests performed in a laboratory setting. Standardized field tests to measure rock strength involve the use a 2-pound hammer to strike a 4-inch-thick sample. The reaction of the rock to the hammer strike allows the geologist to place the rock on the spectrum of strength ranging from very weak to very strong. A very weak rock will crumble when it is pressed with a finger. A moderately strong rock can be hit with a hammer a few times before it breaks. A strong rock can be hit very hard a few times without breaking, and when it breaks, will break into large pieces. A very strong rock can be hit very hard without breaking.

ROCK FRACTURES

A fracture is defined as any break or failure in a rock, whether or not it causes displacement, due to mechanical failure by stress. Fractures include cracks, joints, and fracture cleavage. The defining characteristics of fractures are orientation, width, extent, density, and displacement. These characteristics define the stress history of the host rock, both locally and regionally. Both qualitative and quantitative analyses of fracturing and regional fracture patterns can lead to determinations of localized and regional tectonic events and aid in the reconstruction of complex multi-stage deformational histories of an outcrop or area. Cleavage occurring in deformed but only slightly metamorphosed rocks is called fracture cleavage. It consists of groups or sets of closely spaced parallel joints and fractures.

Fracturing will have an influence on both the compressive and tensile strength of a rock depending on their size, orientation, and number. Fractures also determine the relative physical weatherability of a rock as fracture density and magnitude will affect the degree to which water and freeze-thaw effects can penetrate into a sample. Fracturing also allows chemical weathering to proceed at accelerated rates within a rock sample. Fracturing can affect a rocks ability to hold

31

water and will, along with porosity, determine a rock's ability to act as an aquifer. In similar fashion, fracturing will determine a rocks ability to be impregnated with oil or gas, an important attribute of petroleum exploration. Fracturing is a function of lithology, thermal history, and tectonics.

FIELD METHODS

A *gravity survey* is a collection of measurements made over a region with a gravimeter to determine differences in the earth's gravitational field.

Ground penetrating radar is used for mapping of subsurface materials by sending a radar impulse below the surface.

A *percolation test* is used to determine the rate, expressed as either velocity or volume, at which water percolates through a porous medium.

Rotary drilling is the typical way of drilling a deep well, and is accomplished with a drill bit that has been cooled and lubricated with drilling fluid.

Seismic reflection is a technique to determine the structure of subsurface formations by making use of the times required for a seismic wave to return to the surface after reflection from underlying formations.

Seismic refraction involves seismic waves that travel large horizontal distances along distinct interfaces in the earth.

A *standard penetration test* analyzes the conditions of geologic materials by counting the number of times a hammer must be dropped in order to drive the sample rod 18 inches into the soil.

FIELD INVESTIGATION TOOLS

An *auger* is a drill attachment used to sample loose surficial material.

Casing is a metal pipe placed into a borehole to prevent solid or liquid material from intruding into the hole.

The *cone penetrometer* consists of a cone, typically angled from 30 to 60 degrees, used to determine the force required to thrust downward into silty or fine to medium-coarse unconsolidated materials for the purpose of obtaining information that a foundation or soils engineer may use to calculate load-bearing values.

A *Shelby tube* is a thin-walled soil-sampling tube, 12 to 30 inches long, attached to a special rod adapter or sub by means of machine screws. The device is designed to take soil samples by pressing or pushing the tube down into the formation sampled.

A *split-spoon sampler* is a type of barrel sampler that is used to collect disturbed soil samples.

TEST PITS

A test pit in borehole geophysics is generally used to calibrate instruments before insertion into a drill hole to account for local conditions. For example, before a downhole gamma ray survey, careful calibration of the spectral gamma probe in a test pit of known isotope concentrations permits the process of spectral stripping to be done. Spectral stripping identifies the individual elements contributing to the total gamma count through the comparison of the total spectrum against known standards for individual elements. Test pits are also used to make a preliminary study of the conditions below the surface prior to drilling. The presence of surficial units that may impede drilling are noted. The test pit is an essential prerequisite before committing expensive and delicate instrumentation.

BORING METHODS USED TO SAMPLE SOILS

There are a few different methods utilized in soil sampling. The simplest method for determining soil thickness and composition is with either a metal penetration rod or a hand augur. A flight augur is mechanically driven and escorts samples of soil out of the hole as it drills. These are to be considered disturbed samples but can be logged visually. To obtain an undisturbed sample auguring to the appropriate depth, removing the augur, and manually drawing the sample is the standard technique. A hollow-stem augur is used to obtain undisturbed soil samples without having to remove the augur from the hole. Sometimes, it may be useful to use a rotary-wash drill, which uses a fluid to evacuate loose rock and soil from the hole.

DRILLING FLUID ADDITIVES USED IN BOREHOLES

Drilling fluid, called drilling mud, is used in rotary drilling and is pumped down through the drill stem. Drilling mud is a water-based, chemical or physical suspension that seals off porous zones and suspends and disperses drill cuttings. Drilling fluid also counteracts the pressure of formations encountered in drilling. It consists of various substances in a finely divided state including bentonite and barite. Barite or other weighting materials are used to counterbalance formation pressure and to stabilize the borehole. Calcium carbonate or ground cellulose can be used as bridging agents to seal gaps in very porous formations by allowing the formation of a filtercake against the sides of the borehole. Bentonite, gilsonite, artificial polymers, or asphalt are used as additives to improve filtercake properties. Chemical inhibitors can be used to counteract adverse reactions between drilling fluid and certain formations. This is most commonly used when drilling in shale-rich formations when calcium, potassium, salts, polymers, asphalt, or glycol are added to counteract these reactions.

COLLECTING SOIL SAMPLES

Undisturbed soil samples can be collected with a Shelby tube or other thin-walled-sampler. The technique involves driving hollow tube penetrators into a column of soil and extracting the sampling tube. A sample is thus obtained and examined with all original characteristics intact including: constituents, grain size distribution, horizons, and structure. The following tests can be performed on an undisturbed soil sample: compressibility, compaction, consolidation, density, and shear strength. Soils may also be collected by grab or gridded sampling techniques or from an excavated test pit. These are disturbed samples and can be tested for constituents and some structural elements. Tests on disturbed soils include: grain size distribution, expansion data, bulk density, and Atterberg limits. Original structure can be obtained from pit wall analyses in many instances. Somewhat limited but many times sufficient information can be obtained from disturbed soil samples obtained with hand-powered augers or truck-mounted power augers.

INFORMATION THAT CAN BE GATHERED FROM AN UNDISTURBED SOIL SAMPLE

The following tests can be performed on an undisturbed soil sample: compressibility, compaction, consolidation, density, and shear strength. Undisturbed soil samples can be collected with a Shelby tube or other thin-walled-sampler. The soil material can be extracted from the sampling tube and examined intact. The primary advantage of undisturbed soil samples lies in the fact that original stratigraphic relationships are maintained. This allows for observation and testing of original soil horizons and affords in-situ information not obtainable from disturbed soil samples. Shear strength tests on undisturbed soil samples are especially relevant as this will provide a profile across a desired area. Soils may also be obtained directly by grab or channel sampling from an exposed test pit wall. These are disturbed samples and can be tested for constituents and some structural elements. Tests on disturbed soils include: grain size distribution, expansion data, bulk density, and Atterberg limits.

THIN-WALLED PUSH-TUBE SAMPLER

A thin-walled push tube sampler is best for evaluating a soil that is cohesive and even-grained. Conglomeratic, rocky or extremely non-cohesive soft soils should not be sampled using a thin-walled push tube sampler. One common example of this kind of sampler is the Shelby tube. The sampler typically has a 3- or 5-inch outer diameter, is 12 to 30 inches long, and has a wall thickness of approximately 11 or 14 gauge. The thin-walled push-tube sampler is operated by inserting the tube completely into the material to be sampled and twisting to separate the soil sample from its surroundings. The tube is then carefully removed from the ground, and the sample is removed from the tube hydraulically.

FIXED-PISTON SAMPLER

A fixed-piston sampler forces a short tube-like device into soils, soft rock, or rock material without utilizing sample tube rotation. The tube is driven into the material to be sampled either hydraulically or is pounded in with a drive hammer. A second tube is then forced inside the first tube and is rotated to separate it from the soil column below. Fixed piston samplers are best for obtaining samples of soft, wet soil, or any soil below the water table. A sample in an undisturbed state is generally obtained with the fixed-piston sampler. A fixed-piston sampler is also referred to as a drive sampler. These samplers are typically equipped with a free or a retractable-type piston that recoils up inside the barrel of the sampler while remaining in contact with the top of the soil.

DOUBLE-TUBE CORE BARREL SAMPLERS

The two basic types of double tube core barrel samplers are the Denison sampler and the Pitcher sampler. The Denison sampler features an outer barrel with a serrated leading edge, around an inner barrel with a smooth edge. The Pitcher sampler utilizes a self-adjusting inner barrel. The Denison sampler is used to obtain samples of hard soils or partially consolidated sediments. In the Denison design a smooth inner barrel pushes into the soil, aided by circulating drilling fluid, as the outer barrel slowly rotates dislodging the sample. The Pitcher sampler operates in a similar fashion with the exception that the inner barrel protrudes past the bit and adjusts itself in accordance with the hardness of the soil. Both of these kinds of samplers are suitable for un-cemented, slightly cemented, or extremely fine-grained soils.

CONE PENETROMETER

A cone penetrometer is used to assess the resistance of the soil to penetration by a standardized rod at a constant pressure. This technique can work on all but very dense soils. The penetrometer operates by being pushing through a soil at a constant rate of force. A sensor records the amount of force and time that was required to reach certain distances within the soil. These data obtained through the use of a cone penetrometer can provide information about undrained shear strength, subsurface structure, and soil density. Cone penetrometers consist of a rod with a conical point that is typically angled from 30 to 60 degrees. The diameter of a cone penetrometer is approximately the same size as an A-size diamond-drill rod.

STANDARD PENETRATION TEST

The standard penetration test (SPT) yields data about the geotechnical engineering properties of unconsolidated materials. It is used to determine densities of unconsolidated deposits where it is impractical to obtain an undisturbed sample. The test is performed by driving a thick-walled sampler tube into the bottom of a drill hole with blows from a hammer. The standard hammer weight is 140 pounds, with a hammer fall distance of 30 inches. A counter determines the number of blows required to drive the sampler for each 6-inch interval. If 50 blows are insufficient to advance sampler 6 inches, the distance penetrated at 50 is recorded. Blow counts are totaled for the 2nd and 3rd 6-inch intervals into the N-value, or $C_N = 1/\sqrt{(\sigma'_v)}$, in which σ'_v = the effective overburden pressure (Tons/ft^2), and $C_N * N_{field} = N_{corrected}$. The corrected blow count ($N_{corrected}$) is the number used to compare results from different soils. The SPT is used to assess and compare earthquake liquefaction hazard in sandy unconsolidated materials.

The standard penetration test is used to assess the relative density of subsurface soils. If the soil requires 15 or more blows before allowing 12 inches of sampler penetration, it is considered to be very stiff or hard. If 10 to 15 blows are required, the soil is considered to be stiff. A moderately stiff soil will require only 4 to 10 blows. A moderately stiff soil will allow a person to penetrate to a depth of 1 to 2 inches with thumb pressure. A soil that allows 12 inches of sampler penetration in 4 or fewer blows can be classified as a very soft, and is probably composed of sand, silt, or clay.

BORING LOGS

A boring log, or drill log, is the record of the events and the type and characteristics of the formations penetrated in drilling a core hole. A detailed boring log must contain the following information:

- drilling company and names of drillers
- type of drill rig used
- job location and location sketch
- date, name, and number
- boring number
- ground surface elevation at location of hole
- type of sampler used
- hammer weight and fall
- pressures required
- condition of samples
- water levels at beginning and completion
- completion status
- backfill materials and methods
- monitoring equipment
- perforation intervals and grout intervals
- full summary of the soil and rocks found at the site

The boring log must also contain any specific information pertinent to the day's drilling and/or notations for the following drill shift.

DETAILED SOIL DESCRIPTION

A detailed soil description methodology is outlined in the Unified Soil Classification System (USCS). This classification system divides soils into three major subclasses based on general grain size and also contains provisions for other descriptive attributes of soils. The USCS description is often the initial field description of a soil. Engineering, or geotechnical, soil descriptions are more detailed but include the full USCS attributes. Geotechnical soil descriptions include many other properties of the soil such as moisture content, penetration (density) and shear strength test data, as well as other descriptive elements. This facilitates transition of direct field observation into soil behavior prediction and design engineering of foundations and structures. The color of the soil must be described in relation to a standardized reference for color.

35

Homogeneous, Heterogeneous, Stratified, Laminated, Fissured, Honeycombed, Slickensided, Blocky, Lensed, and Caliche

The following terms are often used to describe and classify the structural characteristics of undisturbed soil samples:

- homogenous: uniform composition throughout the sample, isotropic
- heterogeneous: variable composition, non-uniform throughout, anisotropic
- stratified: contains visible different layers, parallel bedding is evident
- laminated: contains even- and thinly-bedded, parallel layers
- fissured: easily broken along certain planes, fractured
- honeycombed: marked by regular voids, evenly spaced
- slickensided: smooth, polished surfaces due to shearing, indicates displacement direction and history
- blocky: easily breaks down into your regularly shaped granules, which resist further division of soils
- lensed: contains irregularly spaced, non-continuous pockets of material, typically terminated with tapered ends
- caliche: white stained precipitate from groundwater, contains calcium carbonate

Rock Coring and Soil Coring

Core drilling in rock involves the advancement of a 10-ft long barrel inside of the drill rod. The core barrel is attached directly behind the drill bit allowing for collection of a continuous rock sample. The bit is composed of industrial diamonds set in a soft matrix that slowly wears down as the bit advances, exposing new diamonds. Hardness of bit matrix and diamond profile is changed to counteract different drilling condition encountered between formations or rock types. The bit is mounted on a drill stem that is connected to rotary drill on the surface. Diamond bits are usually designed for a specific rock type and contain channels which allow for the evacuation of cuttings. Collecting an undisturbed soil sample requires the use of a cylindrical sampler. Samples are obtained by the extraction of soil cores, typically of the diameter 1-1/2 in or 4 in. The core barrel is detachable and is capped so the core is hermetically sealed for delivery to the laboratory. Individual soil cores, up to 3 ft in length may be obtained by continuous coring if necessary.

Rock Boring Log

A complete rock boring log must contain the following information on the heading: date, location, loggers name, personnel, drill pressure, drilling rate, drilling fluid and bits used, and any other pertinent notes. The actual core logging consists of describing and charting: drill depth, lithologies, facies changes, any veining and faulting encountered, core recovery percentage (missing core), rock color, rock hardness, specific mineralogy, and some general textural/structural characteristics. The textural and structural features that need to be mentioned include the following: formation, lithology, grain size, bedding and foliation, lineation, and fractures. Core samples are then digitally photographed and entered into a computer for detailed analyses and retained so that there can be a record in the event that the rock sample is damaged or misplaced.

Electrical Logs Used in Borehole Geophysics

The specific resistance of the rock walls of the hole to electrical current is measured in the resistivity log. This is done by inserting a drill attachment containing electrodes into the borehole. Electrical resistivity is expressed in ohm-meters. There are two kinds of resistivity log. A normal resistivity log involves the insertion of four electrodes with a standard spacing. A single-point resistivity log, on the other hand, involves the use of only two electrodes, and can therefore only be

performed on a limited area. The spontaneous potential is the measure of the change in DC voltage between the surface and a particular point in the well. In general, differences in electrochemical potentials between formations are responsible for the changes in spontaneous potential.

LOGS USED TO DESCRIBE A BOREHOLE

A caliper log produces a physical profile of the diameter of an un-cased borehole with the use of moveable calipers that record variation in the borehole wall. A gamma ray log is used to assess the type and amount of gamma radiation produced by the rocks in a particular borehole. A neutron log assesses the radioactivity log curve in the borehole by neutron emanation. A neutron log is used to estimate the density and porosity of a rock formation. A well log is a graphic representation that displays a specific characteristic of the rock in the well versus the depth of the well. A well log is a record of the measured physical or chemical characteristics of the rocks encountered in a borehole. Measurements are made by a sonde as it is withdrawn from the borehole by a wire line. Several measurements are usually made simultaneously with the resulting curves being displayed side by side on a common depth scale.

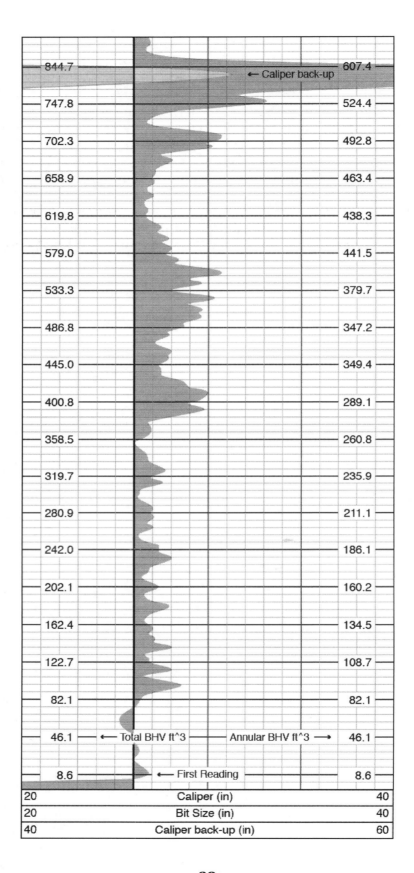

GEOPHYSICAL FIELD INVESTIGATION TERMS

The *invaded zone* is the area affected by the drilling of a borehole in which physical parameters have been altered. The invaded zone lies in between the flushed zone and the un-invaded zone.

When radioactive well logging, gamma rays are measured according to an *American Petroleum Institute (API) unit* standard

Rippability is a measure of the relative ease or difficulty with which an earth material can be dislodged and removed by machine-drawn rippers or rigid steel tines. Rippability refers to the ease with which a material can be excavated mechanically.

Test pits are mechanically excavated surface cuts used to investigate shallow sub-surface conditions. Test pits are used to sample geologic materials in areas of restrictive overburden or vegetative cover. Test pits are also excavated to investigate young faults.

WELL LOG

A *well* log records measurement of the characteristics of the rock and structure encountered in a borehole. The log is graphically plotted, usually as a continuous function of depth. Measurements are collected with a sonde that is withdrawn from the well by a wire line. Several measurements are usually made simultaneously. Measurements include: resistivity studies conducted during electrical logging, acoustic or caliper logging data, gamma ray logging data, neutron logging data, and spontaneous potential logging data. The most common types of well logs are resistivity logs and radioactivity logs. Other well log types commonly produced are specific curve types including sonic logs and gamma-ray logs. A well log can provide information about porosity and permeability, geologic structure (if multiple logs are used), and stratigraphy.

CALIPER LOG

A *caliper* log is a well log that shows the variations with depth in the diameter of an uncased borehole. It is produced by spring-activated arms pressing against the sides of the well bore that measure the varying widths of the hole as the device is drawn upward. The caliper consists of a central core with a potentiometer surrounded by at least three arms. The diameter data for the borehole are recorded by the potentiometer. An acoustic caliper, on the other hand, records the varying diameter of the borehole by means of three ultra-sonic transmitters. It is important to test for changes in borehole diameter, since these are common when different drilling methods are used, or when the surrounding rock has fractures, water, or caving. Borehole diameters change according to lithology and groundwater activity.

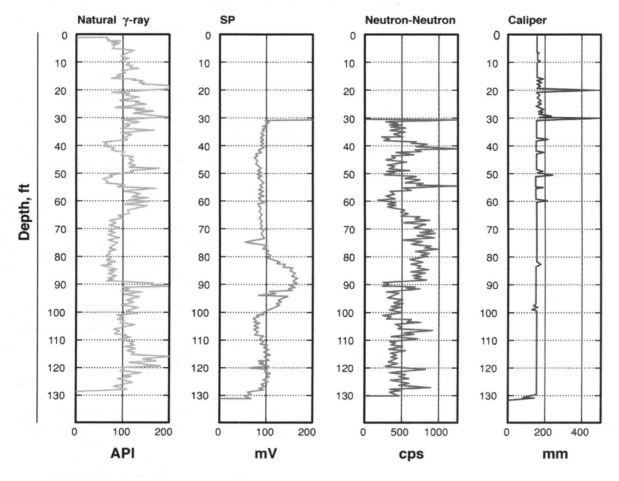

SPONTANEOUS POTENTIAL, RESISTIVITY, AND GAMMA RAY LOGS

Spontaneous potential (SP), resistivity, and gamma ray values are all important parameters of down-hole characteristics collected during electrical and geophysical studies performed in test drilling. These parameters are plotted graphically as a function of depth and displayed on well logs. Relative values for spontaneous potential, resistivity, and the gamma ray logs for common subsurface materials are as follows:

- salt water: low to moderate spontaneous potential, low resistivity
- limestone: low spontaneous potential, high resistivity, low gamma
- sandstone or sand: high spontaneous potential, moderate resistivity, low gamma
- shale or clay: low spontaneous potential, low resistivity, high gamma
- clay: low spontaneous potential, very high resistivity, low gamma
- hydrocarbons: extremely high resistivity
- freshwater: low spontaneous potential, high resistivity

Spontaneous potential (SP) logs and *resistivity* logs are used to obtain information about subsurface structure. Resistivity logging involves electrodes spaced at a constant distance that are moved along a profile (borehole) resulting in vertical variations in resistivity being shown. The test shows the existence of faults that have thrown strata of different resistive properties in different positions. Similar relationships can be used in the identification of an anticline, a syncline, or an underground channel. Spontaneous potential logs can provide insight into the types of fluids present. Caliper logging records the diameter throughout the length of a borehole. Gamma ray logging is a method of logging boreholes by observing the natural radioactivity of the rocks through which the hole is in contact with. It was developed for logging holes that cannot be logged electrically because they are cased with conductive metal. Neutron logging is a method used in boreholes in which a radioactive source provides neutrons that enter rock formations and induce a radioactive response that can be measured.

Electrical resistivity logs are used to obtain information about the composition of materials below the surface, as well as the geologic structures underground. Resistivity measurements can be performed as a downhole survey or from the surface. The method for surface resistivity is to apply electrodes directly to the ground. By comparing the difference in potential voltage between two different electrodes, information about ground water depth, ground water contamination, horizontal extent of conductive contaminants, vertical extent of soil, stratigraphy, and the presence of clay aquitards may be determined.

A *spontaneous potential* log is the record of the naturally occurring potential differences between formations that are found in the borehole. These potentials will tend to develop between the formation water, the surrounding rock materials, and the borehole fluid. Spontaneous potential is measured in DC voltage, and is typically accompanied by a measure of electrical resistivity. Two factors that can affect SP are temperature and quantity of clay. The vertical line drawn through the greatest positive value of spontaneous potential measured is known as the shale line or the baseline, while the vertical line drawn through the most negative value of spontaneous potential measured is known as the sand line. Spontaneous potential logs can determine the thickness of a bed, as well as the amount of salt in the formation water.

A *spectral gamma ray* log is the record of the radiation spectrum and relative intensities of gamma rays emitted by strata penetrated in drilling. Various elements can be differentiated due to the different energies contributed by each type of gamma radiation to the sun total natural gamma ray signature. A standard gamma ray log provides the log curve of the total intensity of natural gamma radiation emitted from the rocks in a cased or uncased borehole. It is used for correlation, and for distinguishing shales, which are usually richer in naturally radioactive elements, from sandstones, carbonates, and evaporates. Amount of gamma radiation induced is also a measure of hydrogen content. Clays and shales tend to have more concentrations of radioactive elements than other types of rock. Volcanic ash increases gamma radiation. The most radioactive rocks are shale, arkose, and granite.

MEASURING GAMMA RADIATION

The basic method for measuring gamma radiation is with a scintillation detector. Scintillometers operate by the use of crystals that emit brief flashes of light when stimulated by radioactivity. These flashes of light are amplified and detected by a meter within the instrument. The more flashes, the higher the level of radiation. Gamma radiation is measured in terms of counts per second, counts per minute, pulses, or API units. Gamma ray logging is used in oil and gas exploration. A gamma ray log produces the radioactivity log curve of the intensity of broad-spectrum gamma radiation emitted from the rocks in a borehole. It is used for correlation, structural analysis, and for distinguishing shales, which are usually richer in naturally radioactive elements, from sandstones, carbonates, and evaporates. Amount of gamma radiation induced is a also a measure of hydrogen content. Gamma ray surveys are also used in uranium exploration, both in regional airborne surveys, and in more focused, propertry-scale ground surveys. Surface gamma-ray anomalies are further investigated for economic uranium mineralization by core drilling.

NEUTRON LOGS

A *neutron* log records secondary radioactivity arising from the bombardment of the rocks around a borehole by neutrons emitted from a source as the tool is raised upward through the borehole. Neutron logs are used in conjunction with other types of logs for the identification of the fluid-bearing zones of rocks. This test also utilizes a neutron source being withdrawn throughout the length of the borehole. A measurement is taken of the energy lost by the neutrons after they come into contact with the subsurface materials. Because this change in energy is largely due to the quantity of water underground, a neutron log is also effective at measuring the porosity of the subsurface materials. Neutrons that enter rock formations induce additional gamma radiation, which is measured by use of an ionization chamber. The gamma radiation so induced is related to the hydrogen content of the rock.

A typical neutron log probe emits neutrons from a source utilizing a mixture of beryllium and americium. Freshly emitted neutrons lose energy as they come into contact with geologic materials and fluids encountered in the borehole. This process is known as moderation. When neutrons are first emitted, they typically possess neutron energy level greater than 10^5 electron volts. After contact with moderators in the borehole, they become epithermal neutrons with an energy level between .1 and 100 electron volts. When a neutron sinks below .025 electron volts, it becomes a thermal neutron. The element that most effectively moderates neutrons is hydrogen and hence, water. Neutron logs are effective in assessing the level of water in the subsurface materials.

A neutron log is a strip recording of the secondary radioactivity arising from the bombardment of the rocks around a borehole by neutrons from a source being caused to move through the borehole. Because hydrogen is such an effective moderator of neutrons, neutron logs are often used to gauge the porosity of subsurface rock. Because resistivity is related to porosity, neutron logs can also give a good reading of this characteristic. A neutron log is also able to provide information about the borehole diameter, ground water temperature, ground water pressure, and the salinity of groundwater. It should be noted that neutron logs are notorious for providing odd results when used to measure the porosity of gypsum, coal, gas-bearing formations of clay, and shale.

USING SEISMIC REFRACTION, SEISMIC REFLECTION, AND 3D SEISMIC REFLECTION OR REFRACTION

Refraction utilizes seismic waves traveling large horizontal distances along distinct interfaces in the Earth. Travel time required for these seismic waves gives information on the velocity and depth of certain subsurface formations. *Seismic reflection* maps the structure of subsurface formations by making use of the times required for a seismic wave to return to the surface after reflection from the formations themselves. The reflections are recorded by detecting instruments which are laid near the site of generation of the seismic pulse. Variations in reflection times can indicate structural features in the rocks below. *Three Dimensional* (3D) *seismic* is obtained through a set of closely-spaced seismic lines that provide a high spatially sampled test of subsurface reflectivity. The resultant data set can be observed in any direction without losing view characteristics of a well sampled seismic section. In a migrated 3D seismic data set all events are placed in their proper vertical and horizontal positions. This provides a much more detailed image than available with 2D seismic technique.

SEISMIC REFRACTION SURVEY

Refraction utilizes seismic waves traveling large horizontal and vertical distances along distinct interfaces in the Earth. Travel time required for these seismic waves gives information on the velocity and depth of certain subsurface formations. The detecting instruments are laid down at a distance from the shot hole that is large compared with the depth of the horizon to be mapped. The seismic waves may be generated with either a small explosion, a hammer, or a specially designed vibration truck. The basic conceptual understanding of the way that seismic waves move through layers of different density is known as Snell's law.

The rippability of Earth materials is defined as a measure of the relative ease with which a geologic or earth material can be dislodged by rippers or rigid steel teeth. It measures the degree of ease with which a material can be excavated. The rippability of Earth materials is dependent on density and degree of weathering to which they have been exposed. Seismic refraction velocity can indicate these parameters. Highly weathered materials will be easier to excavate, because they already contain many voids, fractures, and have been partially decomposed. Rocks that contain very few fractures and discontinuities are extremely difficult to rip, and must be excavated by explosives. The seismic refraction velocity will tend to be the fastest through rocks that have little discontinuity and weathering.

SNELL'S LAW

Snell's Law describes the refraction of seismic waves through subsurface materials of varying density. The formula for Snell's Law is as follows:

$v_1/v_2 = \sin \alpha / \sin \beta$, in which v_1 is the velocity through layer 1, v_2 is the velocity through layer 2, α is the angle of incidence, and β is the angle of refraction. If v_2 is greater than v_1, then the angle of refraction is greater than the angle of incidence. When seismic waves are sent into a two layer material, a portion of the waves will be reflected off the boundary between the layers, while another portion of the waves will be refracted at the next boundary between layers. The composition and weathering (if present) of the subsurface material will determine the velocity at which the refracted waves travel.

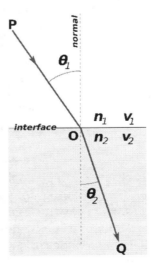

GROUND PENETRATING RADAR

Ground penetrating radar uses radar pulses to image the subsurface. It is a non-destructive method utilizing electromagnetic radiation in the microwave band. Reflected signals reveal subsurface detail. GPR uses transmitting and receiving antennas that radiate short pulses of the high-frequency radio waves into the ground. When the wave encounters a buried object or a boundary with different properties, the receiving antennae receives variations in the reflected return signal. These variations in the return signal are converted into a real-time image displayed on an on-site cathode-ray-tube type television screen. The technique is similar to reflection seismology, but electromagnetic energy is used instead of acoustic energy. The depth range is limited by electrical conductivity of the ground or the presence of other interference causing factors.

Ground Penetrating Radar (GPR) can be used in a variety of geologic and engineering media, including rock, soil, ice, fresh water, pavements and structures. It can detect objects, changes in material, and voids and cracks. Ground Penetrating Radar has many applications in a number of environmental and engineering fields. It is used to study bedrock, soils, groundwater, ice, and also has a number of engineering applications. Non-destructive testing of structures and pavements, locating buried structures and utility lines are included. In environmental remediation GPR is most often performed to delineate landfills and contaminant plumes. In archeology it is used for mapping of excavation sites prior to disruption and digging. Ground Penetrating Radar can reveal near-surface structure in bedrock and soils.

GRAVITY SURVEY

A gravity survey may be conducted as an airborne data collection or as a land-based study. Gravity surveying is a geophysical method that measures irregularities or anomalies in gravity attraction produced by differences in the densities of rock formations. Anomalies are identified based on differences between the observed value of gravity at a point and the theoretically calculated value for that point. Theoretical values are calculated based on a gravity model that assumes a generalized hypothesis of variation in subsurface density as it relates to surface topography. Results are interpreted in terms of lithology and structure. Gravity surveys have application in many earth science-based industries including mineral exploration, oil and gas exploration, engineering geology, and civil engineering. Gravity surveying is also a used in geologic research.

MAGNETIC SURVEY

Magnetic surveys and prospecting are now carried on predominantly with airborne instruments. Magnetic surveys maps variations in the magnetic field of the Earth that are attributable to changes of structure or magnetic susceptibility in certain near-surface rocks. Sedimentary rocks generally have a very small susceptibility compared with igneous or metamorphic rocks, and most magnetic surveys are designed to map structure on or within the basement, or to detect magnetic minerals directly. Magnetic surveys are performed with a geophysical instrument similar to the gravimeter in that absolute magnetic values are not measured, but only the differences in vertical magnetic force between field stations and a selected base station. Magnetic surveys can provide information of subsurface structure of bedrock and location of magnetic lithologies.

AERIAL PHOTOGRAPHY

Aerial photography is very useful in the early stages of geologic investigations for planning and preliminary inspection of surface features. Aerial photography is initially used in geological investigations for terrain analysis. This branch of earth science is known as photogeology. Regional drainage patterns as seen on aerial photographs can reveal information about lithologies of rock. Disruptions in the landscape, such as landslides or sinkhole, are often highly visible on air photos. Many times, these features are indiscernible on the ground without assistance of aerial photos. Stereo-paired aerial photographs are essential in geologic mapping and in the production of topographic maps. Aerial photographs are especially useful in planning traverses and solving access issues prior to a geologic field investigation.

Focal length is defined as the distance from the center of the camera lens to a point where the image is center on the film. The scale of an aerial photograph is determined by the dividing the focal length of the camera by the altitude of the survey platform. The scale of an aerial photograph changes with collection height. In photogrammetric surveying, the platform will maintain a fix altitude over a target area so a relatively consistent scale is maintained. Because of lens distortion and elevation differences, the scale from aerial photography is not consistent from center to edge. A special kind of photo called an orthophotograph is an aerial photograph that has been planimetrically corrected to remove distortion caused by camera optics, camera tilt, and differences in elevation. Unlike an uncorrected aerial photograph, an orthophotograph can be used to measure true distances as it is an accurate representation of the earth's surface.

STEREO-PAIRED LOW ALTITUDE PHOTOGRAPHS

The use of low-altitude stereo-paired photographs is called stereoscopy. Terrain analysis through the use of aerial photography adds preliminary surficial and structural geologic information prior to field studies. Stereo-pair photographs are used in field geology to provide a 3-dimensional image during geologic mapping. Structure, lithologic contacts, and attitude symbols are transcribed directly onto the stereo-pair photos in the field as geology is ground checked. The 3-dimendional view allows the mapper to visualize the ground he is directly mapping. Stereo-pair photos are then directly put into a stereographic plotter, either mechanical or digital, by which field notations can be placed precisely on a topographic base. As most topographic quadrangle maps are prepared using stereo-paired photographs, location of ground features will be optimized on to the topographic base.

SIDE-LOOKING AIRBORNE RADAR

Side-looking airborne radar (SLAR) images are acquired by sending a beam of radar energy to the ground at an angle perpendicular to the aircraft's flight path. Unlike visible and near-infrared wavelengths, radar energy can penetrate most clouds, making it an especially useful tool where persistent clouds cover target areas. With SLAR the terrain is illuminated at an oblique angle to enhance subtle geologic structures such as folds and faults. Light and dark areas on the image are caused by high and low radar reflectivity, respectively. The size of objects discerned from SLAR depends upon the radar return, so the azimuth resolution of 10-15 meters is not necessarily a limiting factor. Side-looking airborne radar is used for terrain analysis in areas with frequent and dense cloud cover that restricts conventional camera-based imagery.

HIGH ALTITUDE LANDSAT PHOTOGRAPHS

The Landsat Program is the longest running enterprise for acquisition of imagery of Earth from space. The first Landsat satellite was launched in 1972, the most recent, Landsat 8, was launched in 2013. Landsat 8 carries eleven spectral band scanners with spatial resolutions ranging from 15 to 100 meters. The wide band of collection allows for the production of varied imagery useful to many industries. Landsat data have been used by government, commercial, industrial, civilian, military, and educational communities throughout the United States and worldwide. The data support a wide range of applications in such areas as global change research, agriculture, forestry, geology, resource management, geography, mapping, water quality, and oceanography. Landsat 8 imagery can be blown up to scales approaching 1:50,000 without extensive distortion due to lack of resolution. Landsat 8 is slated to be replaced by Landsat 9 in the year 2023.

HIGH ALTITUDE COLOR INFRARED IMAGES

High-altitude color infrared images are taken by aircraft flying at extremely high altitudes. The cameras used to take these photographs typically have special filters to block out blue and ultraviolet wavelengths, so that the images will only use the red, near infrared, and infrared portion

45

of the electromagnetic spectrum. Infrared radiation has a longer wavelength than visible light, and when combined with near infrared portion of the visible spectrum, is very effective in thermal mapping. Objects that reflect near infrared wavelengths well will appear red on the photographs, and other objects that do not reflect infrared radiation as well will appear green. This kind of photography is used in both military and civilian applications for determining heat spectrums on the ground. Its uses in geology include mapping of volcanic features and near-surface plutonic activity. False color infrared images are useful in assessing content of moisture in the soil.

SPOT IMAGES (SATELLITE POUR L'OBSERVATION DE LA TERRA)

The SPOT satellite is a high-resolution, optical imaging earth observation satellite system operating from space. The program was initiated by the French in the 1970's. The SPOT program has launched 5 satellites to date. The program was designed to improve the knowledge of the earth by exploring the earth's resources and for detecting and forecasting phenomena involving climatology. The satellites also monitor human activities and natural events. The SPOT system includes a series of satellites and ground control resources for satellite control and programming. SPOT images come in green, red, and near infrared bands. These images can be stereo-paired to produce three-dimensional images. Level 1a images are used for stereo plotting and radiometric studies. Level 1b images are used for thematic studies and photo interpretation. Level 2a images are used for standard cartographic projections. Level 2b images provide slightly more accurate cartographic projections. The images produced by SPOT systems have a resolution of between 10 and 20 m. The satellite used to take these images orbits the Earth once every 26 days.

SHUTTLE RADAR TOPOGRAPHY MISSION (SRTM) IMAGES

The Shuttle Radar Topography Mission (SRTM) is an international research effort for obtaining digital elevation models on a global scale. This was initiated to generate the most complete high-resolution digital topographic database of Earth to date. SRTM consisted of a specially modified radar system that flew onboard the Space Shuttle Endeavor during the 11-day STS-99 mission in February of 2000. Shuttle Radar Topography Mission images are taken using the techniques of radar interferometry. The technique involves radar waves that are sent out from different locations reflecting off the surface. These signals are then picked up by a single detector. The amount of interference in the received waves gives an indication of the topography. SRTM images are capable of providing a three-dimensional topographical view of the Earth. The vertical image resolution of an SRTM image is 90 m.

Mineralogy and Petrology

USING PHYSICAL OR CHEMICAL CHARACTERISTICS TO IDENTIFY MINERALS

A mineral is defined as "a solid inorganic substance of natural occurrence." Minerals can be identified by means of their physical or chemical characteristics. The physical characteristics of a mineral are a direct result of the chemical composition of that mineral. Physical characteristics that can be used to identify a mineral are: crystal habit and symmetry, cleavage, fracture, crystal twinning, specific gravity, color and streak, luster, luminescence, radioactivity, and magnetism. The possible combination of all chemical elements on Earth represents millions of compounds. Despite this fact, only some 2400 minerals have been described to date. All minerals possess a unique internal structure, and most have unique chemical compositions. Minerals are thus highly identifiable by chemical analyses. In chemical analysis of a mineral a determination is made of the relative amounts of elements and their oxidation states. While minerals can normally be identified by physical characteristics, they can also be identified by the color of the flame they produce when burned, a function of chemical composition.

SILICATE MINERALS

Silicate minerals are classified on the basis of the configuration of anions in the mineral structure. The shape of the silicate molecule is a tetrahedron with four large oxygen atoms surrounding a silicon atom. Silicate mineral construction is based on combinations of the silicate tetrahedron. There are seven basic types of silicate mineral:

- Nesosilicates: contains SiO_4; composed of an isolated tetrahedral; includes zircon, olivine, and garnet
- Sorosilicates: contains Si_2O_7: isolated double or linked tetrahedral; includes lawsonite and hemimorphite
- Cyclosilicates: contains SiO_3; includes beryl group and tourmaline
- Inosilicates (single-chain): contains SiO_3; includes pyroxene group and pyroxenoid group
- Inosilicates (double-chain): contains Si_4O_{11}; includes amphibole group
- Phyllosilicates: contains Si_2O_5; forms sheets; includes biotite, talc, and chlorite
- Tectosilicates: contains SiO_2 and Si_3O_8; forms frameworks; includes feldspar and zeolite groups

IGNEOUS ROCKS

Igneous rocks are rocks that are formed from cooling magma or lava. They can be classified in any of several different ways, including mode of occurrence, texture, mineralogy, and geometry. Mode of occurrence is the most common.

Igneous rocks are classified by mode of occurrence as intrusive (plutonic), extrusive (volcanic), or hypabyssal. Intrusive rocks are coarse grained rocks that are formed by slowly cooling magma far below the earth's surface. Extrusive rocks are smooth and fine-grained rocks that are formed by faster cooling magma at or above the earth's surface. Hypabyssal rocks are less common rocks that are formed only slightly below the earth's surface.

In terms of texture, igneous rocks are classified as either phaneritic or aphanitic. The phanerites are igneous rocks in which crystal structure can be identified megascopically (by the naked eye). Fine-grained igneous rocks in which mineralogy cannot be determined megascopically are

47

classified as aphanites. In general, phanerites are intrusive rocks, while aphanites are extrusive rocks.

BOWEN'S REACTION SERIES

Bowen's Reaction Series is based on the theory that basalt is the parent material that gives rise to all other kinds of igneous rock. The diagram below displays the progression in Bowen's Reaction Series showing the order in which minerals precipitate in an igneous melt:

Olivine	Anorthite
Mg pyroxene	Labradorite
Mg-Ca pyroxene	Andesite
Amphibole	Oligoclase
Biotite	Albite
Potassium feldspar	
Muscovite	
Quartz	

The left branch is called the discontinuous reaction series and represents a collection of minerals that interact with magma to create each successive member. On the right side, the continuous reaction series, feldspar crystals perpetually interact with cooling magma. All the minerals atop the diagram are those that crystallize early, while the minerals at the bottom only crystallize once magma has cooled considerably. Bowen realized that both sides of the reaction series operate simultaneously within a cooling melt and can explain many features observed in igneous rocks.

Bowen's reaction series is based on a number of controlled laboratory experiments and provides a generalized progression of mineral precipitation from a cooling magma. It is very useful in describing observed field relationships of igneous rocks and has been repeatedly verified. An important practical use of Bowen's theory is the prediction of mineral weathering. This is based on the fact that the surface of the Earth is a low temperature environment compared to that found during rock formation. Because of this, Bowen's reaction chart also indicates the stability of minerals at the earth's surface with the ones at bottom being most stable and the ones at top being quickest to weather. This is because minerals are most stable in the conditions closest to those under which they had formed.

INTRUSIVE ROCKS AND EXTRUSIVE ROCKS

Alkali-feldspar granite is the end-member of quartz-rich plutonic rocks in terms of feldspar composition with <10% plagioclase (calcium) feldspar, and 90% to 100% alkali-feldspar (K-spar) (sodium/potassium). The extrusive counterpart is alkali-feldspar rhyolite. A progression of plagioclase/K-spar concentration ratios define a series of plutonic rocks from granite (30-90% K-spar; 10-65% Plagioclase), to granodiorite (10-35% K-spar; 65-90% plagioclase), through tonalite (<10% K-spar; 90-100% plagioclase). The extrusive equivalents of these are rhyolite, dacite. Syenitoids are quartz-poor relative to granites. These rocks range from alkali-feldspar syenite (90-100% K-spar; <10% plagioclase), to syenite (65-90% K-spar; 10-35% plagioclase), to monzonite (35 – 65% of both plagioclase and K-spar). The extrusive equivalents of these rocks are trachyte and latite. Most extrusive volcanic rocks are basalt that typically contains only plagioclase feldspars.

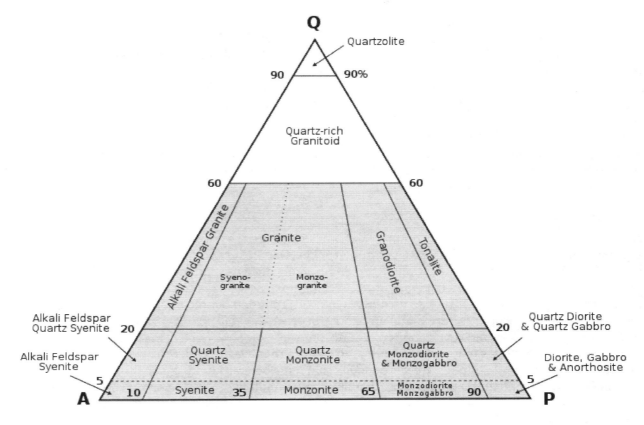

SEDIMENTARY ROCKS

Sedimentary rocks may be deposited physically, chemically, or biologically. Although some chemically precipitated sedimentary rocks are formed as a solid aggregate, most sediments must be lithified by cementation to form a rock. Sedimentary rocks are divided into three main categories: detrital sedimentary rocks, consisting of loose rock and mineral fragments derived from erosion; chemical and biochemical rocks, made up of precipitated minerals; and diagenetic sedimentary rocks, formed as a result of recrystallization, replacement, or other chemical modification of the original sediments. Even though sedimentary and diagenetic rocks comprise less than 10% of the Earth's crust by volume, they cover some 75% of the continental surface. Ninety-five percent of all sedimentary rocks consists of sandstones, mudrocks, and carbonate rocks. Of these, the mudrocks are most abundant, making up about 65% of all sedimentary rocks. Sandstones make up 20 to 25% of all sedimentary rocks, and carbonate rocks account for about 10 to 15% of all sedimentary rocks.

DIAGENESIS

Diagenesis is any change occurring within sediment after its deposition and during and after its lithification, exclusive of weathering. It includes such processes as compaction, cementation, replacement, and crystallization, under normal surficial conditions of pressure and temperature. Compaction and lithification are both considered to be diagenetic processes, but weathering and metamorphism are not as they do not occur between 100 and 300°C. The following are other diagenetic processes: 1) cementation, the diagenetic process by which coarse clastic sediments become lithified or consolidated into hard, compact rocks, usually through deposition or precipitation of minerals in the spaces among the individual grains of the sediment. 2) replacement,

49

change in composition of a mineral or mineral aggregate, presumably accomplished by diffusion of new material in and old material out without breakdown of the solid state.

FACIES

Facies is a term of wide application, referring to such aspects of rock units as rock type, mode of origin, composition, fossil content, or environment of deposition. A facies change refers to a lateral or vertical variation in the lithologic or paleontologic characteristics of contemporaneous sedimentary deposits. It is caused by, or reflects, a change in the depositional environment. Facies may change vertically through a sequence as a result of changing environment through time. Facies may also change laterally through a deposit as a result of changing environments with distance at the same time. The structures and textures found in sedimentary rocks give clues to the environment of deposition, as discussed above, and thus allow geologists to assign parts of a deposit to a particular sedimentary facies. Individual facies are generally described in terms of the environment is which deposition occurred.

CLASTIC ROCKS

Rock fragments and minerals that comprise detrital sediments are derived from pre-existing rocks that have undergone subaerial weathering and erosion. Detrital grains are then transported to be re-deposited as sediment. Lithification or cementation produces a sedimentary rock. The predominant detrital rocks are conglomerates, sedimentary breccias, sandstones, siltstones, and claystones. Conglomerates are made up of 50% or more rounded pebbles, cobbles, or boulders, whereas sedimentary breccias are made up of 50% or more angular pebble-, cobble-, or boulder-sized fragments. Sandstones consist of sandstone deposits that have been cemented or consolidated. Sandstones may be well laminated to thin- to thick-bedded. Quartz is the predominant mineral. Siltstones are silt deposits that have been lithified. Most siltstones occur interbedded with sedimentary sequences that are predominately sandstone or shale. Claystones, mudstone, and shale are made up of clay-sized particles. Mudstones exhibit blocky cleavage as they contain more irregularly shaped particles than shales.

INFORMATION PROVIDED BY GRAIN SIZE AND COMPOSITION FOR SANDSTONE, CONGLOMERATE, AND SHALE

Since most sedimentary rocks are derived by processes of weathering, transportation, deposition, and diagenesis, the textures we find in sediment and sedimentary rocks are dependent on the specific process and the order in which they occurred. These include: the nature of the parent rocks, the strength of the wind or water currents that carry and deposit the sediment, the distance transported or time involved in the transportation process, biological activity with the sediment prior to diagenesis, and the chemical environment under which diagenesis occurs. Grain sizes in conglomerate, sandstone, and shale are directly related to deposition energies of sediments which comprise these rocks. As the energy or velocity of transport decreases, heavier particles are deposited and lighter fragments continue to be transported. This results in sorting due to density.

DOLOMITE, DIATOMITE, CHERT, PYRITE, PEAT, COAL, AND EVAPORATES

Dolomite, known chemically as $CaMg(CO_3)_2$, forms when the porewaters in limestone are enriched through evaporation which causes magnesium to be subsequently exchanged for calcium in the atomic structure. The formation of diatomite, a light-colored soft friable siliceous sedimentary rock consisting chiefly of diatoms, occurs through thick accumulations of diatomaceous material (diatomaceous earth). Chert is a hard, dense, dull to semivitreous, microcrystalline or cryptocrystalline sedimentary rock, consisting dominantly of interlocking crystals of quartz. Chert may also contain amorphous silica (opal). Pyrite is not a sedimentary rock. It is a sulfide mineral. Pyrite frequently occurs diagenetically in marine shales. Peat is formed in swamps from accumulation of dead and partly decomposed marsh vegetation. Peat has a yellowish brown to brownish black color, is generally of the fibrous consistency, and can be either plastic or friable. Coal is a readily combustible rock containing more than 50% by weight and more than 70% by volume of carbonaceous material.

LIMESTONE

There are both clastic and nonclastic limestones. Clastic limestones are made up of calcium carbonate fragments that were deposited in place or were transported from elsewhere within the basin in which they formed. Chemically and biologically precipitated particles are classified according to grain size. Oolites are from 0.2 to 2.0 mm, pellets are particles <2.0 mm, and fossils with no size limit. After lithification limestones are classified by the size of the clasts: calcirudites, calcarenites, or calcilutites. The clastic limestones form predominantly in a marine environment. Nonclastic limestones consist of chemically or biologically precipitated calcite or aragonite material that has not been transported since original deposition. Other limestone rocks in the nonclastic subclass such as reef limestone (stromatolite) and travertine, are named on the basis of texture and mode of formation. These limestones form in both marine and nonmarine environments.

METAMORPHIC ROCKS

Metamorphic rocks are classified genetically by their environment of metamorphism. The three major sub classes are: rocks produced in response to dislocation metamorphism, rocks formed in contact zones around igneous intrusions, and rocks metamorphosed regionally during mountain building episodes. Cataclasites are formed as a result of mechanical breakage and distortions that occur during crustal movements. Cataclasites can be formed from any rock and consist of any mineral assemblage. Contactites form when hot magma is intruded into relatively cooler host rocks, heating and metamorphosing the surrounding country rock. Changes can range from complete recrystallization to minor color changes. Regional metamorphic rocks consist of extensive volumes of rock that undergo textural and compositional changes in response to mountain building. Regional metamorphism involves recrystallization and new mineral growth under increased pressure and temperature.

Geologists often study the facies of metamorphic rocks in order to determine the pressure and the temperatures at which the rocks were formed. During broad and consistent regional metamorphism, all the rocks in an area will experience varying degrees of pressure and temperature. By studying metamorphic grade zones across a region, the metamorphic episode can be fully understood. In contact metamorphism, decreasing metamorphic grade outward due to temperature gradient is useful in identifying ore zones and in describing a metamorphic event. Contact metamorphism typically has a far smaller or no pressure signature compared to regional metamorphism. In dynamic metamorphism, a process in which rocks are fractured by intense pressure, metamorphic facies can aid in interpretation of a faulting event or earth movement.

CONDITIONS THAT DISTINGUISH THE SPECIFIC CATEGORIES OF REGIONAL METAMORPHISM

Regional metamorphism is classified according to temperature and pressure regimes:

- Prehnite-pumpellyite facies: formed deep below water in sediment of greywacke, shale, and mafic rocks; zeolyte appears at a depth of 3000 to 15,000 feet, while prehnite-pumpellyite appears between 10,000 and 40,000 feet
- Blueschist or glaucophane schist facies: formed in subduction zones and other tectonically active environments; temperature between 300 and 400°C, and pressure above 5000 bars
- Greenschist facies: form at slightly greater depth than blue schist; temperature between 300 and 500°C, pressure between 3000 and 8000 bars

- Amphibolite facies: slightly deeper environment than greenschist facies; temperature is between 450 and 700°C, pressure between 3000 and 8000 bars
- Granulite facies: formed in deep regional metamorphism; temperature above 650°C, pressure between 3000 and 12,000 bars
- Eclogite facies: temperature between 350 and 753 degrees Celsius, pressure above 7,500 bars

52

Sedimentology, Stratigraphy, and Paleontology

FOSSIL ASSEMBLAGES, INDEX FOSSIL, AND KEY BEDS

The following terms are commonly used in stratigraphy:

- fossil assemblages: the collective group of fossils occurring in a rock or formation. The fossil assemblage is all flora and fauna existing together in a sample from which relative age determinations are made
- index fossil: an individual fossil with a known and specific age range that is used to identify the particular sequence in which it is found. Frequently use with other index fossils to describe a more specific time range for a particular sample
- key beds: a stratum that is well defined or easily identifiable containing distinctive characteristics that can be used in correlation of surface or subsurface mapping units. A key bed can be lithologic or based on fossils

PARTICLE DEPOSITION AND LAVA FLOW

The geologist can determine the vertical orientation of a rock bed by the orientation of lava flow structures, or by observation of particle deposition. Because these processes are dependent on gravity, rocks displaying these structures can usually be reoriented and can provide a great deal of information about prior vertical orientation. Graded bedding in which large particles give way to particles with decreasing size in individual beds are a common sedimentary feature recognizable and helpful in strata re-orientation. Lava flows contain very indicative internal structures such as crude graded bedding and an alternation of dense flow rock with vesicular flow top rocks. Both of these gravity-related structures can be recognized and used to re-orient lava flows. Packages of successive lava flows display an alternating pattern of dense and vesicular lava that can aide in reorientation.

TOP AND BOTTOM INDICATORS

Features that orient a bed are often referred to as top and bottom indicators. As sedimentary rocks can be deformed by folding and faulting long after the deposition process has ended, it is important to be able to determine which was up in the rock when it was originally deposited. Original depositional features such as cross-bedding, graded bedding, or imbricate bedding can be useful in general reorientation of beds. Other physical structures useful for orientation of bedding include: ripple marks (top of bed), mud cracks (top of bed), raindrop marks (top of bed), load casts (bottom of bed), sole marks (bottom of bed), and tool marks (top of bed). Biological activity after deposition can impart recognizable structures on sedimentary rocks, such as burrows and trails.

STRATIGRAPHIC CORRELATION

Tracing a stratigraphic bed or group of rocks from one area to another involves detailed examinations of field relationships, depositional environments, and chemical and physical composition. Geologists use theories of depositional environments to date, classify, and compare various strata. In the absence of good index fossils, or if contained index fossils do not provide correlation due to poor time resolution, a careful comparison of both the specific and regional geology between correlated areas must be considered. Depositional environments must be correlative and not in opposition to establish a general and valid stratigraphic correlation. Differences in chemical and physical characteristics of stratigraphic units must be explained in establishment of a correlation. Stratigraphic correlation can be based on time or environment such that two very different sedimentary packages can correlate in time. Conversely, two very similar depositional systems may not be time correlative

The discovery of one fossil or paleontological attribute is not sufficient evidence to proclaim a stratigraphic correlation. Any stratigraphic correlation must include an entire model of the formation of all rocks in area of interest. Paleontological evidence is supportable only when cross-referenced to overlapping known fossil assemblages or environments that can be temporally or spatially matched. Modern paleontology defines ancient life by studying how long-term physical changes of global geography, paleogeography, and climate paleoclimate have affected the evolution of life. Paleontology is interested in ecosystem responses to changes in the planetary environment and to evaluating how these responses have affected patterns of biodiversity. For valid stratigraphic correlation based on paleontology, the researcher must establish a level of certainty by describing a fossil assemblage that takes into account flora, fauna, and depositional environments.

SEDIMENTARY ROCK STRATIFICATION

The variation in the thickness of layers in sedimentary rock is quantified by assigning named ranges of bed thicknesses. The following criteria quantify and name standardized bed thicknesses:

$$> 300\text{cm} = \text{massive bedding}$$
$$100 - 300\text{cm} = \text{very thickly bedded}$$
$$30 - 100\text{cm} = \text{thick bedded}$$
$$10 - 30\text{cm} = \text{medium bedded}$$
$$3 - 10\text{cm} = \text{thinly bedded}$$
$$0.3 - 1.0\text{cm} = \text{thickly laminated}$$
$$< 0.3\text{cm} = \text{laminated}$$

Sedimentary rocks will break apart according to their hardness and internal structure. Massively bedded rocks tend to be harder to break and have generally higher compressive strengths when tested in a laboratory setting. Thinly bedded or laminated sedimentary rocks tend to be fissile or friable in general and do not possess breaking resistance or high compressive strengths. Degree of cementation is a very important component as a massive, poorly-cemented sedimentary rock could be quite friable and split easily.

IDENTIFICATION OF FAULTING ON A GEOLOGIC MAP

Identification of faulting on a geologic map is easily accomplished by observing disruption in normal sedimentary outcrop patterns or sections. Even when faults are not marked on the map, it is possible to identify sedimentary outcrop pattern irregularities. Sedimentary rocks units typically produce unbroken polygons on a geologic map, unless they are severely folded. Sedimentary units or groups of units which truncate against each other are a major fault indicator. Conversely, thickening of sedimentary units that cannot be attributable to folding is indicative of faulting. If two beds lie on opposite sides of a fault and have moved along either the strike or dip of the fault, they may either repeat or be absent after erosion. If the strike of the sedimentary beds is cut in a perpendicular fashion by a fault, there will be discontinuities as a result of the offset.

CREATION OF A DIVERSE ARRAY OF SEDIMENTARY PRODUCTS BY WEATHERING AND EROSION

Detritus, consisting of fragments of rocks and minerals, is moved by the surface processes of weathering and erosion. Moving particles drop out when the energy of transportation drops below that needed to carry these particles. This is known as clastic sedimentation. Another common type of sedimentary deposition occurs when material that is dissolved in water precipitates out to form sediment. This type of sedimentation is known as chemical sedimentation. A third process involves living organisms which extract ions in water to construct shells and bones. This material collects after the death of the organism and is described as biogenic sedimentation. Most of all sedimentary rocks (95%) consist of sandstones, mudrocks (made up of silt and clay-sized fragments), and carbonate rocks (made up of mostly calcite, aragonite, or dolomite). Weathering and erosion release all of these materials to be re-incorporated into new sedimentary rocks.

VARVES

Varving involves a two-phase sedimentary package or sequence of beds that were deposited in a body of still water. Varves are specifically characterized by yearly cyclical deposition. A varve includes one set or thin pair of graded layers seasonally deposited in a glacial lake or other body of stillwater. Varves are frequently observed associated with glaciation. A glacial varve sequence consists of a lower layer, formed in summer when relatively coarse-grained, light-colored sediment accumulates through the rapid melting of ice; and a thinner layer consisting of very fine-grained dark sediment slowly deposited from suspension in quiet water while the streams are ice bound. Counting and correlation of varves have been used to measure the ages of Pleistocene glacial deposits.

DEPOSITION OF EVAPORITES

All water bodies on the surface and in aquifers contain dissolved salts. If a body of water becomes restricted in a closed basin and inflow of fresh water is restricted such that it remains below the value of net evaporation, dissolved salts will begin to concentrate. With continued evaporation, dissolved salt concentrations may become oversaturated and minerals called evaporites will begin to precipitate out. The main groups of evaporite minerals are: Halides (halite, sylvite, and fluorite), Sulfates (gypsum, barite, anhydrite), Nitrates (nitratite, niter), Borates (borax), and Carbonates (trona). Evaporite minerals start to precipitate when their concentration in water reaches such a level that they can no longer exist as solutes. These minerals will precipitate out of solution in reverse order of their solubilities. The order of precipitation of the evaporite minerals is: 1) calcite and dolomite, 2) gypsum and anhydrite, 3) halite, and 4) potassium and magnesium salts.

STRATIFORM AND STRATABOUND DEPOSITS

A stratiform deposit is one in which the target rock or mineral is contained in or constitutes layers in a sedimentary, metamorphic or igneous layered sequence. Stratiform deposits are strictly syngenetic deposits, meaning the mineralization formed at the time of the deposition or crystallization of the host layer. This deposit will not necessarily be confined to a single bed or strata but will assume the general tabular shape and aspect of deposits hosted by a particular bed. Stratabound deposits are mineral deposit contained in a single stratigraphic unit. Stratabound deposit refers to a number of differently oriented orebodies contained typically within a sedimentary rock unit. Stratabound mineral deposits are usually epigenetic deposits such as metasomatic replacements. A stratabound deposit is generally controlled structurally and chemically by the strata or horizon which hosts it.

Geomorphology, Surficial Processes, and Quaternary Geology

KARST TOPOGRAPHY AND TERRAIN

Karst topography is a landscape that has been shaped by the dissolution of a soluble layer or layers of bedrock, usually carbonate rock such as limestone or dolomite. These landscapes display distinctive surface features and underground drainage, and in some examples, there may be little or no surface drainage. Some areas of karst topography, such as southern Missouri and northern Arkansas in the United States, are underlain by thousands of caves. Karst landforms are caused by mildly acidic groundwater exposed to soluble bedrock. Carbonic acid causing these features is formed by atmospheric carbon dioxide dissolves in the water. In the United States, karst regions occur in every state. The largest are in central Florida, south central Indiana, and southwestern Mississippi.

The following features are found in the depressions of karst terrain:

- sinkholes: round or roughly elliptical depressions ranging in diameter from a few feet to 100's of feet. Created by bedrock collapse or the dissolution of bedrock by groundwater
- sinkhole pond: the result of clay clogging a developing or existing sinkhole resulting in the formation of a localized perched water table
- swallow hole: the opening at the bottom of the sinkhole through which water can flow into a space below the surface
- polje: A karst field or karst plain. Derives from the Slavic for *field*.
- sinkhole or karst plain: a region characterized by sinkholes or karst topography. Krs, a limestone plateau in the Dinaric Alps of northwestern Yugoslavia and northeastern Italy is the type locality for karst topography.

The karstification of a landscape has the potential to generate many different features both on the surface and beneath it. Following terms all refer to karst-related subsurface disruptions:

- karst window: any opening in a cave, sinkhole, or karst feature that penetrates to the surface
- uvala: a karst window with a length greater than 1000 feet
- solution-subsidence trough: a depression longer than 10 miles caused by subsidence and solution along a fault
- sinking creek: a creek or stream that starts on the surface and disappears underground
- sink: the terminal end of the sinking creek
- blind valley: a valley that terminates in a swallow hole
- solution/karst valley: the type of blind valley located between surface and subsurface drainage

The following structures are formed in karst terrain by the actions of carbonate-rich groundwater seepage and dissolution/precipitation of minerals:

- natural totals and bridges: formed by water that dissolves rock underneath karst terrain
- hum: individual remains of hills left behind after the dissolution of rock
- caverns: interconnected caves with many levels and extending in all directions

56

- travertine: dense, finely crystalline limestone. Frequently massive and concretionary. Typically, white, tan, or cream and commonly displaying a fibrous or concentric banded structure. Formed by chemical precipitation of calcium carbonate from solution in surface and ground waters
- dripstone: any cave deposit of calcite or other mineral formed by dripping water, including stalactites and stalagmites.
- helictite: a small thin structure formed by persistent but small quantities of water trickling out of a hole forming a distorted twig like lateral projection of calcium carbonate

GLACIERS

To be considered a glacier, a snowfield must possess some of the following characteristics: a large mass of ice formed, at least in part, on land by the compaction and recrystallization of snow, moving slowly by creep downslope or outward in all directions due to the stress of its own weight, and surviving from year to year. Glaciers have an upper part that receives most of the snowfall called the accumulation zone. The depth of ice in the accumulation zone exerts a downward force sufficient to cause deep erosion of the rock. On the opposite end of the glacier, at its foot or terminal, is the deposition or ablation zone, where more ice is lost through melting than gained from snowfall and sediment is deposited. The place where the glacier thins to nothing is called the ice front. Due to erosive forces at the edges of the moving ice, glaciers turn V-shaped river-carved valleys into U-shaped glacial valleys. In United States, glacier formations are found in Alaska, as well as in the Rocky, Sierra, and Cascade Mountains.

The following depositional features have been formed by glaciers:

- moraine: a mound, elongate ridge, or other accumulation of unsorted and unstratified glacial drift. Typically composed of till deposited chiefly by direct action of glacier ice. Moraines produce a variety of topographic landforms that are generally independent of control by the buried surface on which the drift lies. Caused through direct deposition.
- valley train: a linear accumulation of boulders and cobbles confined between two rock walls, moraines, or by unmelted ice. Caused through direct deposition.
- lacustrine plain: a large area characterized by lakes and proglacial deposits. Lakes may have dropstones if icebergs once floated in the lake. Other lakes associated with glaciers are supraglacial lakes and kettle lakes
- knob and basin topography: mounds and hillocks of material scattered around small basins, formed by the deposition of glacial drift

The following erosional features are associated with Alpine glaciers:

- cirque: an amphitheatre-like topographic feature formed at the head of a glacier by erosion. Cirques form in conditions which are favorable, for example in the northern hemisphere includes the north-east slope being in shade and away from prevailing winds. These areas are sheltered from heat, and thus, they encourage the accumulation of snow
- tarn: a small but deep lake found in the basin of a cirque; created by the melting of a glacier head
- glacial polish: a smooth surface located on bedrock and the results of abrasion and movement of glaciers
- striations: multiple scratches or grooves, generally parallel, inscribed on a bedrock outcropping or surface by a glacial event

57

The following valley features are observed in alpine glacier regions:

- glacial trough: a valley with precipitous sides coming down from a cirque
- glacial step/stairway: a series of ice steps that connect a cirque with the end of a glacial trough. Steps are created by downhill-moving glaciers that differentially erode layers of bedrock
- paternoster lakes: a group or collection of lakes found on glacial steps
- hanging valley: a tributary glacial valley that has been stranded or had its streambed undercut by the mainstem glacier, producing a steep cliff. After glacial retreat, a waterfall frequently connects hanging valleys to mainstem stream
- fjord: a glacially carved U-shaped valley that has been flooded by seawater and is open at its mouth to the ocean
- trough lake: a glacial trough filled with water, but above sea level

Erosion due to alpine glaciation and cirque development causes some steep landforms at points where cirques intersect. Some of Earth's most spectacular mountain scenery occurs in glaciated areas with these steep and pointed features. The following are pointed features of a glacier:

- arête: a knife-edged rock divide between two glacial cirques
- col: a connection across the rock arête dividing two cirques
- horn: a peak or pinnacle thinned and eroded by three or more glacial cirques. The Matterhorn of the Swiss Alps was formed in this manner
- monument/tind: a horn that has been separated by itself by intersecting cirques
- truncated or faceted spurs: triangular hillside features due to glacial erosion of the headlands between two former streams.

Unlike alpine glaciers which are restricted to valleys, continental glaciers advance along a wide front and cover large areas. As recently as 12,000 years ago, continental glaciers covered much of the northern United States and much if not all of Canada. Some of the features that allow us to recognize areas that were covered by continental glaciation in the past are: end moraines, ablation moraine, large areas covered with glacial till. Also, the following geomorphic features and landforms are indicative of continental glaciation: eskers, drumlins, ground moraine, glacial lakes, kettle ponds, and kames. Fluvial features contributable to continental glaciation include: braided outwash streams and outwash plains. Continental glaciation has occurred cyclically over time. Currently there are active continental glaciers in Greenland and Antarctica.

The following depositional features are associated with continental glaciation:

- till plain: a large area covered with ground or ablation moraine consisting of dominantly unsorted and unstratified drift. This generally unconsolidated material was deposited directly by and underneath a glacier without subsequent reworking by melt water. Consists of a heterogeneous mixture of clay, silt, sand, gravel, and boulders ranging widely in size and shape
- swell and swale topography: a region created by thick deposits of till with clay content. Produces gently rolling topography. A swell is created by the advance of the glacier, while a swale is formed by the retreat of a glacier
- outwash plain: proglacial melt water deposits consisting of unconfined sorted sediments; stream pattern depends upon angle of topography

The following structures are created by deposition associated with continental glaciation:

- **drumlin**: elongated and symmetrically arranged hills of glacial drift which may have been formed by reworking of older glacial sediments. Some drumlins may be cut and formed from sediments that were confined by floating ice
- **esker**: a narrow and sinuous ridge of graded sand and gravel deposited by streams that are supraglacial, englacial or subglacial
- **kettle**: a shallow bowl-shaped depression formed when a large block of ice is stranded in outwash or mixed outwash and till during glacial degradation. Upon melting of the ice block, the ensuing depression may become a kettle-lake
- **kame/kame terrace**: a low steep-sided hill or mound composed of poorly sorted sand and gravel that was deposited by melt water cascading into crevasses near the melting edge of a glacier

WIND EROSION AND DEPOSITION

Wind erosion and deposition are controlled by grain size. It requires less wind energy to move silt than sand. Deposits that occur as a result of wind deposition are termed eolian deposits. Wind erosion removes material light enough to be transported and these particles will therefore be moved to another area and re-deposited. This is called deflation. Wind suspended particles may ultimately impact on solid objects causing erosion termed abrasion. Eolian deposits occur as loess and dune sand and include sedimentary structures such as wind-formed ripple marks. Fine-grained, silt sized eolian deposits can occur at any elevation and wind-borne silt can travel long distances. Eolian sand deposits occur closer to their original source due to less transport potential.

The following features are created by wind erosion:

- **yardang**: a ridge formed by the action of wind-abrasion in cohesive material
- **ventifact**: colluvial material or large cobbles that have been highly polished or shaped by wind abrasion caused by airborne sand
- **pedestal rock**: an isolated erosional remnant of rock supported by a thinner pedestal. Caused by differential erosion
- **blow out**: a small cup- or trough-shaped hollow or depression that is formed by wind erosion on a sand dune or other unconsolidated deposit. Typically occurs in areas of shifting sand or loose soil where protective vegetation is absent, disturbed, or destroyed.
- **desert pavement**: a natural deposit of residual wind-polished pebbles, boulders, and other rock fragments that mantles a desert surface. Typically occurs in areas where wind action or sheet wash have removed all smaller particles.

Dunes are large wind-derived accumulations of sand that are located anywhere there is a source and a mode of emplacement, such as beach or desert environments. There are four basic types of dune:

- **parabolic dune**: U-shaped mounds of sand with convex noses and elongated arms. Sometimes these dunes are called blowout or hairpin dunes and are well known in coastal deserts. Unlike crescent shaped dunes, their crests point upwind. The elongated arms of parabolic dunes follow rather than lead because they have been fixed by vegetation
- **transverse dune**: Barchan dunes
- **longitudinal dune**: longitudinal dunes, also called Seif dunes, elongate parallel to the prevailing wind, possibly caused by a larger dune having its smaller sides blown away. Seif dunes are sharp-crested and are common in the Sahara

- barchan dune: crescent-shaped mounds are generally wider than they are long. The slip face is on the dune's concave side. These dunes form under winds that blow from one direction, and they also are known as transverse dunes.

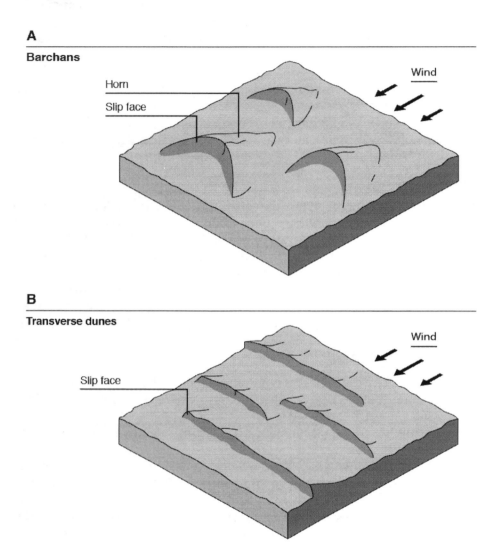

A

Barchans

Horn

Slip face

Wind

B

Transverse dunes

Slip face

Wind

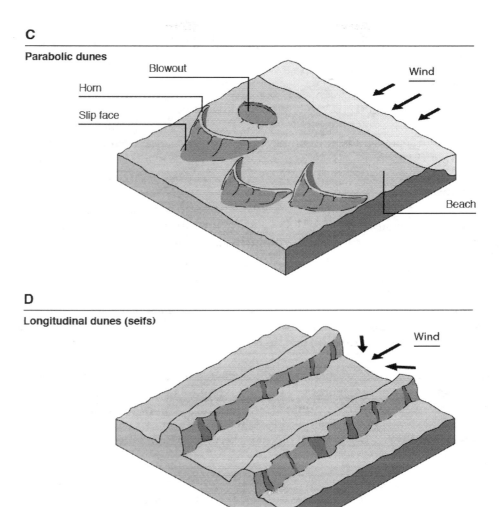

C

Parabolic dunes

Horn

Blowout

Slip face

Wind

Beach

D

Longitudinal dunes (seifs)

Wind

The following are major categories of sand-based depositional feature:

- ripple/ridge: an uneven surface or area constructed of subparallel small-scale ridges formed at the interface between a fluid and unconsolidated sediments. Typically produced by wind action, subaqueously by currents, or by the agitation of wave action. Features trend at right angles or obliquely to the direction of fluid flow.
- sand shadow/sand drift: elongated and tapering sand formations that occur behind obstructions due to deceleration and general diminishment of transport energy
- dune: a hill-shaped deposit of sand attributable to eolian processes. Dunes occur in varying morphologies and sizes based on the dynamics of wind and particle sizes which formed them. Typically, dunes are longer on the windward side where the material is pushed up the dune, and shorter on the leeward side, or slip face
- whaleback or sand levee: a large sinuous ridge or elongated hill that runs parallel or subparallel to the direction of the prevailing wind
- undulation: a small whaleback
- sand sheet: a flat area characterized by ripples

Structure, Tectonics, and Seismology

EARTH'S COMPOSITION

The Earth has an outer silicate solid crust, a highly viscous mantle, a liquid outer core that is much less viscous than the mantle, and a solid inner core. The crust of the Earth is composed of a great variety of igneous, metamorphic, and sedimentary rocks. The oceanic crust is different from the continental crust in that the former is from 3 to 6 miles in thickness and is mostly composed of mafic minerals. The continental crust is from 20 to 30 miles thick and is mainly composed of lighter silicate rocks. Below the crust is the mantle, an approximately 2900 km thick zone that comprises 70 percent of Earth's volume. The distinction between crust and mantle is based on chemistry, rock types, rheology and seismic characteristics. The Earth's liquid outer core surrounds the inner core and is believed to be composed of iron mixed with nickel and trace amounts of lighter elements.

PLATE BOUNDARIES

Three types of plate boundaries occur depending upon the way the tectonic plates move relative to each other. Transform boundaries occur where plates slide past each other along transform faults. The relative motion of the two plates is either sinistral (left side toward the observer) or dextral (right side toward the observer). Transform plate boundaries produce devastating earthquakes. The San Andreas fault in California is currently a transform boundary. Divergent boundaries occur where two tectonic plates are pulling apart, as in mid-ocean ridges and zones of rifting. Convergent boundaries occur when two tectonic plates are being pushed together. Typically, one of the plates will be forced under the other creating a subduction zone. Convergent plate boundaries and subduction zones produce volcanic and plutonic activity.

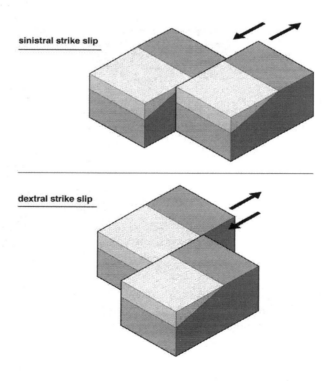

62

Mometrix

SEISMIC WAVES

A seismic wave is a wave that travels through the Earth, most often as the result of an earthquake. Seismic waves are also caused to propagate by the continual pounding of ocean waves against cliffs, or by the wind. The two types of seismic waves are body waves and surface waves. Body waves travel through the interior of the Earth along pathways that are bent by the varying density and stiffness of earth materials encountered. Two individual types of body waves are: P waves, also called longitudinal or compressional waves; and S waves, referred to as transverse or shear waves. P wave propagation involves the ground being alternately compressed and dilated in the direction of propagation. S waves propagate as the ground is displaced perpendicularly to the direction of propagation. Surface waves are analogous to the waves that form in water and travel just under the Earth's surface. They travel more slowly than body waves. Because of their low frequency, long duration, and large amplitude, they can be the most destructive type of seismic wave.

MEASURING EARTHQUAKES

Earthquakes are caused by a sudden release of energy from the Earth's crust. Earthquakes are recorded with a seismometer, also known as a seismograph. There are a few different magnitude scales used to measure earthquakes. The Richter scale, also known as the local magnitude scale, utilizes a single number system to quantify the seismic energy released by an earthquake. It is a base-10 logarithmic scale obtained by calculating the logarithm of the combined horizontal amplitude of the largest displacement from zero on a seismometer output. There are other types of magnitude scale, including individual scales for surface waves and body waves. The Mercalli and Rossi-Forel scales measure the intensity of an earthquake by assessing its effects on structures and human beings. Intensity of shaking is measured on the modified Mercalli scale.

CALCULATING SEISMIC MOMENT, MOMENT MAGNITUDE, AND EARTHQUAKE ENERGY RELEASE

Earthquakes are recorded with a seismometer, also known as a seismograph. Earthquakes are also measured and described by the following physical characteristics: seismic moment (M_0) is calculated with the following equation:

$$M_0 = \mu A u$$

where M_0 is seismic moment in dyne-cm or N/m, μ is the shear modulus of the crustal segment containing the fault, A is the fault area of interest, and u is the average slip along the fault.

Moment magnitude (M) is calculated with the following equation:

$$M = \frac{\log M_0}{1.5} - 10.7$$

Energy release (E_r) is calculated with the following equation:

$$E_r = 1.6M_0 \times 10^{-5}$$

63

EARTHQUAKE HAZARD TERMS

The following terms relate to the hazards of earthquakes and could occur on earthquake hazard maps, reports, or emergency response documents:

- seismic zone factor: the number assigned to every seismic zone on a hazard map corresponding to the estimated highest amount of ground acceleration; these numbers are used when determining locations for structures
- maximum capable earthquake: an estimation of the greatest possible earthquake that could be expected to strike a particular location; expressed as a probability of occurrence
- response spectrum: a graphical depiction of ground motion, in which spectral acceleration is plotted against period
- time history: ground acceleration over time calculated for a particular location during an earthquake event. It is used to develop a response spectrum

ACUTE ANGLE OF A RIGHT TRIANGLE (A) AND ITS NEIGHBORING SIDES (ADJACENT, OPPOSITE, HYPOTENUSE)

In a right triangle, the relationship between the lengths of the sides can be determined with the trigonometric function's sine, cosine, and tangent, if the value of the two acute angles can be determined. By selecting and knowing the value in degrees of one of the acute angles, and the length of one of the sides, the lengths of any of the other sides can be determined. The sine of the known angle is equal to a ratio of the length of the opposite leg of the triangle divided by the length of the hypotenuse of the triangle. The cosine of the known angle is equal to a ratio of the length of the adjacent leg of the triangle divided by the length of the hypotenuse. The tangent of the known angle is equal to a ratio of the length of the opposite leg divided by the length of the adjacent leg of the triangle.

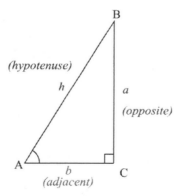

REPRESENTING THE ATTITUDE OF A PLANE IN SPACE OR THE BEARING AND PLUNGE OF A LINE

When describing the orientation of a plane in three dimensions, the two essential components are strike and dip. Strike is defined as the course or bearing of the outcrop of an inclined bed, vein, or fault plane on a level surface. It is the azimuth or bearing of a horizontal line perpendicular to the direction of dip. Dip is defined as the maximum angle at which a bed, stratum, or vein is inclined from the horizontal, measured perpendicular to the strike and in the vertical plane. Collectively, strike and dip constitute bedding attitude. In standard geologic literature, attitude is notated with either a quadrant-based or 360-degree azimuth to display strike direction, followed by the dip azimuth bearing and value. The dip bearing azimuth is required because there are two possible dip directions from any strike line. It is also possible to list only dip and dip direction, assuming that strike will be 90° from the direction of dip.

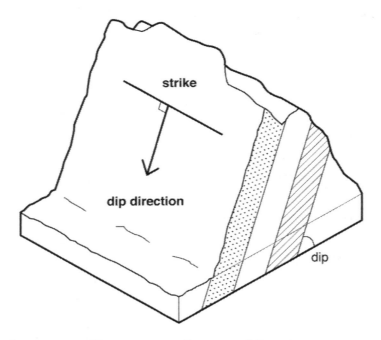

DETERMINING THE STRIKE OF A PLANE WITH GRAPHIC METHODS

The attitude of a plane can be uniquely determined if three points of elevation on the plane are known, provided that we assume a constant dip value. True north direction must also be known to produce an absolute attitude. In many geological situations this involves knowing the depth beneath the surface at three localities for a desired plane. The three points must be plotted on a 2-dimensional map at their precise locations and to scale with each other. A straight line is drawn connecting the deepest and the shallowest points. The point along this line corresponding with the depth of the medium depth point is determined by drawing structure contours along the line. The projection method involves making a fold line and then projecting points as a cross-section. The simplified projection method also involves a fold line, which is drawn between the high and low points and indicates the apparent dip direction. In the proportional method, the map scale is transferred onto the three points, and parallel lines are drawn to calculate strike.

SOLVING A THREE-POINT PROBLEM FOR THE DIP

When you are given three points with different elevation, the north heading, and the map scale, you can choose one of two methods to graph the information. The three-point problem involves plotting the points on a 2-dimensional map at their precise locations and to scale with each other. A straight line is drawn connecting the deepest and the shallowest points. The point along this line corresponding with the depth of the medium depth point is determined by drawing structure contours along the line. A line drawn between the medium-depth point and the new point will define strike direction. Dip can then be calculated trigonometrically. With the projection method, a strike line is run from the lowest point in the fold line made in the dip direction. The dip angle is considered to be the angle between the line connecting the projected points and the fold line.

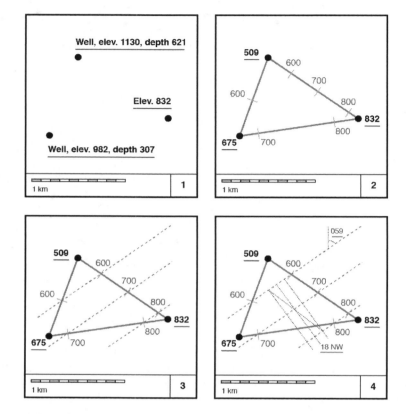

CALCULATING BOTH STRIKE AND DIP

In order to calculate strike, one must contrast elevations with the distances between points. Also, one must be well versed in right angle trigonometry. First, locate a point, expressed here as X, on the line in between the highest and lowest points, A and C, respectively. X should have the same elevation of the middle point B. Then, the equation can be: $(B – C)/(A – C) = (CX)/(CA)$, or (mid-point elevation – low point elevation)/(high point elevation – low point elevation) = (distance from low point to point X)/(distance from low point to high point). The answer is the measure of the distance from C to X along the line CA. The line that runs between X and B is the strike. In order to determine dip, the following equation can be used: $\text{Tan (angle)} = \text{rise/run}$.

FOLD LINE

A useful visual tool in geologic map interpretation involves the use of a fold line. A fold line can be laid out along the direction of the dip of a bed or geologic horizon when strike, dip, and the direction are indicated on the map. One half of the map will then indicate the horizontal map view, while the other half will indicate a cross-sectional, vertical view. The vertical view will contain the dip line, while the map view will include strike line and dip direction. This method of orienting a map can help you to envision the actual geometric relationship between orientation of dip, dip direction and strike. This graphical method is useful in envisioning underground structure or for plotting underground intersections between tabular geologic features or drill hole intercept.

MAPPING THE INTERSECTION OF A TOPOGRAPHIC SURFACE WITH A BEDDING SURFACE

When performing an outcrop pattern problem, the assumption is made that all beds are of uniform thickness and that they have constant strike and dip. Using a topographical map and given strike, the outcrop patterns for inclined beds can be determined graphically or mathematically. Using the graphical method, topographical contours will be drawn along the tip line, in the same direction as the dip. The vertical scale will be drawn perpendicular to the strike. After this is done, the outcrop pattern will be indicated by the intersection of the contours in the dip line. The location of visible outcrop bands will be indicated by lines parallel to the strike lines from those intersections. To use the mathematical method, solve the equation: Tan (angle) = rise/run, thereby calculating the spaces between the contour lines.

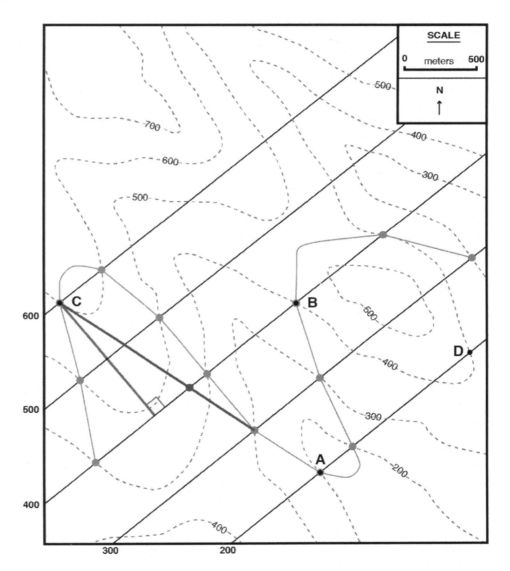

THICKNESS PROBLEMS

There are four basic types of thickness problem. Before any of them can be solved, the cross-section in the dip direction perpendicular to strike must be drawn. The following terms are required in graphical solutions: thickness (t), outcrop width on the ground perpendicular to strike (w), dip angle (δ), angle between strike and traverse direction (β), traverse distance across the outcrop (l), slope angle (σ), and slope angle along the traverse ($σ_1$). The four scenarios are:

- horizontal ground surface, outcrop width perpendicular to strike: t = w sin δ
- horizontal ground surface, outcrop not perpendicular to strike: t = l sin β sin δ
- sloped ground surface, outcrop width perpendicular to strike: t = w sin (angle)
- sloped ground surface, outcrop width not perpendicular to strike: either t = l (sin δ cos $σ_1$ sin β – sin $σ_1$ cos δ), if the slope and dip are in the same direction, or t = l (sin δ cos $σ_1$ sin β + sin $σ_1$ cos δ), if the slope and dip are in opposite directions

DEPTH PROBLEMS

In order to solve a depth problem, you must be provided with a point, strike, scale, and north heading. The easiest method of solving a depth problem is by constructing a geologic map projection utilizing trigonometry. There are four basic categories of depth problem:

- horizontal ground surface, distance from surface to where depth has been measured is perpendicular to strike along dip direction
- horizontal ground surface, distance from surface to where depth is measured not perpendicular to strike along dip direction
- sloped ground surface, transverse from outcrop to location of depth measurement is not perpendicular to strike
- sloped ground surface, transverse from outcrop to location of depth measurement is perpendicular to strike along dip direction

The easiest method of solving a depth problem is with trigonometry. There are two ways of doing this:

- scaled cross-section method: strike, dip direction, and perpendicular line from outcrop to the point of interest should be drawn. Relationship between strike and traverse direction indicates the type of depth problem. Scale is used to measure the distance between dip angle, which is measured at the intersection of outcrop with traverse, and the point of interest, which is marked by a perpendicular line from the traverse direction intersecting the line of the dip angle
- projection method: find a point where strike line projects under the point of interest. Then, subtract strike elevation from the elevation of the point

SOLVING APPARENT DIP/TRUE DIP PROBLEMS

When the dip of a plane in relation to the horizontal is not measured perpendicular to the strike of that plane, the resulting value is known as apparent dip. The angle between strike and apparent dip direction (β) indicates the relationship between apparent dip angle (α) and dip (δ). Apparent dip and true dip problems can be solved with the following four methods: graphic projections, alignment diagram, trigonometric calculation, and the use of an equal area stereonet. The trigonometric method involves right angle geometry and the equation tan α = tan δ sin β. The graphic method requires the use of fold-line diagrams in which right triangles are constructed using the dip angle and the apparent dip direction. The equal area stereo net allows the user to calculate dip and apparent dip from a graphical representation of interaction of planes upon a sphere.

68

Hydrogeology and Geochemistry

GROUND WATER LOCATION TERMS

The vadose zone is the area between the ground surface and the saturated water table. The vadose zone is commonly known as the unsaturated zone. As the water in the vadose zone is less pressurized than atmospheric pressure, this water is retained through the combined processes of adhesion and capillary action. Capillary action supports the vadose zone above the saturated water table. The capillary fringe is the zone in which groundwater seeps from the water table to fill pores upward into the vadose zone. In areas with good soil development with a wide range in pore size, the unsaturated zone can be several times thicker than the saturated zone. The water table is defined as the surface between the zone of saturation and the zone of aeration. The water table is the surface of a body of unconfined ground water at which the pressure is equal to that of the atmosphere.

AQUIFER, CONFINED AQUIFER, AND UNCONFINED AQUIFER

An aquifer is defined as an underground stratum or zone below the surface of the Earth capable of producing water. The zone must yield water in sufficient quantity to be of value as a source of supply. In an unconfined aquifer the system is open to exchange as the upper boundary of the aquifer is at the water table or phreatic surface. Usually the shallowest aquifer at a given location is unconfined, meaning it does not have a confining layer (an aquitard or aquiclude) between it and the surface. Unconfined aquifers are readily recharged by rainfall, streams and lakes which are in hydraulic connection with it. A confined aquifer has the water table above its upper boundary (an aquitard or aquiclude), and are typically found below unconfined aquifers.

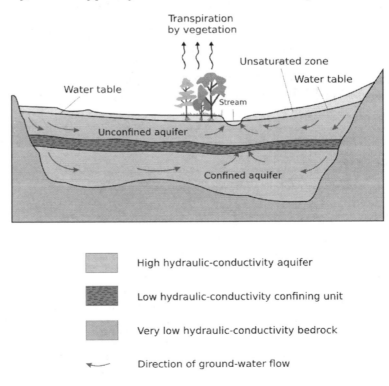

69

POROSITY VS. PERMEABILITY

Porosity, expressed as the letter n, is the percentage of a soil or rock that is occupied by pore space. The effective porosity (n_e) is the proportion of the volume of a rock or soil that is comprised of interconnected pores through which fluid may flow. Effective porosity is the ratio of the volume of liquid that a given mass of saturated rock or soil will yield by gravity compared to the volume of that mass. Permeability, expressed with the letter k, is defined as the capacity for a rock or soil to transmit a fluid. Degree of permeability depends upon the size and shape of the pores, and the nature and extent of interconnections. It is measured by the rate at which a fluid of standard viscosity can move a given distance through a given interval of time. The unit of permeability is the Darcy. The intrinsic permeability (k_i) of a rock or soil is the ease with which fluid flows through it at a specific hydraulic gradient.

WATER'S POTENTIAL ENERGY TO ITS PRESSURE AND HEIGHT

Head, or hydrostatic head, is defined as the pressure exerted at any given point in a body of water at rest. The hydrostatic pressure of ground water is generally due to the weight of water at higher levels in the zone of saturation. A potentiometric surface is an imaginary surface representing the total head of ground water. It is defined by the level to which water will rise in a well. The water table is a particular potentiometric surface. Hydraulic gradient is the difference in potential energy between two points on the body of water, divided by the horizontal distance between the two points. The hydraulic gradient describes and quantifies the slope of the water table or potentiometric surface.

WATER WELL TERMS

The area of influence of a water well is the area surrounding the well within which the piezometric surface has been lowered when pumping has achieved the maximum steady rate flow.

The piezometric surface is an imaginary surface representing the total head of ground water defined by the level to which water will rise in a well.

The cone of depression is a conical area that is produced in a water table or in the piezometric surface by pumping. It forms because water must flow through progressively smaller cross sections as it nears a well, steepening the hydraulic gradient.

Drawdown is a change in the hydraulic head at a well due to pumping relative to background conditions.

Well efficiency refers to yield and recharge characteristics of a well.

AQUIFER PROPERTIES THAT AFFECT THE FLOW OF GROUND WATER

Aquifers are typically saturated regions of the subsurface which produce an economically feasible quantity of water. Many quantified aquifer parameters affect the flow of groundwater while others describe aquifer volume and storage capacity. Specific storage, storativity, specific yield, and specific capacity are aquifer properties that measure of the ability of an aquifer to release groundwater from storage due to a decline in hydraulic head. These properties are related to groundwater flow in aquifers but do not directly affect groundwater flow. Other aquifer properties such as porosity have to do with the ability of the aquifer to store water. The parameters that describe the ability of ground water to flow through an aquifer are transmissivity, hydraulic conductivity, and intrinsic permeability. These factors are regulated by the differences in the potential energy of the groundwater, which in turn are a factor of the water distribution. These and several other attributes are used to derive the groundwater flow equation, a mathematical relationship used to describe the flow of groundwater through an aquifer.

CONTAINMENT OF WATER IN UNDERGROUND STRUCTURES

The following terms relate to the containment of water in underground structures:

- field capacity: The quantity of water held by soil or rock against the force of gravity.
- hydraulic conductivity: the ability of a porous rock or soil to transmit water. It is a factor of the rock or soil's permeability, as well as the viscosity of the fluid
- transmissivity: the quantitative assessment of the ability of an aquifer to transmit water. It is the amount of water that can travel through one unit of aquifer with one unit of hydraulic gradient. Transmissivity (T) is related to prevailing kinematic viscosity, which is calculated $T = Kb$, where b is the saturated thickness of the aquifer and K representing hydraulic conductivity.

CATEGORIES OF WATER IN HYDROGEOLOGY

The following categories of water are designated in hydrogeology:

- connate water: water that was incorporated into the interstices of a sedimentary rock at the time of sedimentation and deposition.
- juvenile water: water originating from the interior of the Earth that has never been introduced or circulated in the ground water system.
- perched groundwater: unconfined ground water separated from an underlying aquifer by an intervening unsaturated zone.
- runoff: that part of precipitation appearing in surface streams. May be caused by direct precipitation or by cyclical processes such as seasonal thaw of snow pack.
- underflow: groundwater that flows below the alluvial plane of a surface stream or beneath the stream bed. Common in arid environments.

HYPOTHETICAL PATHS THAT WATER MOLECULES CAN TAKE THROUGH THE HYDROLOGIC CYCLE

Water moves throughout the Earth through different pathways and at different rates. Evaporation of water from the ocean forms clouds that drift over the land and produce rain. The rainwater flows into lakes, rivers, or aquifers. The water in lakes, rivers, and aquifers either evaporates back to the atmosphere or eventually flows back to the ocean, completing a cycle. A water molecule may be taken up by vegetation and stored, eventually to be released back into the atmosphere in a process known as transpiration. Water that infiltrates the ground may eventually wind up in an aquifer, or it may end up as a constituent of sedimentary rock. Water included in sedimentary rocks or in small fluid inclusions in igneous rocks can be preserved for long periods of time.

INPUTS OF GROUNDWATER

A model of groundwater inventory can contain multiple different inputs of groundwater.

- The underflow beneath the bed of streams in the area is one way the groundwater can be introduced to an aquifer.
- An aquifer may receive water from irrigation or from a recharge well.
- Precipitation or other runoff can end up in an aquifer through percolation or as infiltration.
- Groundwater inputs can come from the water that flows into a stream or river when this recharge reaches the water table.

71

- The confining bed around a perched aquifer or barrier between two aquifers may become altered, causing groundwater inflow.
- Groundwater inputs could also come from glacial and bedrock sources, depending upon yields and drawdown and transmissivity characteristics.

LOSSES OF GROUNDWATER

A model of groundwater inventory will necessarily contain a number of different possible losses of groundwater.

- Groundwater losses are caused directly by location and pumping capacity of specific facilities as well as by aggregate agricultural water use and consumptive use by townships.
- Water can be lost to evaporation from storage facilities and from surface waters.
- Groundwater may also be lost due to uptake by vegetation in a process known as evapotranspiration. The aquifer may seek a bit of water, especially if it has a nonzero hydraulic gradient or is pressurized itself.
- Drawdown from individual wells and infiltration galleries may artificially remove water from an aquifer.
- Leakage from the confining beds that surround an aquifer may decrease groundwater inventory.

FILLING AND EMPTYING OF AQUIFERS

An unconfined aquifer is by definition an aquifer that has an open upper boundary coinciding with the water table. Thus, unconfined aquifers are often referred to as water table or phreatic aquifers as they do not have confining aquitard or aquiclude layer between them and the surface. An unconfined aquifer receives recharge water directly from surface precipitation, or from a body of surface water, such as a lake or stream, that is in hydrologic conductivity with it. Unconfined aquifers have relatively high storativities and hence release water from storage by the mechanism of actually draining the pores of the aquifer, releasing relatively large amounts of water. This can occur through extraction from surface or underground wells and/or loss to a deeper confined aquifer through seepage.

CONFINED AQUIFERS

Confined aquifers have the water table above their upper boundary and are typically found below unconfined aquifers. Usually some impermeable layer, such as an aquitard or aquiclude, prohibits hydrologic conductivity between confined aquifers and the open, phreatic aquifers above. Frequently a confined aquifer can best be recognized through the aquifer test which yields a low storativity value. This indicates that the aquifer is storing water using the mechanisms of aquifer matrix expansion and the compressibility of water, both of which are relatively quite small compared to unconfined aquifers. Discharge and recharge for confined aquifers is typically much slower than for unconfined aquifers. It is typical for the pressure inside a confined aquifer to be higher than the atmospheric pressure.

DISSOLVED MATERIALS IN GROUNDWATER

Absorption is the assimilation, the taking up, the incorporation of one substance into another. An example is the absorption of a liquid into a solid or the absorption of a gas into a liquid. Adsorption is the adherence of gas molecules to the surface of solids with which they are in contact. The assimilation of gas, vapor, or dissolved matter on the surface of a solid or liquid is also defined as adsorption. Adsorption can also occur as an attachment of a thin film of liquid or gas, commonly of monomolecular thickness, to a solid substrate. The term sorption refers to any type of retention of a material on the surface of another material when the mechanism is unknown or not specified. Ion

72

exchange refers to the migration of ion across a boundary such as the fluid-solid boundary. Ion exchange is typically reversible but can be non-reversible.

THE SPREADING OF DISSOLVED MATERIALS IN GROUNDWATER

Infiltration is the flow of a fluid into a solid substance through pores or small openings. In groundwater issues it is the movement of water into soil or porous rock. Retardation refers to any effect or remediation technique that is aimed at slowing down or stopping the dispersion of ground water contaminates. Diffusion is the net movement of particles or dissolved materials from an area of high concentration to an area of low concentration. Molecules will diffuse in a random fashion between areas of high and low concentration. As time progresses, the gradient will grow increasingly shallow until the concentrations are equalized. Dispersion is the fairly permanent suspension of finely divided but undissolved particles in a fluid. Advection is transport in a fluid. The fluid is described mathematically for such processes as a vector field, and the material transported is described as a scalar concentration of substance, which is present in the fluid.

GROUND WATER STUDY TERMS

The following terms are used in groundwater studies:

- hardness: the degree to which water contains concentrations of dissolved magnesium and calcium in ionic form
- hardpan: a hard, impermeable layer close to the surface of the soil, caused by cementation and mineral precipitation; typical of acidic soils
- leachate: a solution obtained by leaching. Water that has percolated through soil or rock containing soluble substances and that contains certain amounts of these substances in solution
- sodium absorption ratio: the measure of the degree to which calcium in soil has been replaced by sodium. Expressed as a ratio. A soil with a high ratio is not appropriate for vegetation
- tracers: chemical compounds that are introduced into groundwater flow that lend themselves to being detected, either chemically or visually. Used to document flow rates and flow pathways

DISSOLVED MATERIALS IN GROUNDWATER STUDIES

The following terms are used to quantify the dissolved materials when performing groundwater studies:

- milliequivalents per liter (meq/L): defined as concentration in milligrams per liter divided by equivalent weight. It is used to measure the concentration of all the solutes in a solution
- parts per billion (ppb): parts per billion is a value representing concentration of a dissolved substance in a solution. One part per billion is equivalent in concentration to 1 microgram/liter (ug/l). Used to measure the mass of a solute as related to the total mass of the solution
- parts per million (ppm): parts per million is a value representing concentration of a dissolved material in a solution. It is orders of magnitude more concentrated than ppb. One part per million is equivalent in concentration to 1 milligram/liter. Used to measure the mass of the solutes within the total mass of the solution
- picocuries per liter (pCi/L): used to measure radioactive decay; 1 pCi per liter is the amount of material necessary to create 2.22 nuclear transformations every minute

GROUND WATER QUALITY TERMS

The following terms are related to the quality of groundwater:

- effluent: treated or untreated wastes that are released into the environment. May be a liquid, solid, or gaseous product discharged or emerging from a process
- maximum contaminant level (MCL): the maximum amount of contaminants allowed in water being reintroduced into a source of public water. The established MCL levels are based on health risks
- reference dose: the amount of a chemical a human can be exposed to on a daily basis without suffering any adverse health consequences
- secondary maximum contaminant level: the maximum amount of dissolved material in water that can have an effect on taste, appearance, or smell. Generally, not subject to legislation

WATER QUALITY FOR AGRICULTURE

The major water quality issues for agriculture involve potential problems and restricted use due to salinity, rate of water infiltration into the soil, and specific ion toxicity. Salinity is a factor due to a reduction in soil-water availability to crops. Recent research findings on plant response to salinity within the root zone have been updated and crop tolerance values have become available. A water infiltration problem related to water quality is usually associated with both the salinity and sodium content of the water. The potential water quality issue which causes an infiltration problem is based on a combination of the salinity (EC_w) and sodium adsorption ratio (SAR) of water used for irrigation. Specific ion toxicity is a regional or site-specific problem which must be addressed on an individual basis.

EVALUATING SODIUM BUILDUP IN SOILS

Plants are detrimentally affected, both physically and chemically, by excess salts in some soils and by high levels of exchangeable sodium in others. Soils containing accumulations of exchangeable sodium are typically of poor tilth and low permeability. These attributes render these soils unfavorable for plant growth. Simply measuring the level of sodium in a soil does not give an accurate picture of the effect of this sodium on the soil. This is because high levels of sodium in soil can be rendered more harmful and augmented by correspondingly high levels of calcium and magnesium. Soil scientists gauge the effects of sodium on the soil with the equation for sodium absorption ratio (*SAR*):

$$SAR = \frac{Na}{\sqrt{\frac{Ca + Mg}{2}}}$$

where *Na*, *Ca*, and *Mg* represent the amount of sodium, calcium, and magnesium, respectively, in the soil. If the SAR value is lower than 10, the level of sodium in the soil is not considered to be very harmful.

TOTAL DISSOLVED SOLIDS

Total dissolved solids (TDS) refers to the content of all dissolved substances in a liquid. TDS also includes all material in colloidal suspension, including all organic and inorganic material. The requirement is that the solids must be small enough to pass through a filtration system utilizing a sieve size of two micrometers. The two methods used to measure total dissolved solids are gravimetry and electrical conductivity. Gravimetric methods are more accurate than conductivity. Gravimetry involves evaporating the liquid solvent to leave a residue which can weighed with an

74

analytical balance. Electrical conductivity is an estimation of TDS based on a solvents ability to conduct a current. TDS is expressed in units of parts per million (ppm). The largest component of the total dissolved solids is inorganic salt, so TDS is often referred to as salinity. Any water that has a TDS of less than 500 ppm can be consumed by humans. Livestock should not drink water with a TDS of more than 7,100 ppm.

The groundwater classifications based on total dissolved solids (TDS) are as follows: Freshwater is defined as any water with a TDS of less than 500 parts per million (ppm). This value corresponds with the safe drinking water threshold for human beings. Groundwater with TDS values between 500 ppm and 35,000 ppm is considered brackish water. Saline groundwater contains total dissolved solid values between 35,000 and 50,000 ppm. Any groundwater with a TDS greater than 50,000 ppm is considered to be brine. Only three percent of the water on Earth is fresh water, and about two-thirds of this is frozen in glaciers and the polar ice caps. Of the remaining one-third, only 0.3 percent is represented by surface water. The remainder is represented by groundwater.

WATER HARDNESS

Water that is classified as hard has elevated levels of dissolved metals, usually calcium and magnesium. These ions end up in the water because of the rock content of the surrounding aquifer. Calcium usually enters the water as either calcium carbonate ($CaCO_3$) in the form of limestone and chalk, or calcium sulfate ($CaSO_4$) in the form of evaporite mineral deposits. The predominant source of magnesium is dolomite ($CaMg(CO_3)_2$). Hard water does not produce soap lather readily and typically forms a scale in containers in which it has been allowed to evaporate. Total water hardness (including both Ca^{2+} and Mg^{2+} ions) is reported in units of parts per million (ppm) or weight/volume (mg/L) of calcium carbonate ($CaCO_3$) in water. Standard hardness tests typically measure only the total concentrations of calcium and magnesium. In some locations, iron, aluminum, and manganese may also be present at elevated levels. Water is considered slightly hard if concentrations are in the 40 to 60 mg/L range and very hard if concentrations exceed 120 mg/L.

It is possible to remove hardness from water. Temporary hardness can be removed from a water by boiling it which causes the calcium and magnesium to precipitate out of the solution as bicarbonate or carbonate. However, a certain amount of calcium and magnesium will remain in the solution. These ions, along with other iron and manganese ions, constitute non-carbonate hardness. Methods to reduce the hardness of water include distillation, use of a reverse osmosis system, or the use of water softeners. Water softeners utilize a technique called ion exchange in which calcium and magnesium ions are exchanged for sodium ions. Commercially, hard water problems are addressed through the addition of chemicals and by large-scale softening with zeolite and other ion exchange resins.

Because it is the precise mixture of minerals dissolved in the water, together with the water's pH and temperature that determines the behavior of hardness, a single-number scale does not adequately describe hardness. Descriptions of hardness correspond roughly with ranges of mineral concentrations. Hardness concentration is described in the unit's milligrams per liter (mg/L). Water with dissolved mineral concentrations from 40 to 60 mg/L is classified as slightly hard. If dissolved mineral concentrations increase to the 60 to 80 mg/L range the water is classified as moderately hard. Hard water contains concentrations in the range 80 to 120 mg/L. Very hard water contains dissolved mineral concentrations exceeding 120 mg/L. Hard water causes scaling, which is the precipitation of minerals to form a deposit known as limescale. Scale will clog pipes, ruin water heaters, coat the insides of tea and coffee pots, and decrease the life of toilet flushing units.

WATER QUALITY TEST

A water quality test quantifies nine parameters leading to a water quality index. The parameters quantified in a water quality test are: temperature, pH, dissolved oxygen, turbidity, fecal colliform bacteria, biochemical oxygen, total phosphates, nitrates, and total suspended solids (TSS). The National Sanitation Foundation (NSF) surveyed 142 people representing a wide range of positions at the local, state, and national level about 35 water quality tests parameters available for possible inclusion in this index. The above mentioned nine factors were chosen and some were judged more important than others, so a weighted mean is used to combine the values. The information obtained from a water quality tests may be presented in a table or a graph. The graphs that are used to display this kind of information include bar graphs, pie charts, trilinear charts, and Stiff diagrams.

GROUNDWATER POLLUTION

Groundwater pollution may be attributable to natural as well as anthropogenic (human-caused) sources. Water quality of aquifers is affected by the geology from which the groundwater is abstracted. Groundwater pollution caused by man includes: industrial discharge of chemical wastes; discharge of inadequately treated human waste; surface runoff containing fertilizers, pesticides, and spilled petroleum products; underground fuel storage tank leakage; and surface runoff from construction sites or other impervious areas such as parking lots. Many chemicals undergo reactive decay or chemically change especially over long periods of time in groundwater reservoirs. A noteworthy class of such chemicals are the chlorinated hydrocarbons such as trichloroethylene, used in industrial metal degreasing, and tetrachloroethylene, used in the dry-cleaning industry. Both of these chemicals, which are carcinogens themselves, undergo partial decomposition reactions, leading to new hazardous chemicals.

TESTS USED IN HYDROGEOLOGICAL INVESTIGATIONS

The following types of tests are used in hydrogeological investigations:

- packer test: used to assess the permeability of a section of rock. A short expansible-retractable device is deliberately placed in a well bore at a set interval to prevent upward or downward fluid movement.
- percolation test: assesses the appropriateness of a region for a septic sewage system or structure. It is performed by digging a hole of known dimensions and filling it with water. Time needed for drainage is then recorded.
- pumping test: used to define aquifers. Involves pumping a well for a defined period of time and measuring the change in the hydraulic head of the aquifer
- slug test: assesses transmissivity, conductivity, and storage capacity of wells through water being adding or removing from a well. The well response is then observed.

SPECIFIC RETENTION, SPECIFIC STORAGE, SPECIFIC YIELD, AND STORATIVITY

The following terms refer to the capacity of a well:

- specific retention (S_r): The ratio of the volume of water that a body of rock or soil will hold against the pull of gravity to the volume of the body itself. It is usually expressed as a percentage
- specific storage (S_s): the amount of water which a volume of aquifer will produce when a unit change in hydraulic head is applied to it.

76

- specific yield (S_y): is the ratio indicating the volumetric portion of the bulk aquifer volume that an aquifer will yield when all the water is allowed to drain out of it with only the forces of gravity.
- storativity, also known as the storage coefficient (S): the volume of water that any permeable rock or soil releases or draws in for one unit of the surface area of the aquifer, for a unit change in head.

CALCULATING THE TOTAL HEAD FOR AN UNCONFINED AQUIFER VS. A CONFINED AQUIFER

There are differences in calculation of the total head for unconfined aquifers as opposed to calculation of total head for confined aquifers. In using the Bernoulli equation to calculate the total head in an unconfined aquifer, the pressure value must be set to zero. This is due to the fact that unconfined aquifers exist at atmospheric pressure and that there will not be any compressive energy to drive out the water. Since the velocity is also small for most aquifers, elevation head can be calculated with the following equation:

$$h = z_1 - z_2$$

where h is the head loss, z_1 is the higher elevation head, and z_2 is the lower elevation head.

HYDROLOGIC BUDGET EQUATION

The following equation, known as the hydrologic budget equation, has been developed to summarize the inflow and outflow of water in a specific basin:

$$dS_T = P - E \pm R \pm U$$

where dS_T is the change in total storage, P is precipitation, E is evapo-transpiration, R is runoff, and U is underflow.

Underflow is calculated as groundwater inflow minus groundwater outflow. Runoff is calculated as stream inflow minus stream outflow. Because changes in soil moisture are so miniscule, it is usually neglected in this kind of summary. Geologists use the hydrologic budget equation (occasionally known as the water balance equation) to assess changes over time in a water basin or aquifer or for modeling and planning studies.

GROUNDWATER INVENTORY EQUATION

The groundwater inventory equation can be regarded as a stripped-down version of the hydrologic budget equation. In the groundwater inventory equation, the only terms that are used are groundwater input and output:

$$dS = I - O$$

where dS is the change in aquifer storage (usually reported in acre-feet or gallons per year), I is the input to an aquifer, and O is the output or discharge from the aquifer.

In order for this equation to be effective, input and output must be expressed in the same units. If the change in aquifer storage is positive, this indicates that the aquifer is growing. The groundwater inventory equation is used to assess on-going health of an aquifer or for annual monitoring.

CALCULATING THE TOTAL ENERGY OF AN AQUIFER

The total energy of an aquifer can be calculated using the Bernoulli equation:

$$E = \frac{v^2}{2g} + z + \frac{P}{\gamma}$$

where E is the total energy loss or head loss (with units of length representing the energy from a column of water with that height), v is the velocity of groundwater flow, g is the acceleration due to gravity, z is the elevation of ground water above a reference mark, P is the pressure, and γ is the specific gravity of water.

Velocity head is a measure of energy relative to the amount of energy contributed by the motion of the groundwater. Elevation head is a measure of potential energy and is defined as the amount of energy that would be realized if the water was released from a given elevation. Pressure head is also a measure of potential energy reflective of the compressive energy stored within the water.

CALCULATING POROSITY

Porosity is calculated with the following equation:

$$n = \frac{V_V}{V_T}$$

where n is the porosity, V_V is the volume of void space, and V_T is the total volume of the material (including the void space).

A number of different types of porosity are recognized in geology. Primary porosity is the main or original porosity system in a rock or unconfined alluvial system. Primary porosity is a function of grain size, sorting, void spaces as a percentage of the whole, and hydrologic conductivity. Secondary porosity is a subsequent or separate porosity system and can add or subtract from primary porosity. Secondary porosity relates to chemical leaching of minerals or fracture system development. Secondary porosity includes fracture porosity and vuggy porosity, the latter formed when constituents such as fossils in rocks dissolve.

POROSITIES OF COMMON SEDIMENTS AND ROCKS

As grain size increases and sorting decreases, porosity tends to decrease. For this reason, materials like clay and silt are considerably more porous than materials like glacial till. Consolidation of geologic materials into rock tends to decrease porosities as rocks grains are cemented together during diagenesis. Thus, shale has a porosity of between 0 and 10% and fractured crystalline rock has a porosity of between 0 and 10%. Limestone has a porosity of between 1% and 20%. Sandstone has a porosity of between 5% and 30%. Glacial till has a porosity of between 10% and 25%. Sand has a porosity of between 25% and 40%, as does gravel. Silt has a porosity of between 35% and 50%. Clay has a porosity of between 45% and 55%.

EFFECTIVE POROSITY VS. TRUE POROSITY

Effective porosity of a geologic material is expressed as the ratio of the volume of liquid that a given mass of saturated rock or soil will yield by gravity to the volume of that mass. True porosity is the measure of all the existing voids in a rock or soil. Effective porosity is simply the measure of those voids through which a fluid can flow. In all cases, effective porosity will be lower than true porosity. The equation used to calculate the effective porosity is as follows:

$$n_e = \frac{W_s - W_r}{W_s - W_0} \times \frac{V_V}{V_T}$$

where n_e is the effective porosity, W_s is the weight of a saturated soil sample, W_r is the weight of the sample after gravity drainage, W_0 is the weight of the air-dried sample, V_V is the volume of void space, and V_T is the total volume of the material (including the void space).

SPECIFIC YIELD VS. EFFECTIVE POROSITY

Both specific yield and effective porosity are expressed as the ratio of the volume of water that drains from a saturated rock or soil to the total volume of that rock or soil. Specific yield is very similar to effective porosity in an unconfined aquifer. The main difference is that specific yield is found by measuring the amount of water that drains from the rock, rather than measuring the weight of the rock after drainage. Specific retention is a ratio reflecting the amount of water a soil can retain after drainage. Specific yield and specific retention can be calculated with the following equations:

$$S_y = \frac{V_W \text{drained}}{V_T}$$

$$S_r = \frac{V_W \text{retained}}{V_T}$$

where S_y and S_r are the specific yield and specific retention, $V_{W(drained)}$ and $V_{W(retained)}$ are the volumes of water drained and retained after gravity drainage of saturated soil or rock, and V_T is the total volume of the material (including the void space). S_y and S_r can also be added to yield porosity:

$$S_y + S_r = n$$

VALUES OF SPECIFIC YIELD

Specific yield refers to a volume of water that a mass of saturated rock or soil will produce, solely by gravity, compared to the total volume of the rock or soil. Specific yield is represented as a percentage. As the relative grain size of a rock or soil increases, so should the specific yield of that rock or soil increase. Also, some geologic materials contain charged ions that cause an increase in adhesion of water. Shale and limestone both have a specific yield of between 0.5% and 5%. Clay has a specific yield of between 1% and 10%. Sandstone has a specific yield of between 5% and 15%. Sand has a specific yield of between 10% and 30%. A mixture of sand and gravel has a specific yield of between 15% and 25%. Finally, gravel has a specific yield of between 15% and 30%.

CALCULATING STORATIVITY FOR AN UNCONFINED AQUIFER

Storativity, otherwise known as the storage coefficient, is the volume of water released per unit area in an aquifer per unit decline in hydraulic head. It represents the vertically integrated specific storage value for an aquifer or aquitard. Storativity of an unconfined aquifer is the average amount of water that the aquifer either releases or stores for each unit area in response to a change of the hydraulic head by one unit. The following equation is used to calculate storativity:

$$S = \frac{\pm V_W}{A \times dh}$$

where S is storativity, V_W is the amount of water in storage, A is the area of the aquifer, and dh is the change in head.

In general, the storativity values for unconfined aquifers are between 0.01 and 0.3.

CALCULATING STORATIVITY FOR A CONFINED AQUIFER

In a combined aquifer, there is a more complex interplay between the potentiometric surface, water release, and hydrostatic head. Even if the release of water from a confined aquifer lowers the head, the aquifer will remain saturated if the potentiometric surface remains above the aquifer. When water evacuates a confined aquifer the pressure within the aquifer decreases and the remaining water expands. The storage coefficient, or storativity, of a confined aquifer is calculated with the following equation:

$$S = b \times S_S$$

where S is the storativity, b is the saturated thickness of the aquifer, and S_S is the specific storage, or the amount of water per unit volume of the aquifer that is lost or gained due to compressibility.

Storativity values for a confined aquifer range between 0.001 and 0.00001.

HYDRAULIC CONDUCTIVITY

Hydraulic conductivity is defined as that property of soil or rock that determines the relative ease or difficulty with which a fluid, typically water, can be transported through that medium. It is dependent upon the intrinsic permeability of the material and on the degree of saturation of that material. Hydraulic conductivity is the proportionality constant in Darcy's Law. Hydraulic conductivity can be calculated with the following equation:

$$K = k_i \times \frac{\gamma}{\mu}$$

where K is the hydraulic conductivity, k_i is the intrinsic permeability of the medium, γ is specific weight, and μ is the dynamic viscosity.

As the number of fractures or voids in a material increases, so do the values for intrinsic permeability and hydraulic conductivity. Geologists evaluate hydraulic conductivity values with pumping tests, computer models, and laboratory simulated flow tests. Hydraulic conductivity is a logarithm, so the values are expressed in orders of magnitude rather than on a linear scale.

TRANSMISSIVITY

Transmissivity is defined as the relative amount of water that can be transmitted horizontally in an aquifer to a pumping well or draw point. The aquifer value for hydraulic conductivity will influence the degree of transmissivity. Transmissivity is also directly dependent upon aquifer thickness. Transmissivity is calculated with the following equation: T = Kb, in which T is transmissivity, K is hydraulic conductivity, and b is the saturated thickness of the aquifer. For a confined aquifer the transmissivity value remains constant because the saturated thickness remains constant. For unconfined aquifers, the thickness is measured from the base of the aquifer to the top of the water

table. As the water table in an aquifer can fluctuate, the transmissivity value for unconfined aquifers can vary.

BAILER TEST

A bailer test is one of 3 available single-well hydraulic tests that yield estimates of the hydraulic conductivity of aquifer materials around a single well. These single-well tests are less accurate than multiple-well pumping tests but are an efficient option for obtaining an inexpensive estimate of relative hydraulic conductivity. The bailer test, also referred to as a slug test or falling-head test, involves the rapid addition or subtraction of a known volume of water from a monitoring well. The predetermined volume of water that is added or removed is referred to as a slug. Observations and measurements of the well characteristics are then collected with careful documentation of required recovery times. The essential requirement is that the slug be added or removed as quickly as possible. Well water level or pressure is then monitored. This test is also used to determine transmissivity and storativity.

PUMP-IN TEST AND SLUG TEST

A pump-in test, also known as a constant-head test, involves a measured discharge of water into a monitoring well to maintain a constant water level within the well. The method is more commonly used where the aquifer materials have moderate to high hydraulic conductivity. The pump-in test is a single-well hydraulic test used to obtain order-of-magnitude values of hydraulic conductivity. It is used to determine the measure of the horizontal hydraulic conductivity of an aquifer. A slug test is a particular type of single-well test in which a known amount of water is quickly added or removed from a groundwater well and the change in hydraulic head is monitored through time. A slug test does not require pumping. The slug test determines the near-well aquifer characteristics of the material the well is completed in. Slug test can determine transmissivity and storage coefficient.

CONSTANT-RATE PUMPING TEST VS. BAILER TEST

A constant-rate pumping test stimulates an aquifer or well through pumping and by observing the aquifer's response in observation wells. The constant-rate pumping test is performed in order to measure the hydraulic conductivity, storativity, or specific yield of an aquifer or well. The constant-rate pump test is a multi-well test. A bailer test is one of 3 available single-well hydraulic tests that yield order-of-magnitude estimates of the hydraulic conductivity of aquifer materials around a single well. These single-well tests are less accurate than multiple-well pumping tests but are an efficient option for obtaining an inexpensive estimate of relative hydraulic conductivity. The bailer test does not require pumping. The bailer test is used if the transmissivity of the material the well is completed in is too low to realistically perform a proper pumping test.

STEP-DRAWDOWN TEST

The step-drawdown test provides information about storage coefficient and transmissivity of a well that describes the specific capacity of the well and its fluctuations during increased yields. The overall efficiency of the well is often measured with a step-drawdown test. The test is performed by gradually increasing the rate at which water is pumped out of a well. Drawdown is measured during each incremental increase in the rate of pumping. A constant-rate pumping test stimulates an aquifer or well through pumping and by observing the aquifer's response in observation wells. The constant-rate pumping test is performed in order to measure the hydraulic conductivity, storativity, or specific yield of an aquifer or well. A slightly different test is the variable-rate drawdown test, in which the rate of withdrawal is manually changed. In this test, the optimum pumping rate and well depth can be determined more quickly.

81

THEIS METHOD

Geologists who wish to use the Theis method to analyze the results of an aquifer test will plot the drawdown versus time on log-log paper. When the data from more than one well is plotted, the plot axes should be drawdown versus t/r^2, in which r = distance between the pumping and observation wells. After this is done, the paper should be laid over a curve of $W(u)$ versus $1/u$. The field data plot is then moved in order to overlap the $W(u)$ vs. $1/u$ curve allowing for an arbitrary match point to be chosen. Obtained from that point are all of the values of drawdown, time (or t/r^2), $W(u)$ and $1/u$. At this point, the values of $W(u)$, drawdown, and pumping rate can be entered into the first Theis equation to calculate transmissivity. T, time (or t/r^2), and u can subsequently be entered into the second Theis equation to calculate storativity.

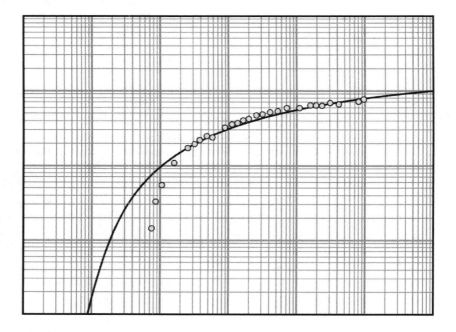

The Theis equations are:

$$s = \frac{Q}{4\pi T} W(u)$$

$$u = \frac{r^2 S}{4Tt}$$

where s is the drawdown, Q is the volumetric discharge rate, T is the transmissivity, $W(u)$ is the well function, u is a dimensionless time parameter, r is the distance from the well to the point of measurement, S is the storativity, and t is the time since pumping began.

The Theis equations are used to determine transmissivity (T) and storativity (S) by inverse modeling. All parameters except T and S are measured or observed from the well. A mathematical analysis is then performed to determine the best-fit values of S and T for the well.

TIME-DRAWDOWN METHOD (JACOB STRAIGHT-LINE METHOD)

When only one well is being observed, the time-drawdown method may be preferred to the more complex Theis method. In this method, the drawdown is plotted on the linear side of a semi log paper against time and the linear portion of the data from the last bits of the experiment should be

82

extrapolated backwards to the zero-drawdown axis. Assuming that the cone of depression will not reach a steady state during the first 10 minutes of the experiment, the data from this period can be thrown out. The characteristics of the aquifer may then be calculated with the following equation:

$$s = BQ + CQ^2$$

where s is drawdown, Q is the pumping rate, B is the aquifer loss coefficient, and C is the well loss coefficient.

DISTANCE-DRAWDOWN METHOD

One variation of the Jacob straight-line method is called the distance-drawdown method. This technique is used to consider data from three or more observation wells. The drawdown is plotted versus distance from the drawdown well on the linear side of semi-log paper, and the linear portion of the data from the closest wells is extrapolated backwards to zero-drawdown axis. The following equations are used to determine the characteristics of the aquifer:

$$T = \frac{35Q}{ds}$$

$$S = \frac{Tt_0}{640r^2}$$

where T is transmissivity, Q is pumping rate, ds is the change in drawdown (over one log cycle from the plot), S is storativity, t_0 is the time at the zero-drawdown point from the plot, and r is the distance between the pumping and observation wells.

TIME-DRAWDOWN TEST EQUATIONS FOR CALCULATING TRANSMISSIVITY AND STORATIVITY

For calculating transmissivity in square feet per day:

$$T = \frac{35Q}{ds}$$

For calculating transmissivity in gallons per foot per day:

$$T = \frac{264Q}{ds}$$

For calculating storativity in square feet per day:

$$S = \frac{Tt_0}{640r^2}$$

For calculating storativity in gallons per foot per day:

$$S = \frac{Tt_0}{4790r^2}$$

where Q is pumping rate, ds is the change in drawdown (over one log cycle from the plot), t_0 is the time at the zero-drawdown point from the plot, and r is the distance between the pumping and observation wells.

DISTANCE-DRAWDOWN TEST EQUATIONS FOR CALCULATING TRANSMISSIVITY AND STORATIVITY

For calculating transmissivity in square feet per day:

$$T = \frac{70Q}{ds}$$

For calculating transmissivity in gallons per foot per day:

$$T = \frac{528Q}{ds}$$

For calculating storativity in square feet per day:

$$S = \frac{Tt}{640r_0^2}$$

For calculating storativity in gallons per foot per day:

$$S = \frac{Tt}{4790r_0^2}$$

where Q is pumping rate, ds is the change in drawdown (over one log cycle from the plot), t is the time since testing began, and r_0 is the distance from the pumping well at the beginning of testing.

WELL EFFICIENCY

Well efficiency is a ratio that compares the theoretical well draw down to the actual well draw down. The following factors may influence the efficiency of a well: borehole size, soil conditions, gravel packing, casing characteristics, and screening characteristics. Well efficiency is calculated with the following equation:

$$WE = \frac{s_t}{s_a}$$

where WE is well efficiency, s_t is theoretical drawdown, and s_a is the actual drawdown.

An inefficient well will require greater drawdown in order to achieve the same output as an efficient well. Well efficiency is sometimes calculated by comparing the measured fraction of laminar head loss to the total head loss. Both of these approaches are flawed theoretically and practically. A more rigorous method of evaluating well efficiency involves comparing the functional relationships between the actual discharge drawdown curve and the curve produced by a properly developed well. Well efficiency is an important parameter in the accuracy of aquifer tests. It is potentially important in spacing and completion depths for commercial and residential water wells.

If it is assumed that the entire vertical extent of an aquifer has been screened, it is possible to use a distance-drawdown graph to estimate well efficiency. The screen should be made of some material that allows the water from the aquifer to flow into the borehole, while still preventing the well from collapsing. Well efficiency can be calculated on the distance-drawdown graph by extrapolating the line backwards towards the pumping well. It is essential that the borehole not contain any elements that will interfere with the slow suction of water from the well. In the best-case scenario, wells can only provide about 80% efficiency. A more rigorous method of evaluating well efficiency involves comparing the functional relationships between the actual discharge drawdown curve versus the curve produced by a properly developed well.

HYDRAULIC GRADIENT

The hydraulic gradient is the change in hydraulic head per unit of distance along the flow path between two points. As such, hydraulic gradient represents the slope of the water table between two wells. Hydraulic head is a specific measurement of water pressure or total energy per unit weight above a datum. Hydraulic head is usually measured as a water surface elevation and indicates the energy at the bottom of a piezometer. The hydraulic gradient between two points can be calculated with the following equation:

$$i = \frac{dh}{l} = \frac{h_1 - h_2}{l}$$

where i is the hydraulic gradient, dh is the difference in head (h) between points 1 and 2, and l is the distance between the two points.

Hydraulic gradient measurements are important in defining changing aquifer characteristics through time.

DARCY'S LAW

Darcy's Law is an equation that describes fluid flow through a porous medium. Darcy's Law forms the scientific basis of fluid permeability in earth sciences. Darcy's law is essentially a proportion between the instantaneous discharge rate through a porous medium and the viscosity of the fluid and the pressure drop over a given distance. The equation for Darcy's law is as follows:

$$v_d = K \frac{h_1 - h_2}{l} = \frac{Q}{A}$$

where v_d is the specific discharge or discharge velocity, K is the hydraulic conductivity, $(h_1 - h_2)/l$ is the hydraulic gradient, Q is the volumetric discharge rate, and A is the cross-sectional area of the open space of the pipe.

This law is used to calculate the speed with which water can move through an aquifer, especially a confined aquifer. Darcy's Law can only be used in situations of low turbulence and slow flow.

Darcy's Law is used to establish ground water flow equations essential for calculating fluid movement in confined aquifers. These groundwater flow equations are valid for three-dimensional flow only. In unconfined aquifers, the solution to the 3D form of the equation is complicated by the presence of a free surface water table boundary condition. Problems arise because in addition to solving for the spatial distribution of heads, the location of this surface is also an unknown. This is a non-linear problem, even though the governing ground water flow equation is linear. Hence, Darcy's Law must be modified using the Dupuit assumption.

LAMINAR FLOW AND TURBULENT FLOW

Flow of water in which the flow path remains distinct and the flow direction at every point remains unchanged with time is referred to as laminar flow. Laminar flow is characteristic of the movement of ground water. Water flow in which the flow lines are non-distinct, confused, and heterogeneously mixed is referred to as turbulent flow. Turbulent flow is characteristic of surface-water bodies. In turbulent flow fluid motion occurs in which random parts of the fluid are superimposed upon other random parts of the fluid, impeding a simple laminar pattern of flow.

When laminar flow is occurring, all the molecules of water are basically moving in the same direction at the same rate. Turbulent flow, on the other hand, is when the water molecules move in an irregular fashion, usually because of drag either within the fluid or between the fluid and the objects that surround it. Turbulent flows are more likely to occur at high speeds, and in thinner fluids.

DUPUIT ASSUMPTIONS

The Dupuit assumptions are used in ground water investigations and address unconfined consistent flow above a solid boundary. The Dupuit assumptions consist of the following premises: direction of groundwater flow is horizontal; hydraulic gradient is the same as the water table slope; and equipotential lines are vertical. These assumptions are then combined with Darcy's law to generate the following equation for flow in an unconfined aquifer:

$$Q = \frac{1}{2}K\frac{ht_1^2 - ht_2^2}{l} \times w$$

where Q is the flow rate, K is the hydraulic conductivity, ht_1 and ht_2 are the water table heights above the bottom boundary of the aquifer at the first and second wells, l is the distance between the two wells, and w is the width of the aquifer.

The Dupuit assumption holds that groundwater moves horizontally in an unconfined aquifer, and that the groundwater discharge is proportional to saturated aquifer thickness.

GROUNDWATER VELOCITY

The equation for groundwater velocity is derived from Darcy's law and the equation for calculating velocity of discharge through a pipe. Combining the two equations provides the expression:

$$v_d = Ki$$

where v_d is the discharge velocity, K is the hydraulic conductivity, and i is the hydraulic gradient.

When an area with a high groundwater velocity is subjected to a group of contaminants, these contaminants will tend to separate more quickly than they would in an area with low groundwater velocity. Dispersivity is an empirical factor which quantifies how much contaminants stray away from the path of the groundwater which are carrying them.

SEEPAGE VELOCITY

Seepage velocity is a parameter measured in soil mechanics more so than in groundwater studies. The seepage velocity of groundwater is the actual velocity with which groundwater moves through a porous medium. Groundwater is seldom discussed in terms of seepage velocity. Because no underground medium is perfect for fluid motion, seepage velocity is always lower than discharge velocity. Seepage velocity is calculated with the following equation:

$$v_s = \frac{Ki}{n_e}$$

where v_s is the seepage velocity, K is the hydraulic conductivity, i is the hydraulic gradient, and n_e is the effective porosity.

Seepage is the flow of a fluid through pores. After measuring or estimating the intrinsic permeability (κ), one can calculate the hydraulic conductivity (K) of a soil, and the rate of seepage can be estimated.

NUMBERING WELLS USING THE STANDARD SYSTEM BASED ON THE PUBLIC LAND SURVEY
NUMBERING WELLS IN SQUARE PLOTS

In the Public Land Survey all areas are divided by the Township and Range system, based off a meridian or reference baseline. Each square township has a width of 6 miles, and is further subdivided into 36, 1 square mile sections. The PLS Township numbering system is such that Townships are numbered from north to south away from a meridian. Ranges are numbered east to west on either side of E-W meridians. Sections within a township are numbered, 1 through 36, in a contiguous, descending pattern, beginning at the upper right corner of the township. Each section is further divided into 16 parcels of 40 acres each. These parcels are referred to as quarter-quarter (¼ ¼) sections. These parcels are given letters A through R (I and O are skipped). When more than one well is drilled in a parcel, the designation of the well will include a number.

			RANGE					TOWNSHIP
	T4N R2W	San Bernardino Meridian	T4N R1E	T4N R2E	T4N R3E	T4N R4E		
	T3N R2W		T3N R1E	T3N R2E	T3N R3E	T3N R4E		
	T2N R2W		T2N R1E	T2N R2E	T2N R3E	T2N R4E		
	T1N R2W		T1N R1E	T1N R2E	T1N R3E	T1N R4E		
	T1S R1W	Baseline			T1S R3E	T1S R4E		

MODIFYING THE STANDARD WELL NUMBERING SYSTEM FOR IRREGULARLY SHAPED SECTIONS

The usual system for well numbering assumes a square land division. The system used is the Township and Range system of the Public Land Survey. In many situations based on terrain irregularities or distortions in the PLS grid, sections of land or portions of townships will not be completely square. When section lines are not square, the standard 16 parcel quarter-quarter (¼ ¼) section grid is put into alignment on the map by superimposing the lower right corner of the grid on the lower right corner of the section. Using this method some or all of the quarter-quarter (¼ ¼) section parcels will be less than 40 acres and will not be perfectly square. The positions of

Mometrix

all lettered parcels will be located based on skewing of the overlay off right hand corner. However, it should be easy to determine the location of the parcel.

SALT WATER INTRUSION

Salt water intrusion is a naturally occurring phenomenon in coastal aquifers. Because of the dissolved solute load, seawater has a higher density than fresh water. This higher density has the effect that the pressure beneath a column of saltwater is larger than that beneath a column of the same height of freshwater. If these columns were connected at the bottom, then the pressure difference would trigger a flow from the saltwater column to the freshwater column. Saltwater intrusion is limited to coastal areas. Inland the freshwater column gets higher and the pressure at the bottom also gets higher. This compensates for the higher density of the saltwater column and intrusion stops. The Ghyben-Herzberg ratio states, for every foot of fresh water in an unconfined aquifer above sea level, there will be forty feet of fresh water in the aquifer below sea level. The Ghyben-Herzberg ratio is calculated with the following equation:

$$Z = 40 \times ht$$

where Z is the depth of the freshwater/saltwater interface below sea level, and ht is the height of the potentiometric surface above sea level.

The natural balance between freshwater and saltwater in coastal aquifers is disturbed by ground-water withdrawals and other human activities that lower ground-water levels, reduce fresh ground-water flow to coastal waters, and ultimately cause saltwater to intrude coastal aquifers. A common approach for managing saltwater intrusion has been to reduce the rate of pumping from coastal wells or to move the locations of withdrawals further inland. Other alternative solutions for reducing ground-water withdrawals involve artificially recharging freshwater into an aquifer. This acts to increase ground-water levels and to hydraulically control the movement of the intruding saltwater. In addition to more conventional methods, innovative approaches are now being used to manage saltwater intrusion including aquifer storage and recovery systems, desalination systems, and blending of waters of different quality.

FLOWNET

A flownet is a graphical representation of two-dimensional steady-state groundwater flow through aquifers. A flownet is often used for solving groundwater flow problems where the geometry makes analytical solutions impractical. The method is used as a first check for problems of flow under structures such as dam or retaining walls. The method consists of the construction of a graphical flow area with stream and equipotential lines, which are everywhere perpendicular to each other, making a curvilinear grid. Mathematically, the process of constructing a flownet consists of contouring the two harmonic or analytic functions of potential and stream function. These functions both satisfy the Laplace Equation and the contours represent lines of constant head (equipotentials) and lines tangent to flowpaths (streamlines). The construction of a flownet only provides an approximate solution to the flow problem, but it can be quite good even for problems with complex geometries.

QUALITY ASSURANCE VS. QUALITY CONTROL

Quality assurance (QA) is the act of providing evidence needed to establish confidence that a task or analysis is being performed in the most effective manner. It refers to all planned and systematic actions necessary to provide a targeted level of confidence that a product or service will achieve or satisfy designated standards of quality. QA covers all activities from design, development, production, installation, and servicing to documentation. Quality control, on the other hand, is the

88

system of ensuring that all the procedures involved in the performance of a project serve the goals of the customer. Quality control (QC) basically involves calibrating, fine tuning, and ensuring the longevity of the processes that have been put into place by the quality assurance program. QA/QC are essential business management practices for all chemical sampling and chemical analysis operations to maintain confidence levels in complex data sets.

STIFF DIAGRAM

Stiff water quality diagrams are a useful tool in understanding groundwater chemistry. Stiff diagrams are also called butterfly diagrams. They are used to show the concentrations of abundant anions and cations plotted against each other graphically with the cations on the left and anions on the right. The centerline in a Stiff diagram is the baseline from which graphic representations of the proportions are graphed in millequivalents of each ion. Values for ions that were not detected are plotted as the detection limit or zero if no detection limit was reported. This graphical display of major ion chemistry is used for visualization of aquifer water populations and dynamics. Alternative constituents can be substituted into the diagram to illustrate many differing groundwater issues. The Stiff diagram is a powerful graphic-based tool for investigating various relationships between major ions and trace elements in a groundwater system. The diagram can be enhanced by adding constituents of concern, physical measurements such as pH or temperature, and non-chemical values such as water level.

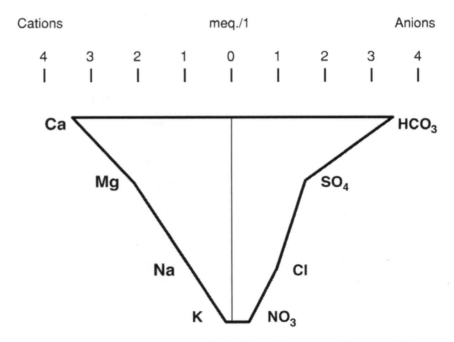

TOP 10 HAZARDOUS SUBSTANCES ON THE CERCLA PRIORITY LIST OF HAZARDOUS SUBSTANCES

The following 10 substances have been deemed the most hazardous by the Comprehensive Environmental Response, Compensation, and Liability Act (CERCLA or Superfund) Priority List of Hazardous Substances for 2005 (in descending order):

- arsenic: inorganic, originates in nature, pesticides, and herbicides
- lead: inorganic; originates in nature, mining, and manufacturing
- mercury: inorganic; originates in nature, combustion, and manufacturing
- vinyl chloride: organic; originates in manufacturing

- polychlorinated biphenyls: organic; originates in coolants and lubricants
- benzene: organic; originates in petroleum and chemical manufacturing
- polycyclic aromatic hydrocarbons: organic; originates in incomplete combustion
- cadmium: inorganic; originates in manufacturing and cigarette smoke
- benzo(A)pyrene: organic; originates in incomplete combustion and manufacturing
- benzo (B) fluoranthene: organic; originates in incomplete combustion and manufacturing

COMMON INORGANIC CONTAMINANTS

The following are the most common types of inorganic contaminants:

- arsenic: originates in nature, pesticides, herbicides, insecticides; can result in cancer and enzyme malfunction
- lead: originates in nature, manufacturing, mining, fossil fuels; can result in damage to the central nervous system and death
- mercury: originates in nature, manufacturing, mining, and volcanic activity; can result in damage to a fetus and to an adult central nervous system
- cadmium: originates in batteries, welding, and cigarette smoke; can result in long-term kidney and digestive system damage
- chromium: originates in manufacturing; can result in high tissue damage and cancer
- white phosphorus: originates in nature and manufacturing; can result in liver, heart, and kidney damage
- selenium: originates in nature and in the refining of copper; can result in damage to the central nervous system
- nitrate: originates in fertilizer, manure, and sewage; can result in infant blood disorders
- perchlorate: originates in rocket fuel; can damage the function of the thyroid gland

DISINFECTION BYPRODUCTS

Disinfection byproducts are chemical substances that form during reactions between disinfectants and organic matter in groundwater. Chemical disinfection of drinking water with substances such as chlorine has been practiced for more than a century. Disinfection byproducts have been deemed to be harmful to human health. The types of disinfection byproducts that form depend on a number of factors. Interaction of different types of disinfectants, and residence times within groundwater aquifers are determining factors in byproduct speciation. Temperature and pH of groundwater also affect byproduct formation. High residence times of disinfectants produce more byproducts. With shorter residence times, higher concentrations of trihalomethanes (THM) and halogenic acetic acids (HAA) are formed. When residence times are longer the temporary forms of disinfection byproducts may become disinfection endproducts, such as tribromine acetic acid or bromoform.

BIOLOGICAL CONTAMINANTS

The two most commonly occurring types of biological contaminants found in groundwater and in drinking water are the protozoa Cryptosporidium and Giardia lamblia. Cryptosporidium is typically found in lake and river water and in groundwater. Ingestion of this protozoa results in stomach cramps, nausea, and damage to the immune system. This protozoa is related to animal or human waste contamination of groundwater. It cannot be eliminated through chlorination, but only through boiling. Giardia lamblia is a protozoa commonly found in water, food, or soil that has been contaminated by animal feces. Contact with this protozoa can cause intestinal disorders like diarrhea, vomiting, and nausea. The following methods are appropriate for eliminating Giardia: boiling, micro-filtering, or introduction of iodine.

LIGHT AND DENSE NON-AQUEOUS PHASE LIQUIDS

Organic contaminants are either described as light non-aqueous phase liquids (LNAPLs), or dense non-aqueous phase liquids (DNAPLs). The designations depend upon whether their density is greater or less than that of pure water. The density of pure water is established at 1 g/cm^{-3}. LNAPLs mainly originate in petroleum products, and are soluble in water. These liquids can only be cleaned up through venting, bioremediation, excavation, and barrier construction. DNAPLs, on the other hand, include coal tar, chlorinated solvents, and creosote. These liquids are slightly soluble in water, and tend to accumulate at the bottom of aquifers. Cleanup of DNAPLs includes biodegradation, physical barrier construction, or pumping. Both LNAPLs and DNAPLs are characterized by their solubility, vapor pressure, viscosity, and wettability.

COMMON ORGANIC CONTAMINANTS

Persistent organic pollutants (POP's) appearing in surface water and groundwater, some that can be resistant to biodegradation, are an environmental threat due to long-range transport, bioaccumulation in humans and animals, and biomagnification in the food chain. Organic pollutants that are commonly at issue are aldrin, chlordane, DDT, dieldrin, endrin, heptachlor, hexachlorobenzene, mirex, polychlorinated biphenyls (PCB's), polychlorinated dibenzofurans, and toxaphene. Many of these chemicals are characterized by low water solubilities, high lipid solubilities, semi-volatility, and high molecular mass. One important factor of their chemical properties that is problematic arises from their ability to pass through biological membranes and accumulating in the fatty tissues of living organisms. These compounds originate from numerous industrial and agricultural sources as primary and secondary pollution.

COMMON PESTICIDE CONTAMINANTS

Pesticides can be classed as synthetic pesticides or biological pesticides, although the distinction can sometimes blur. There are three major routes through which pesticides can reach a groundwater aquifer: it may percolate, or leach, through the soil, it may be carried to the water as runoff, or it may be spilled, for example accidentally or through neglect. The most common pesticide contaminants found in groundwater are as follows: DDT, DDE, DDD, chlordane, aldrin, and dieldrin. DDT, when it decomposes, becomes DDE and DDD. Aldrin and dieldrin adhere to the particles of soil, and frequently leach into aquifers. For human beings, the greatest risk associated with pesticides has to do with eating food that has become contaminated with one or more of these compounds. Consumption and assimilation of pesticides by humans can result in damage to the nervous system, reproductive system, and can be carcinogenic.

BROWNFIELD SITES

A Brownfield site, or Brownfield, is an abandoned, idle, or under-utilized industrial or commercial site that is a challenge to city planners due to complications caused by pollution. Brownfield sites have the potential to be reused once they are cleaned up. Land that is more severely contaminated and has high enough concentrations to qualify as a Superfund area would not classify as a Brownfield site. Many contaminated Brownfield sites sit idle and unused for decades because the cost of cleaning them to safe standards is more than the land would be worth after redevelopment. The requirements for becoming a Brownfields site are summarized in a Brownfields Revitalization and Environmental Restoration Act of 2001. There are three phases of Brownfields redevelopment. In phase 1, the degree to which the site has been contaminated, and the possible financial or legal consequences of development are examined. In phase 2, more comprehensive investigations are performed severe cases. In phase 3, the site is cleaned up.

RCRA

The Resources Conservation and Recovery Act of 1976, known by the acronym RCRA, is designed to protect the public from the disposal of hazardous wastes. Specifically, this law promotes waste reduction, reuse, and recycling. Hazardous waste is defined as waste that poses substantial or potential threats to human health or the environment and generally is flammable, oxidizing, corrosive, toxic, or radioactive. Hazardous wastes are incorporated into lists published by the Environmental Protection Agency organized into three categories. The categories are: non-specific source (F-List) wastes, source specific (K-List) wastes, and discarded wastes (P- and U-List). It is essential that geologists know that there are many exempted hazardous wastes such as mining overburden returned to the mine site, oil and gas wastes, and wastes from the beneficiation and extraction of ores and minerals, including coal.

TEGD GUIDELINES

The Technical Enforcement Guidance Document (TEGD) was composed by the Environmental Protection Agency (EPA) in order to describe the process for monitoring the supply of groundwater. This document is designed to facilitate and maintain purity standards laid out in the Resource Conservation and Recovery Act of 1976 (RCRA). The document includes instructions for well design and overarching parameters for groundwater well construction, operation, and management. The TEGD also includes lists of acceptable materials in the drilling of groundwater wells. It also prescribes a method for analyzing and monitoring groundwater wells and describes the statistical analyses that should be performed to maintain quality during the drilling of groundwater wells.

The TEGD documents best management practices (BMP's) for appropriate methodology of site characterization. The document is designed to alert the designers and drillers of a groundwater well to the potential risks of contaminating an aquifer relating to well construction and operation. In a site characterization, the uppermost aquifer is considered to be those interconnected pockets of water that have the potential to carry contamination further. In order to complete a comprehensive site characterization, the subsurface geology and hydrology must be studied. The range of data collection methods for this document include the following: soil borings, subsurface material tests, slug tests, pump tests, geophysical surveys, piezometer tests, and location of monitoring wells.

The TEGD provides an outline of accepted array design, placement, and construction of monitoring wells. The document stipulates that the monitoring well system should have at least three down gradient wells and one up gradient well. The three down gradient wells should be placed in order to intercept any contaminants moving through the system. According to the TEGD placement of monitoring wells should be based on dispersivity, hydrogeology, and seepage velocity. The targeted stratigraphic horizon or horizons containing the flow and the physical and chemical aspects of perceived hazardous materials will determine the vertical sampling intervals of the wells.

According to the TEGD, the best management practice for the drilling of a monitoring well is with drilling techniques and tools that cause the least disruption to the borehole, and have the least potential to introduce contamination. The document stipulates the use of rotary, cable tool, and auger-based drilling techniques specifically. The document mandates that under no circumstances should drilling additives such as barium sulfate, polymer mud, or bentonite be used. As a general rule, a well should be designed to last at least 30 years. An analysis of the soil and rocks surrounding the well will indicate which filter packs and screen slots should be used. All monitoring wells should have an apron and a concrete cap, with the apron extending from the surface to below the frost line.

According to the TEGD, monitoring wells must adhere to the following specifications: the borehole must be between 10 and 12 inches in diameter with the well completed in the rocks below the aquifer. A well casing made of Teflon or stainless steel should be screened in the saturated zone, with 2 feet or less of filter pack above the screen. This filter pack should be made of clean quartz sand or glass beads. The well casing should be made out to cement in bentonite below the frost line, with the concrete cap and well apron above the frost line. This apron should be at least 4 inches thick and 6 feet in diameter, with a surveyor's pin embedded.

The TEGD emphasizes that all test and monitoring wells should be comprehensively logged. Geophysical logging shall be conducted and documented in accordance with TEGD requirements. The following logs are required: one successful natural gamma ray or gamma-gamma log for the full depth, (top to bottom of test hole); one successful neutron log in the fluid filled portion of the hole, (top to bottom of test hole); one successful (top to bottom of test hole) spontaneous potential (self-potential) log; and one successful (top to bottom of test hole) resistivity log. Log interpretations shall be made by a qualified person. TEGD requirements also call for a detailed geological log of all monitoring wells.

In accordance with the TEGD mandates for the sampling and analysis of monitoring wells, a record must be kept of the methods of sample collection, analysis, preservation, shipment, chain-of-custody, and quality control. The static water level must be measured to within 0.01 feet before a water sample is collected. Before and after collection, the temperature, specific conductance, and pH of the well should be measured. Any contaminating materials that lie atop the water column should be recorded. If there are any contaminants on top of the water column, the well should be evacuated between one and three times. At no time should the sample be shaken. Sample blanks, standards, lab blanks, spiked samples, and duplicates can be used to maintain quality control.

According to the TEGD, after a number of years of operation of a monitoring well program, it should be possible to determine mean and variance for each monitoring well in the system. Data from down gradient and up gradient wells should be compared annually to that of background wells. The TEGD stipulates that if an exceptional amount of variation occurs, it should be investigated and rectified. If the well sampling program is large, it can be analyzed using Cochran's Approximation to the Behrens-Fisher (CABF) t-test. Cochran's approximation is based on Cochran's theorem, a statistical method of analyzing variance. If the well sampling program is small, it can be analyzed using the Averaged Replicate (AR) t-test.

NATIONAL PRIMARY DRINKING WATER REGULATIONS

The National Primary Drinking Water Regulations (NPDWR), or primary standards, are designed to maintain a high quality of water in the public drinking water supply. The NPDWR's are legally enforceable. They set the level of harmful contaminants that can be allowed in drinking water, and categorize contaminants in terms of inorganic and organic chemicals, disinfectants, disinfectant byproducts, microorganisms, and radionuclides. Maximum contaminant levels for inorganic, organic, and disinfectant byproduct chemicals are established. Also, certain treatment techniques for reducing the levels of disinfectants and microorganisms are described. The National Secondary Drinking Water Regulations (NSDWR) are non-enforceable guidelines regulating contaminants that may cause cosmetic effects (such as skin or tooth discoloration) or aesthetic effects (such as taste, odor, or color) in drinking water. EPA recommends secondary standards to water systems but does not require systems to comply.

Engineering Geology

ATTERBERG LIMITS

The Atterberg limits are a measure of the nature of a fine-grained soil. Soil occurs in four states that are dependent on the water content: solid, semi-solid, plastic and liquid. In each of the four states the consistency and behavior of a soil is varied. Also affected are the soil's engineering properties. The following terms relate to the designation of Atterberg limits:

- Atterberg limits: the boundaries between the four levels of soil consistency: liquid, plastic, semi-solid, and solid
- A-line: the division mark between clay and silt on the Atterberg plasticity chart
- plastic limit: lower boundary of plasticity, upper boundary of semisolid
- liquid limit: upper limit of plastic state, lower limit of liquid state
- plasticity index: range in water content between liquid and plastic boundaries
- U-line: mark or line dividing the upper limit of plasticity from the lower limit of liquidity

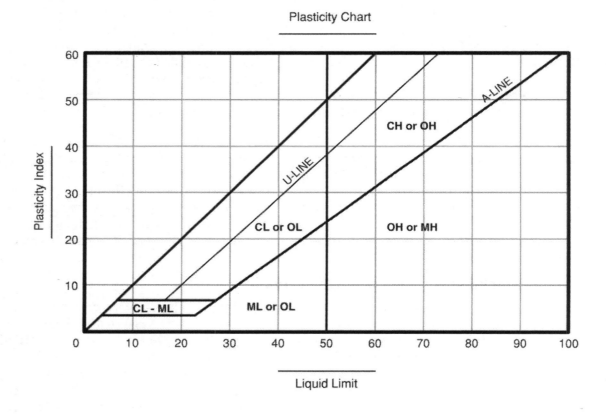

Plasticity Chart

SOIL CHARACTERISTICS IN ENGINEERING GEOLOGY

The following terms are used to describe soil characteristics in engineering geology:

- bulk density (ρ): the weight of a soil for every unit of volume
- dry density (ρ_d): weight of a unit volume of dry soil after sample has been heated to 103 degrees Celsius
- relative density (RD): the ratio of the difference between the maximum and actual void ratios for a soil; calculated with the equation:

$$RD = \frac{e_{max} - e}{e_{max} - e_{min}}$$

  where e_{max} is the void ratio of a soil at its loosest state, e is the in-situ void ratio, and e_{min} is the void ratio of the soil at its densest state. Synonymous with specific gravity

- Specific gravity (G_s): the ratio of the mass of a soil to the mass of an equal volume of distilled water at 4 degrees Celsius

SOIL CHARACTERISTICS TERMS

The following descriptive and quantitative terms are used to describe the characteristics of soil. Some of these terms also refer to the characteristics and interaction of pore fluid with containing soils:

- toughness: the degree of stress that soil can suffer before fracturing
- unit weight (γ): weight of a soil plus water for every unit of volume
- void ratio (e): the ratio of the volume of evacuated space to the volume of the solids in a sample of soil
- degree of saturation (S_R): the ratio of the volume of water to the total volume of void space
- porosity (n): the percentage of the total volume of a rock or soil sample that is made up of void spaces

DETERMINING PERCENTAGES OR RATIOS RELEVANT TO SOIL PHASE RELATIONSHIPS

Water content, porosity, and degree of saturation are typically expressed as a percentage. The equations for water content are: $w = W_w/W_s * 100\%$ (weight of water / weight of solids) and $w = M_w/M_s * 100\%$ (mass of water / mass of solids). The equation for porosity is: $n = V_v/V * 100\%$ (total volume of void spaces / total volume). The equation for degree of saturation is: $SR = V_w/V_v * 100\%$ (volume of water / volume of voids). Void ratio, bulk density, and unit weight are ratios not expressed as a percentage. The equation for void ratio is: $e = V_v/V_s$ (volume of voids / volume of solids). The equation for bulk density is: $\rho = M/V$ (total mass / total volume). The equation for unit weight is: $\gamma = W/V$ (total weight / total volume, usually in pounds/ft^3).

SOIL COMPRESSION TERMS

The following terms and measurements are used to discuss the compression of soil materials:

- compaction: involves increasing soil density by mechanically diminishing the spaces between particles. Natural compaction is also possible
- consolidation: a gradual decrease in the volume of a soil combined with an increase in the density of the soil. Induced by compaction, crystallization, and cementation
- relative compaction: the amount of compaction that occurs in relation to the moisture-density curve. This curve is also known as the compaction curve

- settlement: the slow downward movement of constructed foundations caused by the slow compression of the soil underneath the foundation.
- shrinkage limit: the water content at which the volume of the soil is lowest

SOIL STRESSES AND STRAINS TERMS

The following terms are used to describe the stresses and strains on soils:

- stress (σ): force per unit of area placed on a soil
- strain (ε): an alteration in the shape or volume of a soil related to stress. It is calculated as the ratio of the new shape compared to the original shape
- effective stress (σ'): the total amount of stress placed on a soil minus the pore-water pressure
- normal stress (σ_n): the component of total stress that acts perpendicular to the plane
- shear stress (τ): the component of total stress that acts parallel to any plane in question
- shear strength (s): the degree to which a soil can resist shear stress; this is dependent on the cohesion of soil particles and friction

VOLUME CHANGES IN SOILS

The following terms are used to describe volume changes in soils:

- dilatancy: the tendency of a material to increase in volume when subjected to a shape change. Also refers to material which can assume a close-packed structure from a open-packed structure
- dry strength: the resistance that a dry soil possesses to being crushed. A soil that is composed of clays and gravels will have relatively high dry strength
- quick condition: the tendency of some soils that lack cohesion to allow water to flow rapidly between grains and to liquefy the material. Such a soil does not possess significant bearing capacity. Bearing capacity is the ability of soils to support the loads imposed by buildings or structures

TYPES OF MODULUS

There are three different kinds of modulus, or ways to measure the stiffness of the material:

- bulk modulus (K; otherwise known as incompressibility modulus): a measure of a substance's resistance to uniform compression. It is defined as the pressure increase needed to affect a given relative decrease in volume
- shear modulus (G; also known as rigidity modulus): refers to the deformation of a solid when exposed to a force parallel to one of its surfaces as its opposite face is exposed to an opposing force. This will cause an object that is shaped like a rectangular prism to be deform into a parallelpiped
- Young's modulus (E; also known as the modulus of elasticity): a measure of the stiffness of a given material. Defined as the ratio, for small strains, of the rate of change of stress with strain

QUANTIFYING ENGINEERING PARAMETERS OF SOILS

The following tests are designed to quantify engineering parameters of soils:

- triaxial test: a common method to measure the mechanical properties of many deformable solids. The test is used for soil, sand, clay, and other granular material. Test involves a cylinder of soil which is subjected to uniform fluid pressure from all sides. After being checked for deformation, the sample is then subjected to a vertical load. Drainage conditions are controlled
- direct shear test: laboratory tests to measure the shear strength of soil in which the soil or rock sample is surrounded with sand and subjected to a series of mechanical stresses which are analyzed by computer. The sample is normally saturated before the test is run, but can be run at the in-situ moisture content
- unconfined compressive strength test: similar to a triaxial test but without external confining pressure applied

SOIL GRAIN SIZE

The following terms are used to describe the grain size of soil:

- well-graded soil: soil or unconsolidated sediment consisting of particles of several different sizes and having a uniform or equal distribution of particles from coarse to fine. A graded sand or sandstone containing coarse, medium, and fine particle sizes is an example
- effective size: corresponds with the weight percentage of material equal to a certain size amount. Measures the distribution of grain sizes; for example, a grain with an effective size of D_{30} would be finer than 70% of the other grains in the sample
- gap-graded soil: any soil that is missing distinct particle size ranges.
- coefficient of curvature (C_C): a measure of the curve on a grain size distribution plot
- coefficient of uniformity (C_U): a measure of the degree to which grain sizes are uniform. Found by determining the ratio of particle sizes

SOIL STRENGTH INVESTIGATIONS

The following terms are related to soil strength investigations:

- bearing capacity: the maximum load per unit area that a particular soil can be subjected to before it collapses. Bearing capacity is the ability of soils to support the loads imposed by buildings or structures
- consistency: the general amount of cohesion in soil particles
- critical void ratio: the void ratio of soil that stays the same even during shearing events
- Mohr circle: a graph showing all of the individual stresses that act on a single point on a plane. The x-axis will indicate normal stress, while the y-axis will indicate shear stress
- Mohr-Coulomb equation: calculates the amount of shear stress that causes a material to fracture

STRUCTURE OF MOISTURE CONTENT IN SOIL

The following terms are used to describe the structure of the moisture content in soil:

- liquefaction: Soils that transform from the solid state to a consistency of a heavy liquid as a consequence of increasing porewater pressure. Liquefaction is caused by the tendency of a soil to decrease in volume when subjected to cyclic undrained loading

- optimum moisture content: the level of moisture required to reach the maximum dry density level of the soil. At this point any further addition of moisture increases the density of the soil
- piping: erosion by percolating water in a layer of subsoil which results in caving and in the formation of narrow conduits, tunnels, or pipes through which soluble or granular soil material is removed. An example is the movement of material from the permeable foundation of a dam or levee by the flow or seepage of water along underground passages
- seepage: the flow of a fluid through soil pores

PHASES OF MATTER FOUND IN PARTIALLY SATURATED SOILS

Partially-saturated soils will contain matter in the solid, gas, and liquid phases. The volume of a partially-saturated soil can be calculated with the equation: $V = V_a + V_w + V_s$, in which V_a is the volume of air, V_w is the volume of water, and V_s is the volume of solids. When soil water content is reduced below saturation the interface between air and water within pores are curved because of surface tension. As the water content is reduced, drainage occurs from progressively smaller openings, and the interface radius decreases. On occasion, it will be necessary to simply calculate the volume of air and water, which is expressed as V_v. It can be assumed that the gaseous constituents of a partially-saturated soil do not have any weight.

WEIGHT OF SOLIDS, DRY DENSITY, UNIT WEIGHT OF DRY SOIL, POROSITY AND VOID RATIO

Soil is usually composed of three phases: solid, liquid, and gas. Mechanical properties of soil directly depend on the way these phases interact with each other and with applied potentials. The following equations all have the same denominator and are used to calculate the above-mentioned properties (w is the percentage of water content). The equation for the weight of solids is: $WS = W / (1 + w)$, in which W is total weight. The equation for dry density is: $\rho_d = \rho / (1 + w)$, in which ρ is bulk density, calculated as mass divided by volume. The equation for unit weight of dry soil is: $\gamma d = \gamma / (1 + w)$, in which γ is unit weight. The equation for porosity is: $n = e / (1+e)$, in which e is void ratio. Finally, the equation for void ratio is: $e = n / (1-n)$, in which n is porosity.

CALCULATING THE DEGREE OF SATURATION

There are two different equations that can be used to express the degree of soil saturation. One equation is a rendering of the definition of degree of saturation:

$$S_r = \frac{V_w}{V_v}$$

where S_r is the degree of soil saturation, V_w is the volume of water in the soil, and V_v is the volume of void space in the soil.

The other way to calculate degree of saturation is as follows:

$$S_r = \frac{w G_s}{e}$$

where w is the ratio of water content ratio, G_s is the specific gravity, and e is the void ratio. These three quantities are themselves calculated as follows:

$$w = \frac{m_w}{m_s}; \quad G_s = \frac{m_s}{V_s \rho_w}; \quad e = \frac{V_v}{V_s}$$

where m_w is the mass of water in the soil, m_s is the solid mass of the soil, V_s is the volume of the solid, and ρ_s is the density of the solid.

TESTING DENSITY

Density is a property of particulate materials defined as the mass of the particles of a given volume divided by the volume that they occupy. There are a number of different techniques to test for density in soils. The Proctor Compaction Test and the similar Modified Proctor Compaction Test are utilized to ascertain the maximum achievable density of soils. The Proctor Compaction Test (ASTM D698) uses a 4-inch diameter mold holding 1/30th of a cubic foot of soil. The soil is compacted in three separate lifts using 25 blows by a 5.5 lb hammer falling 12 inches. This delivers an effective compactive effort of approximately 12,400 ft-lb/ft^3. The Modified Proctor Compaction Test (ASTM D1557) utilizes the same mold as the Proctor Compaction test, but differs in the use of a 10 lb. hammer falling through 18 inches with 25 blows on each of five lifts. This achieves an effective compactive effort approaching 56,000 ft-lb/ft^3. There is also a test (ASTM D4253) which uses a vibrating table using standard vibrations for a standard time to densify the soil.

COMPACTION TESTING

Compaction is the process of increasing the bulk density of a soil or aggregate by driving out air. For any soil the density obtained through compaction depends on the moisture content. At very high moisture contents, the maximum density is achieved when the soil is compacted to saturation with most or all of the air being driven out. At low moisture contents, the soil particles interfere with each other and the addition of some moisture will allow for a greater bulk density. Peak density occurs at the point at which this effect begins to be counteracted by the saturation of the soil. The procedures for compaction testing include: The Proctor Test, which uses a 4-inch diameter mold holding 1/30th of a cubic foot of soil that is compacted in three separate lifts of soil using 25 blows by a 5.5 lb hammer falling 12 inches; and the Modified Proctor Test, which uses the same mold, but uses a 10 lb. hammer falling through 18 inches, with 25 blows on each of five lifts.

DETERMINING DRY STRENGTH, DILATANCY, AND TOUGHNESS OF SOIL SAMPLES

There are three tests performed to determine the basic characteristics of a soil sample:

- In the toughness test, the sample is rolled into a cylinder about an eighth of an inch in diameter. The sample is then folded and re-rolled again. This process is repeated several times. When the plastic limit of the sample has been reached, it will become rigid and lose plasticity.
- In the dilatancy test, the sample is made slightly moist and is shaken latterly in the hand. If water beads up on the surface of the sample, it is considered dilatant.
- In a dry strength test, the soil is moistened until it has a consistency similar to putty. The sample is then dried out and broken. A soil with a high degree of plasticity will also have a high degree of dry strength.

CLASSIFICATION OF ORGANIC SOILS AND BOUNDARY SOILS

In the Unified Soil Classification System (USCS), highly organic soils are labeled Pt (peat). There are organic subdivisions in the silt and clay divisions, both those with high and low liquid limit. Organic soils are those that have an organic content above 18%. If the organic content is between 18 and 36%, the soil is most likely an organic clay or an organic silt. If the sample has an organic content between 36% and 90%, it is classified either as peaty. A boundary soil is one that has characteristics of two different soil types. Boundary soils will typically have a liquid limit value close to 50 so that they straddle the dividing line between the two subdivisions of silt and clay.

STRESS

Stress is a measure of force per unit area within a body. It is a body's internal distribution of force per area that reacts to external applied loads. Stress is often broken down into its shear and normal components as these have unique physical significance. In short, stress is to force as strain is to elongation. When discussing soils, stress is defined as the amount of force that needs to be applied per unit area in order to cause a certain amount of deformation. A normal or compressive stress is considered positive when it points in the direction of the object; a parallel or shear stress is considered positive when it tends to place the object in a counterclockwise rotation. When drawn, stresses are divided into three vectors, one for each of the three dimensions.

EFFECTIVE STRESS AND TOTAL VERTICAL STRESS

The concept of effective stress is one of the most important contributions to soil mechanics. It is a measure of the stress on the soil skeleton (the collection of particles in contact with each other), and determines the ability of soil to resist shear stress. Effective stress (σ') on a plane within a soil mass is the difference between total stress (σ) and pore water pressure (u). The total stress σ is equal to the overburden pressure or stress, which is made up of the weight of soil vertically above the plane, together with any forces acting on the soil surface (e.g. the weight of a structure). The e equation used to calculate total vertical stress (σ_v) is:

$$\sigma_v = z\gamma$$

where z is the depth, and γ is the total unit weight of soil.

MOHR CIRCLE

Coulomb's hypothesis determines the combination of both shear and normal stress required to cause the fracture of a material. Mohr's circle is used to determine which principal stresses that will produce this combination of shear and normal stress, and the angle of the plane in which this will occur. Normal stresses are plotted on the x-axis while shear stresses are plotted on the y-axis. The center point of the circle is the normal stress, and the radius is the maximum shear stress. A Mohr circle is formed by drawing a diagram of the object and all the stresses that are acting upon it. The diameter of the Mohr circle is determined by the maximum and minimum principal stresses. Any plane that is drawn through the object in question will lie in some relation to the major principal plan; the angle of relation is called the Mohr circle plot. The Mohr's circle is used to find the planes of maximum normal and shear stresses, as well as the stresses on known weak planes.

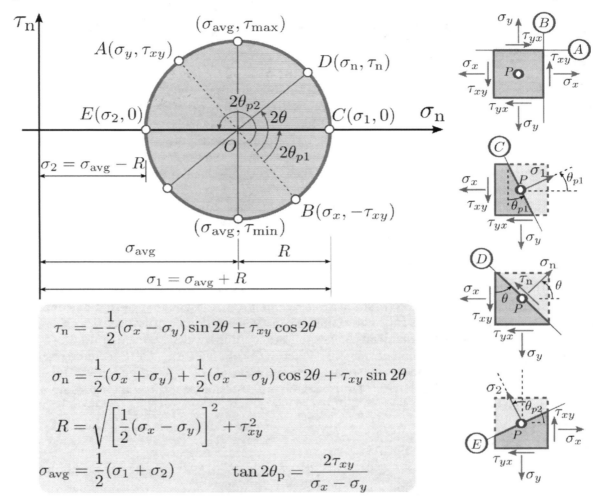

$$\tau_{\mathrm{n}} = -\frac{1}{2}(\sigma_x - \sigma_y)\sin 2\theta + \tau_{xy}\cos 2\theta$$

$$\sigma_{\mathrm{n}} = \frac{1}{2}(\sigma_x + \sigma_y) + \frac{1}{2}(\sigma_x - \sigma_y)\cos 2\theta + \tau_{xy}\sin 2\theta$$

$$R = \sqrt{\left[\frac{1}{2}(\sigma_x - \sigma_y)\right]^2 + \tau_{xy}^2}$$

$$\sigma_{\mathrm{avg}} = \frac{1}{2}(\sigma_1 + \sigma_2) \qquad \tan 2\theta_{\mathrm{p}} = \frac{2\tau_{xy}}{\sigma_x - \sigma_y}$$

STRAIN THAT A MATERIAL CAN EXPERIENCE BASED ON DIFFERENT TYPES OF SHEAR

In any branch of science dealing with materials and their behavior, strain is the geometrical expression of deformation caused by the action of stress on a physical body. When an object is subjected to pure shear stress, this is known as volumetric strain. Volumetric strain is quantified as the ratio of the change in volume to the original volume. Shear strain, on the other hand, is the result of either simple or simple rotational shear. Sheer strain is calculated as the maximum displacement divided by either the tangent of the angle of displacement or the link between the bottom and top planes of the object. Axial strain, otherwise known as normal strain, is a compressive force that acts along one axis of the object. It is calculated as the ratio of the change in length divided by original length.

ELASTIC PROPERTIES

An elastic material is one that changes shape in response to any stress, but immediately reverts back to its original shape when the stress ends. The relationship between stress and strain can be quantified with Poisson's ratio, Young's modulus, the shear or rigidity modulus, or the bulk or incompressibility ratio. Poisson's ratio is the comparison of the change in length divided by the change in diameter. Young's modulus is calculated as normal stress divided by axial strain in cases where the stress-strain ratio is constant. The bulk or incompressibility modulus is calculated as hydrostatic pressure divided by volumetric strain, and is used in cases where pressure is uniform on the object in all directions. Bulk modulus is the inverse of compressibility, and shear modulus is calculated as shear stress divided by shear strain.

SHEAR STRENGTH

Shear strength describes the maximum physical ability of a soil to deform before a point of significant plastic deformation or yielding occurs due to an applied shear stress. Two theories are commonly used to estimate the shear strength of a soil depending on the rate of shearing as a frame of reference. The Tresca theory applies to short term loading and is also referred to as the undrained strength or the total stress condition. The Mohr-Coulomb theory applies to long term loading of soil and is known as drained strength or the effective stress condition. In modern soil mechanics, including building design for earthquake protection, the above-mentioned classical techniques are frequently superseded by critical state theory. The factors controlling shear strength in soils are: soil composition, state (or void ratio), structure, and loading conditions. Shear strength is determined and quantified through the following tests: cone penetration test, direct shear test (ASTM D3080), triaxial shear test, and the unconfined compression test (ASTM D2166).

BEHAVIOR OF COHESIONLESS SOILS OR SOILS

Cohesion is the component of shear strength of a soil that is independent of interparticle friction. In soils, true cohesion is caused by electrostatic forces, cementing, or through cohesion by contained plant roots. Apparent cohesion is caused by capillary pressure and pore pressure. Depending on the initial void ratio of a soil, the material can respond to loading by either strain-softening or strain-hardening. Strain-softened soils may be triggered to collapse if the static shear stress is greater than the ultimate or steady-state shear strength of the soil. In this case, liquefaction occurs. Soil liquefaction describes the behavior of loose saturated cohesionless soils which go from a solid state to having the consistency of a heavy liquid as a consequence of increasing porewater pressures.

MOHR-COULOMB FAILURE ENVELOPE

The Mohr-Coulomb theory is used in soil engineering to define shear strengths of soils at different effective stresses. Coulomb's friction hypothesis describes and determines the combination of both shear and normal stress that will cause a material to fracture. A soil failure envelope, also known as a strength envelope, is an indication of the maximum amount of shear stress that a soil can withstand before fracturing. This level can be determined by plotting the experimental results of a strength test on a Mohr plot axis.

Failure envelope can be calculated with the following equation:

$$s = c + \sigma_n \tan \varphi$$

where s is shear strength, c is cohesion, σ_n is normal stress at failure, and $\tan \varphi$ is the coefficient of internal friction.

EXPANSIVE SOILS

Expansive soils, referred to as swelling soils, are those that assume a general volume increase when subjected to moisture. Swelling soils always contain clay minerals that readily attract and absorb water. Another type of swelling material is known as swelling bedrock, containing rock called claystone. When water is absorbed these clays or bedrock experience a large increase in internal pressure or an expansion of volume. In many cases, expansive soils are buried under a layer of topsoil or dense vegetation and cannot be identified at the surface. Test holes can be drilled by geotechnical and civil engineering firms or by some construction companies to collect samples. After the samples are taken, they are sent to a laboratory where the swelling potential is determined. In areas where there is a high concentration of swelling soils, laboratory analysis of the soil is required by law. Mitigation of expansive soils involves dewatering foundations in existing and designed structures.

UNIFIED SOIL CLASSIFICATION SYSTEM AND THE MODIFIED WENTWORTH SCALE

The Unified Soil Classification System (USCS) is a soil classification system used in the engineering and geology disciplines to describe the texture and grain size of a soil. The classification system can be applied to most soils and unconsolidated materials, and is represented by a two-letter symbol. The first letter in the classification system describes the grain size of the particles in the soil or aggregate as follows: (G) gravel, (S) sand, (M) silt, (C) clay, (O) organic. The second letter designation describes particle size and grading, (P) poorly graded (uniform particle size), and (W) well graded (diverse particle size), or (H) high plasticity, and (L) low plasticity. Soils can be classified into fairly small groups based on this two-letter system.

Under the Unified Soil Classification System (USCS) coarse grained soils will have more than 50% of total material retained on a No.200 (0.075 mm) sieve. The two subdivisions of coarse-grained soils are: gravel, with a requirement that greater than 50% of coarse fraction be retained on No.4 (4.75 mm) sieve; and sand, required to have 50% of its coarse fraction pass a No.4 sieve. Gravel can consist of clean gravel up to gravel with greater than 12% fines. The group divisions of gravel are: well graded gravel, fine to coarse gravel, poorly graded gravel, silty gravel, and clayey gravel. Sand can consist of clean sand up to sand with greater than 12% fines. Sand group subdivisions are: well graded sand, fine to coarse sand, poorly graded sand, silty sand, and clayey sand.

FINE-GRAINED SOILS AND HIGHLY ORGANIC SOILS

Fine grained soils will have more than 50% of their content pass through a No.200 sieve. The subdivisions are: silt and clay with a liquid limit less than 50; and silt and clay with a liquid limit ≥ 50. Both are further subdivided in organic and inorganic components. Inorganic silts and fine sands will have a very small dry strength, no toughness, and either a quick or slow dilatancy. Inorganic clay has a low to medium plasticity and will have a medium to high dry strength, a moderate amount of toughness, and little if any dilatancy. Organic silts and organic silt-clays with a low plasticity will have a slight to medium dry strength, slight toughness, and a slow dilatancy. Inorganic silts and fine sandy or silty soils will have a low level of toughness, a slight dry strength, and a slow dilatancy. Inorganic clays with a high level of plasticity will have a high dry strength, a high degree of toughness, and no dilatancy.

UNIFIED SOIL CLASSIFICATION SYSTEM VS. MODIFIED WENTWORTH SCALE

Particle size, also called grain size, refers to the diameter of individual grains of sediment, or the particles in clastic rocks. There are two different scales used to classify the grain size of soils: the Unified Soil Classification System (USCS), and the Modified Wentworth (MW) scale. The USCS scale is typically used for soils, while the MW scale is more commonly used for rocks. In the Modified Wentworth scale size ranges define limits of classes that are given names. The classes: coarse, medium, and fine, are augmented by the qualifying term "very" for further distinction. The use of this scale relies on observation, rather than the sieve analysis used in the USCS scale. The USCS system relies more on specifications based on sieve analyses. The classification system can be applied to most soils and unconsolidated materials, and is represented by a two-letter symbol

TYPES OF DOWNWARD MOVEMENT OF SOIL OR ROCK

The following five kinds of downward movement of soil or rock can occur:

- avalanche: a large mass of snow, ice, soil, or rock, or mixtures of these materials, falling, sliding, or flowing very rapidly under the force of gravity
- fall: the free falling or precipitous movement of a detached segment of bedrock of any size from a cliff or other very steep outcrop or slope
- rotational slide or slump: a slide of homogeneous earth or clay in which the slip surface of failure closely follows the arc of a circle
- topple: an overturning slope movement with a turning point below the center of gravity of the falling unit
- translational slide: landslide displacement in which the components have not rotated relative to one another, so that features that were parallel before movement remain so afterwards

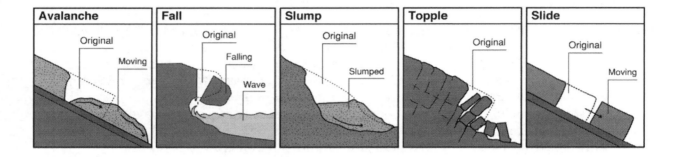

TYPES OF DOWNWARD MOVEMENTS THAT MAY OCCUR IN GEOLOGY

There are six kinds of downward movement that may occur in geology:

- settlement: natural compaction or re-compaction in disturbed sediments
- differential settlement: general downward movement or subsidence that occurs in differing areas of a structure at differing rates
- hydrocompaction: the collapse or densification of soil due to the effects of saturation or wetting
- subsidence: the vertical settling of the surface of the Earth without or with only minimal horizontal motion
- soil creep: the gradual, steady downhill movement of soil and loose rock material on a slope that may be very gentle but is usually steep
- triggered creep: any slow movement downhill that occurs as a result of an externally applied force. For example, an earthquake

LANDSLIDES

The term landslide covers a wide variety of mass-movement and other gravity-driven downslope transport processes involving the movement of soil and rock material en masse. Typically, displaced material in landslides will move over a relatively confined zone or surface. Wide ranging slope angles and diversity of geologic materials of varying properties that affect resistance to shear, result in a great range of landslide morphologies, slide rates, and sizes. Landsliding is often preceded and followed by perceptible creep along the surface of sliding and/or within the slide mass itself. Terminology used to classify and describe landslide types generally includes the

104

landform or material involved, as well as the process responsible for it. Some examples are: rockfall, translational slide, block glide, avalanche, mudflow, liquefaction slide, and slump.

When describing landslides, geologists typically used a system of two-word descriptors: the first describing the material that is fallen, and the second describing the movement that has occurred. A landslide may contain a number of different materials ranging from soil to rock. A fall is defined as the relatively free falling or precipitous movement of a newly detached segment of bedrock (usually massive, homogeneous, or jointed) of any size from a cliff or other very steep slope; it is the fastest form of mass movement and is most frequent in mountain areas and during spring when there is repeated freezing and thawing of water in cracks in the rock. A topple is an overturning slope movement, with a turning point below the center of gravity of the falling unit. A spread is a simple dry landslide. A flow is defined as a mass movement of unconsolidated material that exhibits a continuity of motion and a plastic or semifluid behavior resembling that of a viscous fluid. Water is usually required for most types of flow movement.

The following terms are related to landslides:

- crown: the practically undisturbed material still in place and adjacent to the highest parts of the scarp along which a landslide moved
- head scarp/main scarp: a relatively straight, cliff like face or slope of considerable linear extent which breaks the general continuity of the land. Separates surfaces involved in the landslide from those at higher elevations that were not involved in the event.
- toe: the farthest reaches of the bottom of a landslide. The zone of maximum extent of runout
- flow: a mass movement of unconsolidated material that moves in a plastic or semi fluid motion resembling a viscous fluid. Examples are: creep, solifluction, earthflow, mudflow, debris flow, and sturzstrom. Water is usually required for most types of flow movement

ELEMENTS OF LANDSLIDE INVESTIGATION

A geologist will perform a landslide investigation in order to determine whether a landslide is likely to occur in some location where a structure is to be placed. A landslide investigation has a number of steps. The first step in performing such an investigation is to assemble historical information on the natural and human history of the region. The following sources are useful for acquiring this information: municipal files, notes from other geological projects, aerial photos, reports, and maps. A full investigation of the subsurface conditions, including topography, drainage, geological structure and weathering, and faults, should be performed before any construction is initiated. In general, all the data should be aimed at locating any weak regions in the location.

LANDSLIDE STABILITY ANALYSIS METHODS

As part of a landslide investigation, a landslide and stability analysis will be performed in order to calculate what is known as the factor of safety (F). The factor of safety is simply the ratio of the forces that will resist a landslide divided by the forces that will promote a landslide. The factor of safety (F) is the likelihood of a landslide occurring in a particular area. In order to perform this analysis, a geologist will need to have an equilibrium slope analysis, a measure of the sheer strength of local soil, and the general idea of the orientation and angle of internal friction of the subsurface materials. In many cases, it will be possible to perform a landslide stability analysis by using a general slope stability chart.

PREVENT LANDSLIDES

There are a few basic ways to mitigate the possibility of landslide. Extremely steep grades can be minimized by recontouring and moving material from the crown to toe area, thus reducing the chance of a landslide. Decreasing saturation and pore-pressure of soils by diverting surface water or adding dewatering wells, horizontal drains, or trenches, can minimize the risk of landslide. Monitor wells and piezometers can be installed to monitor interior dynamic of potential slide areas and to alert for potential landslide events. Architecturally, buttresses and retaining walls can be put in to stabilize unsteady slopes. Rocks that are considered to be unstable may be shored up with rock bolts, and soil can be hardened through thermic treatment or grouting.

EXPRESSING THE STEEPNESS OF A SLOPE

There are a few different ways to express the steepness of a slope. The most common way to express slope is as the ratio between the horizontal and vertical. It is commonly expressed, for example, as three-to-one (3:1), or two-to-one (2:1), with the vertical component of slope as one. Another way to express slope is as a grade, or as a ratio between vertical and horizontal slope; this is typically expressed as a percentage. The third and final way to express slope is to consider the angle of the slope as compared to the horizontal as measured with a slopemeter. The slope angle is calculated by considering the arctangent of the vertical extent divided by the horizontal extent.

SUBSIDENCE

Subsidence is the sudden sinking or gradual downward settling of the Earth's surface with little or no horizontal motion. The movement is not restricted in rate, magnitude, or area involved. Subsidence is many times caused by the activity of humans. Human-caused subsidence can be related to subsurface mining, oil extraction, or the pumping of groundwater. Underground and near-surface coal mining is especially susceptible to subsidence as the sedimentary host rocks are seldom competent. Hard-rock mining related subsidence can be severe near stoped areas or buried shafts/adits. Removal of large amounts of oil or gas from a section can cause subsidence. Occasionally urban or suburban planners are challenged by subsidence from abandoned mines. Subsidence may also be caused by natural geologic processes, such as dissolution, thawing, compaction, slow crustal warping, or withdrawal of fluid lava from beneath a solid crust.

MATERIALS USED IN AN ENGINEERED STRUCTURE

The following terms relate to the different materials that may be used in an engineered structure:

- grout: a pumpable slurry of cement or a mixture of cement and sand that is forced into boreholes or crevices in a rock to prevent ground water infiltration. Frequently it is used to seal crevices below a dam or to consolidate and re-cement together broken or brecciated rock formations. Also called cement grout
- gunite: a mixture of portland cement and sand that is applied through pressure using a specially adapted hose. It is frequently used in a sealing technique to preserve mine timbers and roadways, and as a fireproofing agent
- riprap: a layer or series of layers of durable and angular rock fragments placed or fitted together. Its purpose is to secure a slope or to prevent erosion of a slope or face by waves or the action of water currents. If riprap is secured with concrete it is called grouted riprap
- shotcrete: a mixture of portland cement and sand that commonly includes coarse aggregate (up to 2 cm).

TYPES OF GROUND MATERIALS

The following terms relate to the different types of ground materials:

- flowing ground: liquefied soil that is emplaced or propelled by seepage into a tunnel or excavation due to a lack of soil cohesion or adequate sealing
- raveling ground: rock that breaks into small round pieces when being drilled that tends to cave into the hole when the drill string is pulled. Rock or soil that forms agglomerated particles that bind a drill string by becoming wedged between the drill rod and the borehole
- running ground: soil that is cohesionless. May be semiplastic or plastic and is typically seen in wet clays. These soils readily deform under pressure and squeezing into openings and crevices. These soils may enter a mine tunnel once the roof and wall supports have been removed
- squeezing ground: any soil or rock that after entering a mine excavation or tunnel which is seen to maintain a constant volume
- swelling ground: any rock or soil which undergoes a volume increase after excavation. Typical of many clay-rich soils or formations

DAMS

Dams are walls to hold back water. They are typically secured at either side by an abutment. The main part of the dam will be constructed of some impervious material, with pervious areas on either side of the dam's core. The water in the reservoir being held back by the dam will be able to penetrate the pervious areas upstream. Below the dam, a cutoff trench will be dug that prevents seepage from emerging from the reservoir. In order to prevent the dam from leaking, the phreatic line must curve down and away from the reservoir heights on the upstream side, in the direction of the dams based on the downstream side. Water pressure relief can be furnished by blanket and toe drains at the base of the pervious zone, as well as by further relief wells beyond the toe drain.

Building a dam to hold back a water reservoir is an enormous engineering endeavor. A river diversion is typically required involving coffer dams and construction site de-watering before construction of the dam can begin, a major project in itself. Rock scaling and wall preparation must be performed upon the canyon walls where the dam is located. Beforehand, geologists spend many hours analyzing aerial photographs, geologic maps, photogrammetric data, core drill data and logs, and results of engineering tests on the rocks hosting the dam site. Test would include shearing and compression tests on rock near the dam and fracture and detailed structural analyses of rocks in and around the dam site. Any dam investigation must contain a very detailed and specific earthquake and prior tectonic evaluation of the dam site and environs.

TYPES OF DAMS BUILT IN THE UNITED STATES

Large dam in the USA are typically masonry arch dams. In the arch dam, stability is obtained by a combination of arch shape and gravity action. The large dams such as Hoover Dam are concrete gravity arch dams. Gravity dams are designed to ensure that their stabilities are secured by size and shape. This guarantees that they will resist overturning, sliding and crushing at the toe. Embankment dams are made from compacted earth, and have three main types, rock-fill, earth-fill, and asphalt-concrete core dams. Embankment dams rely on their weight to hold back the force of water. A cofferdam is commonly made of wood, concrete, or steel sheeting, and is a (usually temporary) barrier constructed to exclude water from an area that is normally submerged.

CAUSES OF DAM FAILURES

The main causes of dam failure are: spillway design error; geological instability caused by changes to water levels during filling or poor surveying; poor maintenance of outlet pipes; extreme rainfall;

107

and human or computer design error. Dam failures are generally catastrophic if the structure is breached or significantly damaged. Routine monitoring of seepage from drains in, and around, larger dams is necessary to anticipate any problems and permit remedial action to be taken before structural failure occurs. Most dams include a mechanism that permits the reservoir to be lowered in the event of such problems. Embankment dams are probably the most susceptible to failure as they are generally constructed of unconsolidated or grouted material. Concrete gravity arch dams are less prone to catastrophic failure due to their concrete construction.

USING FLOW NETS TO HELP DESIGN A DAM

A flow net is a graphical representation of two-dimensional steady-state groundwater flow through aquifer. Construction of a flownet is often used for solving groundwater flow problems where the geometry makes analytical solutions impractical. These diagrams are often used in the design of dams, to determine where water pressure will tend to accumulate. On such a diagram, the maximum equipotential line will be the horizontal line at the base, while the minimum equipotential line will be the horizontal line at the base of the downstream area. Flow lines will then be drawn to show the possible paths of water beneath the structure. The shortest flow line will be the curve that joins the intersection of the dam and the upstream ground with the intersection of the dam and the downstream ground; the line drawn along the impervious boundary beneath the ground at the base of the dam will be the longest flow line.

The following terms refer to dams:

- abutment: a surface or mass provided to withstand thrust as in the end supports of an arch or bridge or the terminal of a dam
- cut off: an impermeable wall or other structure placed within the abutments or beneath the base of a dam to prevent or reduce seepage loss. Typically developed in porous or fractured strata beneath or adjacent to a dam. It may be made of concrete, interlocking sheet piling, or grout injected in a pattern
- dam crest: a dam's flat top
- freeboard: the distance between the crest of a dam and the top of the water reservoir below
- pressure-relief well: a well drilled at the base of a dam that prevents seepage underneath the dam and relieves water pressure
- random zones: any area within a dam where excavated materials are stored
- spillway: a venue for the flow of water in the reservoir, which serves to reduce water pressure by allowing some water to go over or around the dam

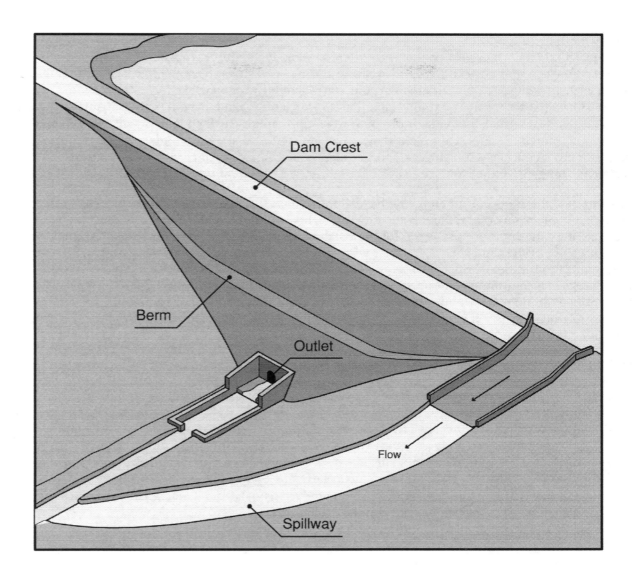

TYPES OF ENGINEERED STRUCTURES

The following terms are types of engineered structures:

- berm: a bench built into the sloping wall of an open pit or quarry to break the slope angle of an acceleration slope and to prevent and arrest rock fall or slide material
- grout curtain: a pattern or grid of intersecting drill holes into which grout has been injected to form a barrier. Used around an excavation or under dams to form a zone through which ground water cannot seep or flow
- lagging: used to secure the roof and sides behind the main timber or steel supports in a mine or excavation. This provides early resistance to pressure to discourage displacement of roof materials.
- phreatic line: the line or level of seepage. The upper water surface of the zone of seepage
- slaking: crumbling and disintegration of rocks upon exposure to weathering related to air or moisture. Also refers to the breaking up of clay or soil when saturated with water, or of the effect observed in coal or clay-rich sedimentary rocks when exposed to air

109

TUNNELS

A tunnel should be oriented such that it cuts across geology and intercepts desired zones of interest. Rock competence and ground stability at the portal site and available space for tailings are of concern. In general, areas with high groundwater and weak subsurface formations should not be tunnel sites. If at all possible, a tunnel should not cross a large fault or void in the subsurface unless it is a targeted zone such as a vein or ore body. Pre-tunneling core drilling data will assist in layout of planned tunnels. Tunnel siting should maximize efficiency of access to underground target, environmental concerns, and storage and site plan issues. A major concern in tunnel siting is avalanche danger. Tunnels must be sites out of direct and recurrent avalanche zones.

Conventional methods of tunneling involve drilling and blasting. After each shot, the broken rock (muck) at the face must be removed and any timbering completed before the next shot can be drilled. These methods are preferred for hardrock mining. After the tunnel has been established structures like arches and rock bolts must be created to maintain the tunnel structure. In continuous mining a machine cuts or rips coal from the face and loads it onto conveyors or into shuttle cars in a continuous operation. This eliminates the drilling and shooting operations of conventional mining. Continuous mining provides a continuous flow of ore and eliminates the need for multiple heading in conventional technique to achieve the same. This method is more applicable to coal mining.

The following parts of a tunnel all relate to the ground surface:

- shaft: A vertical excavation, driven from the surface, that is typically of limited area compared to its depth.
- adit: a horizontal or nearly horizontal tunnel constructed into a hillside, typically at a level below a known ore body or coal seam, for accessing working or for dewatering of a mine.
- stope: any excavation in a mine designed for removing ore. Shape and size are determined by, and are directly related to, the physical dimensions or shape of the orebody
- raise: a vertical opening in a mine driven upward from a tunnel level to connect with the level above. Typically, does not connect to the surface
- drift: an entry constructed into the slope of a hill that is usually driven horizontally into an ore body or coal seam
- winze: a vertical shaft connecting two underground levels in a mine. Does not reach to the surface
- crown: the curved roof of a tunnel excavation
- invert: the floor or bottom of a closed water conduit, aqueduct, tunnel, or drain

ROCK QUALITY DESIGNATION

The designation of rock quality, known by the initials RQD, is performed by analyzing the rock core. In order to be suitable for analysis, the rock core must be at least 2 inches in diameter. RQD is the total length of all pieces of core that are twice the diameter of the core divided by the total length of the core; this value is expressed in terms of a percentage.

- A rock in good condition has an RQD of between 75 and 90%.
- A rock in fair condition has a RQD of between 30 and 75%.
- A rock in poor condition has a RQD between 25 and 30%.

Another way of designating rock quality is with Terzaghi numbers, which place a rock on a scale of one to nine: nine is a swelling rock, and one is a hard rock.

110

GROUT

Grout is a mixture of cement and fine sand that is commonly forced or pumped into boreholes to prevent ground water seepage from flowing into an excavation or underground working. Grouting is utilized to seal crevices in a dam foundation, or to consolidate and cement together rock fragments in a brecciated or fragmented formation. Grout is often used to stabilize abandoned mine related subsidence hazards in areas of near-surface mining. Pressure grouting is used to re-densify vuggy ground and to re-level structures damaged by subsidence or settling. Grout is typically prepared with very high slumps and most often does not contain a coarse aggregate faction. It is usually a combination of cement, sand, fly ash, and water. Some grout is prepared so as to be non-shrinking in order to insure competent seals.

In dam construction, grout can be used to prevent seepage and to enhance stability of the overall dam. It should be applied after the site has been excavated but before dam construction begins. Often times, engineers will use so-called grout blankets, which are broad expanses of relatively thin grout, in order to limit permeability on the upstream side of the dam. In order to increase the strength of surrounding rocks, engineers might use off pattern grouting techniques, which involve forcing grout into specially arrayed boreholes.

ENGINEERING CEMENT AGGREGATES TO GAIN THE MAXIMUM STRENGTH AND LONGEVITY

In its simplest form, concrete is a mixture of paste and aggregates. The paste is composed of portland cement and water and acts to coat the surface of both the fine and coarse aggregates. Through the chemical reaction known as hydration the paste hardens and gains strength to form a rock-like mass called concrete. Typically, a mix is about 10 to 15 percent cement, 60 to 75 percent aggregate and 15 to 20 percent water. Entrained air in many concrete mixes may also take up another 5 to 8 percent. It is a good rule of thumb to keep water as minimal as possible. As for the aggregates, they should be chosen with an eye towards size and grade. Materials that are likely to become corrupted during multiple freeze and thaw sessions should be avoided. The following materials should never be used in a cement aggregate: coal, alkali, mica, or clay.

Economic Geology and Energy Reserves

CLASSIFICATION OF ORE DEPOSITS

Mineral deposits are classified in a number of different ways. The most basic classification system utilizes mineralogy. In this system the economic minerals contained in the deposit are designated, such as: massive sulfide, lead/zinc, or gold/silver deposit. This method does not designate mode of formation, temperature, or field habit. Mineral deposits are often classified by their temperatures of formation. These designations, epithermal, mesothermal, and hypothermal, refer to low-temperature, medium-temperature, and high-temperature respectively, and are useful as certain minerals or groups of minerals are recognizable by their temperature environment. The most common classification system utilizes mineralogy and field habit. In this system, the field habit of the deposit is modified by listing the minerals of the deposit such as: narrow vein gold/silver, lead/silver replacement, or disseminated gold/sulfide.

MAGMATIC SEGREGATION DEPOSITS

Magmatic deposits are related genetically with magmas that are emplaced into the crust. These deposits occur within the lithologies derived from the crystallization of such magmas. The most economically important magmatic deposits are related to mafic and ultramafic melts. These important deposit types include chromite deposits, nickel-copper deposits, and platinum group metal (PGM) deposits. Chromite deposits form as the product of the separation of the earliest crystallized solid phases, including chromium-rich spinels, which settle out from a differentiating melt. Chromite deposits can be either stratiform or podiform in habit. Nickel-copper deposits form as the end member of a process known as liquid immiscibility. This process involves the separation of a sulfur-rich liquid, containing Fe-Ni-Cu, from a parental magma. The sulfur-rich liquid produces an immiscible sulfide phase that segregates and settles to the base of the intrusive body. PGM deposits are similar in formation to nickel-copper segregation deposits.

SUBAERIAL VOLCANIC DEPOSITS

The predominant economic deposit associated with subaerial volcanism are industrial minerals and construction products. The most important industrial mineral deposits associated with volcanic events include kaolin, bentonite, zeolites, and scoriaceous cinders. All of these mineral resources occur as alteration products of volcanic rocks associated with subaerial eruptions. Kaolin it is found in pyroclastic flows and ash-flow tuffs. Bentonite occurs as stratiform mineral bodies within poor welded pumice-rich and ash-rich layers. Zeolites deposits are distal to volcanic vents. Volcanic cinders and other scoriaceous products of subaerial volcanic eruption are important as filler for cinderblocks and other uses. Epithermal hot-spring type gold/silver and base metal deposits are sometimes related to subaerial volcanism and are somewhat less economically important, although a few deposits are of exceptionally high grade. These deposits can also contain native mercury.

VOLCANOGENIC DEPOSITS

Volcanogenic massive sulfide ore deposits are a type of metal sulfide ore deposit, mainly Cu-Zn, which are associated with and created by volcanic-associated hydrothermal events in submarine environments thermal springs and volcanoes. They are predominantly stratiform accumulations of sulfide minerals that precipitate from hydrothermal fluids on or below the seafloor in a wide range of ancient and modern geological settings. Volcanogenic massive sulfide deposits are distinctive in that ore deposits are formed in close temporal association with submarine volcanism and are formed by hydrothermal circulation and exhalation of sulfides which are independent of

112

sedimentary processes. The temperature will be between 25 and 350°C. The rocks formed will contain sulfur, nickel, zinc, lead, copper, iron, tungsten, antimony, and tin. The largest deposits of sulfides are found close to the volcanogenic site, while iron and manganese oxides are typical of the areas farther away from the vent.

SEDIMENTARY ORES

Sedimentary ores occur when normal sedimentary rocks attain ore grade or are concentrated by normal processes. Some examples of sedimentary ore deposits include saline residues, phosphatic deposits, or bog iron ore of the Clinton type. Sedimentary ores are formed both by mechanical aggregation and through chemical precipitation operating syngenetically with the formation of the surrounding rock. The nature and tenor of sedimentary mineral deposits has changed throughout Earth's history in relation to changes in the oxidation (redox) state of the ocean-atmosphere system and biological evolution. Mechanical accumulation or aggregation occurs when surficial geologic and geomorphic processes concentrate minerals by specific gravity or by size. Some of the most common types of mechanical accumulation deposits are alluvial placers are gold and platinum.

FORMATION OF WEATHERING DEPOSITS

Important ore deposits associated with the weathering of rocks include aluminum/bauxite deposits, oxide deposits, and supergene enrichment of precious/base metal deposits. Weathering of aluminum-rich bedrocks, such as granite, gneiss, basalt, syenite, and shale in tropical lateritic environments produces important ore deposits of aluminum. The predominant minerals in bauxite deposits are gibbsite, boehmite, and diaspore. Weathering produces some economically important oxide deposits including conversion of primary magnetite minerals into secondary hematite. These accumulations of secondary hematite gravels are referred to as pisolites. Supergene enrichment involves the in-situ concentration of precious/base metal deposits in the near surface zone of weathering. In the supergene zone of an ore deposit, weathering will cause the formation of complex oxide minerals that are frequently very much enriched in the target metals of the deposit.

REGIONAL METAMORPHIC DEPOSITS

Regional metamorphism occurs in areas of convergent plate tectonics. Subduction and continent-continent collision result in orogensis and metamorphism. Convergent boundary plate movements result in thrusting, folding, and faulting in the upper parts of the Earth's crust, and plastic folding, metamorphism, and plutonism (formation of magma chambers at depth) at greater depths. Metamorphism is the mineralogical, chemical, and structural adjustment of solid mineral assemblages to changing physical and chemical conditions. Metamorphism may occur due to increasing temperature, pressure, or both. Minerals of economic importance are associated with regional metamorphism. Some examples include: fine quality gemstone rubies (red corundum), from Burma (Myanmar), formed through the regional metamorphism of impure carbonate rocks. These pigeon-blood rubies are the most valuable gemstones in the world. Most beryls, or emeralds and aquamarines, either crystallize from pegmatites (igneous processes) or through regional metamorphism of aluminous rocks to form talc and mica schists.

ANTICIPATING DEPOSITS TO FORM FROM SOLUTION-REMOBILIZATION

Mineral deposits related to solution and remobilization are called hydrothermal ore deposits. Cells of thermally heated groundwater near igneous intrusions, and in other areas of increased thermal gradients, circulate convectively dissolving metallic elements from country rocks. These metal-laden hydrothermal fluids rise upward or outward from source and fill fractures and weak zones in the rocks above. When temperature decreases sufficiently, or chemical conditions change due to interaction with wallrocks, dissolved metals in these fluids will precipitate out forming metallic veins or replacement deposits. Hydrothermal deposits are divided into the following classifications based on temperature of formation: epithermal (50° to 200° C), mesothermal (200° to 300° C), and hypothermal (300° to 500° C). Different mineral assemblages are associated with each temperature range and hence, the presence of desired mineral species can be anticipated if the mineralogy and field characteristics of the occurrence can be classified.

EPIGENETIC DEPOSITS

Epigenetic ore deposits are those that were formed subsequently after the rocks which host them. The term is the opposite of syngenetic deposits which were formed at the same time as the host rocks containing the deposits. Seafloor exhalative deposits or magmatic segregation deposits are examples of mineral occurrences that are syngenetic as the minerals were laid down at the same time as the host rocks. Epigenetic deposits are not directly related to the formation of the rocks which host them but frequently are due to some secondary connection to host rock formation. An example would be cooling history of a granite that controls fracturing to be later filled with hydrothermal minerals. Some examples of epigenetic deposits include: hydrothermal deposits and sediment hosted uranium deposits.

MINING METHODS USED TO EXTRACT RESOURCES OF INTEREST FOR ECONOMIC GEOLOGY

Mining methods are directly related to ore body configuration, ore grade, structure of host rocks, and economics. The mining method is designed to maximize recovery of ore and safety. Many ore bodies are amenable to surface mining and will be mined through the use of open-pit mining. Open pit mining is perhaps the least expensive mining method and allows for the mining of large high-tonnage, low-grade deposits. Underground mining methods consists of: drift mining, slope mining, shaft mining, drift and fill, sublevel caving, block caving, shrinkage stopping, longwall mining, room and pillar, and retreat mining. In situ mining, also known as solution mining, involves the pumping of reactive fluids from the surface down into a mineral deposit to dissolve the desired constituent. The mineral-laden fluid is then recovered and the desired commodity is recovered from the pregnant solution.

COAL

Coal is organic material that has been lithified by being pressurized and heated without oxygen over a long period of time. In general, higher degrees of metamorphism produce higher degrees of coal. The types of coal are: lignite, sub-bituminous, bituminous, and anthracite. Lignite is coal of low rank with a high inherent moisture and volatile matter content. Lignite is subdivided into black lignite, brown lignite, and brown coal. Sub-bituminous coal is of intermediate rank between lignite and bituminous. Bituminous coal ranks between sub bituminous coal and anthracite and contains more than 14% volatile matter (on a dry, ash-free basis) and has a calorific value of more than 11,500 Btu/lb. Anthracite is coal of the highest metamorphic rank, in which fixed-carbon content is between 92% and 98%. Anthracite is hard and black, and has a semi metallic luster and semi conchoidal fracture.

The largest collections of coal are in areas that used to be coastal plains, estuaries, or deltas, and subsequently became fresh or brackish swamps. Such swamps tend to accumulate huge amounts of organic matter, which over time becomes covered by water and other material to create a heated and pressurized environment for the formation of coal. The amount of time required for the formation of coal depends on climate and other factors. In North America, extensive inland seas during the Cretaceous era with repeated cycles of advance and retreat created the conditions for extensive coal deposits. Extremely thick beds of coal occur in Colorado and Wyoming in Cretaceous coal sequences. Coal can occur in very unusual places such as interbedded with old lava flows.

ESTIMATING COAL TONNAGE IN A RESERVE

Coal reserves are that part of the reserve base that could be economically extracted or produced at the time of determination. The term reserves need not signify that extraction facilities are in place and operative. Reserves include only recoverable materials. The tonnage of coal in a reserve is calculated with the following equation: Tonnage = t x w x A, in which t is the weighted average thickness of coal, w is the weight of coal per unit volume, and A is the area of the coal deposit. Available coal in the United States as reported by the The United States Department of Energy is 1,081,279 million short tons (9.81×10^{14} kg), which is about 4,786 BBOE (billion barrels of oil equivalent).

MAIN COAL-PRODUCING LOCATIONS IN THE UNITED STATES

The major coal producing regions of the United States are: the Appalachian Mountain region of eastern USA, the Midwest, and the Rocky Mountains. The Appalachian Mountain region is the major producer of bituminous coal in the USA. Large field of bituminous coal also occur in the Midwest and along the Rocky Mountains. Most of the coal that comes from the Western states is lower grade sub-bituminous and lignite. In the Rocky Mountains, Wyoming produces the most coal of any state; however, Montana has the most coal reserves. The largest coal mine in the United States is in Wyoming. One of the largest deposits of anthracite coal is in northwestern Pennsylvania. Current coal reserves in the United States are 270 years.

PETROLEUM

Petroleum, or crude oil, is a naturally occurring liquid found in formations in the Earth consisting of a complex mixture of hydrocarbons (mostly alkanes) of various lengths. The approximate length range is C_5H_{12} to $C_{18}H_{38}$. Any shorter hydrocarbons are considered natural gas or natural gas liquids. In its naturally occurring form petroleum contains other nonmetallic elements such as sulfur, oxygen, and nitrogen. It is usually black or dark brown (although it may be yellowish or even greenish) but varies greatly in appearance, depending on its composition. Petroleum is composed of long-chain and short-chain hydrocarbons. Petroleum is turned into the following fuels: ethane, diesel, fuel oil, gasoline, jet fuel, kerosene, liquid petroleum gas (LPG), and natural gas. Derivative products of petroleum include: alkenes, lubricants, wax, sulfuric acid, asphalt, and paraffin.

LOCATION OF PETROLEUM DEPOSITS

Hydrocarbons are less dense than rock or water causing them to migrate upward through adjacent rock layers until they either reach the surface or become trapped beneath impermeable rocks. Because of this fact, petroleum deposits are generally found associated with large packages of sedimentary rocks. Anywhere sedimentary rocks occur is a potential source of petroleum. This includes the thick sequences of continental sedimentary rocks known from numerous areas around the globe. Offshore deltaic and continental shelf sediments are also a strong location for petroleum discovery. Hydrocarbons are typically found in traps within large sedimentary packages. Traps include both structural and stratigraphic traps. Structural traps can be very effective in concentrating hydrocarbons over a large area. Important structural traps include domes, anticlines, and folds. Fault-related features also act as structural traps. Stratigraphic traps are formed when impermeable barriers or beds seal a reservoir bed or when permeability changes within the reservoir strata itself.

NECESSARY CONDITIONS

A petroleum pool is a field or deposit with similar pressure and reservoir characteristics. A petroleum pool that has a common petroleum/water contact and a distinctive pressure regime is a fundamental unit of petroleum accumulation, and can be treated as a natural object. A petroleum pool is a naturally occurring and quantifiable accumulation of oil. The conditions necessary for the formation of a petroleum pool are: source of hydrocarbon, permeability and porosity of available host rocks, stratigraphic or structural traps available, and a transporation path from source to reservoir. Structural traps are formed by a deformation in the rock layer that contains the hydrocarbons. Fault-related features also act as structural traps. Stratigraphic traps are formed when impermeable barriers or beds seal a reservoir bed or when permeability changes (facies change) within the reservoir bed itself.

CHARACTERISTICS OF RESERVOIR ROCKS

Conventionally, in order for a reservoir to be capable of storing petroleum, the rocks comprising the reservoir must be porous. Porosity is defined by the ratio, P, expressed as a percentage of the volume, V_p, of the pore space in a rock to the volume, V_r, of the rock, the latter volume including rock material plus the pore space; $P = 100 \, V_p/V_r$. It is typical for a reservoir rock to have a porosity value between 10 and 20%. It is possible for some reservoir rocks to have secondary porosity. The permeability rating of a reservoir rock must be between five and 1000 millidarcies. Permeability (or perviousness) of rock is its capacity for transmitting a fluid. Degree of permeability depends upon the size and shape of the pores, the size and shape of their interconnections, and the extent of the latter. It is measured by the rate at which a fluid of standard viscosity can move a given distance through a given interval of time. The unit of measure for permeability is the Darcy.

FORMATION OF PETROLEUM TRAPS

Hydrocarbons migrate upward through adjacent rock layers until they either reach the surface or become trapped beneath impermeable rocks. This process occurs because hydrocarbons are less dense than rock or water, forming accumulations called reservoirs. This process is not simple as it is influenced by underground water flows and by the structure of confining rocks. Typically, oil may migrate hundreds of kilometres horizontally, vertically, or even short distances downward before becoming trapped in a reservoir.

Hydrocarbon traps include both structural and stratigraphic traps. Structural traps are formed when sedimentary strata are deformed by folding, faulting, or diapirism, creating an impediment to upward oil migration. Anticlines are very effective hydrocarbon traps as they produce downward-flexing pockets in packages of sediments in which oil can accumulate. Salt dome diapirism is the vertical emplacement of plastic salt bodies upward into higher stratigraphic sections of strata. The impervious nature of these salt bodies creates an aquitard within the sediments they have pierced, facilitating the trapping of mobile hydrocarbons. Faulting can bring impermeable strata against reservoir rocks, trapping hydrocarbon against the fault. Stratigraphic depositional traps are created when relatively impermeable strata, such as shales or mudstones, occur either horizontally (facies change) or vertically adjacent to reservoir rocks. Hydrocarbon migrating horizontally or vertically will become trapped as impermeable strata (aquitards) are encountered.

RESERVES VS. RESOURCES

Reserves are an estimate within specified accuracy limits of the valuable metal, hydrocarbon, or mineral content of known deposits that may be produced under current economic conditions and with present technology. Typically, reserves are subdivided into three groups: proven, probable, and possible, all associated with a degree of confidence or upper limit of knowledge. Proven and probable reserves are essentially in hand. Possible reserves are yet to be defined and quantified. Resources, on the other hand, are all those known and unknown deposits, whether that can be extracted using existing technology or not. In order to calculate petroleum reserves, it is necessary to determine the volume of the reservoir rock as well as the degree to which this rock is filled with oil. Also, one must determine to what degree or efficiency the oil within the rock can be recovered.

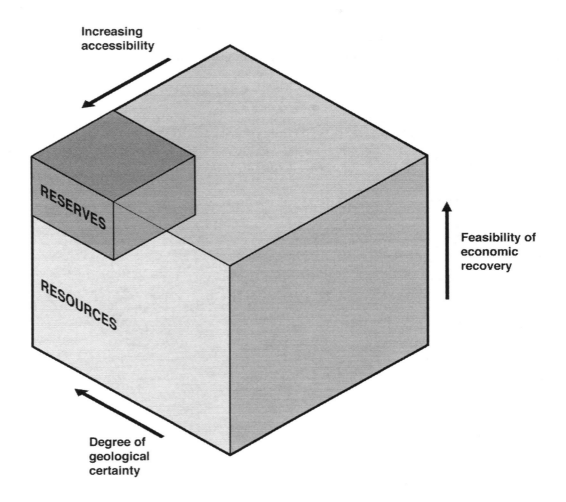

ARCHIE'S FORMULA

Calculation of oil reserves requires determination of reservoir oil holding abilities and extraction dynamics. This involves the calculation of the water/oil percentage utilizing Archie's Formula. Archie's Formula is used to determine the water saturation of oil reserves. It is a function of porosity, resistivity, and various coefficients, and is expressed as follows:

$$S_w^n = \frac{aR_w}{\varphi^m R_t} = F_R \frac{R_w}{R_t}$$

where S_w is the water saturation, a is a constant (often 1), φ is the porosity, R_w is the resistivity of formation water when 100% saturated, R_t is the true formation resistivity, m is the cementation component, n is the saturation exponent.

If water saturation is less than 60%, their reservoir will mostly provide water; with a water content of between 35 and 90%, however, the reservoir may produce oil.

CALCULATING THE RECOVERABLE STOCK-TANK OIL (STO)

Oil in place is the total hydrocarbon content of an oil reservoir and is often abbreviated STO. Oil in place is a different term from oil reserves. Geologists use the recoverable stock-tank oil (STO) reserve equation to calculate the amount of oil that can be recovered from a reservoir with existing technology. The amount of oil that can be recovered will depend on the viscosity, the permeability of the reservoir, the production system, and the ratio of gas to oil. The equation is as follows:

$$N = \frac{CV_b\varphi(1 - S_w)R}{FVF}$$

where N is the stock-tank oil in place, V_b is the bulk rock volume, C is a constant that depends on the units used for volume, φ is the fluid-filled portion of porosity, S_w is the water saturation, R is the percentage of oil that is recoverable, and FVF is the formation volume factor.

ASBOG Practice Test

Want to take this practice test in an online interactive format?
Check out the bonus page, which includes interactive practice questions and
much more: **https://www.mometrix.com/bonus948/asbog**

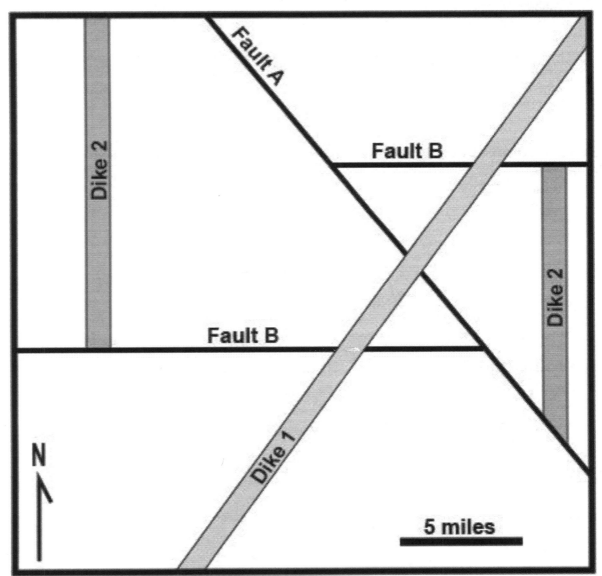

Figure 1

1. The map in Figure 1 shows two vertical dikes (Dike 1 and Dike 2) and two faults (Fault A and Fault B). What is the correct sequence of events, listed from oldest to youngest?

a. Emplacement of Dike 1, emplacement of Dike 2, movement of Fault A, movement of Fault B
b. Movement of Fault A, emplacement of Dike 1, emplacement of Dike 2, movement of Fault B
c. Movement of Fault B, emplacement of Dike 2, movement of Fault A, emplacement of Dike 1
d. Emplacement of Dike 2, movement of Fault B, movement of Fault A, emplacement of Dike 1

2. A rock described as arkosic

a. is frequently a basalt.
b. contains >90% olivine.
c. is sandstone containing ≥25% feldspar.
d. is a type of carbonate.

3. If the scale of a map is 1:24,000, what does 1 inch on the map represent?

a. 240 feet
b. 2,000 feet
c. 24,000 feet
d. 1,000 feet

4. In a region eroded by glaciers, what are bowl-shaped depressions at the head of a glacial valley?

a. Cirques
b. Kames
c. Arêtes
d. Drumlins

5. Which two-letter symbol is commonly used for a fat clay?

a. CH
b. OH
c. CL
d. ML

6. For a dip-slip fault, what is the area above the fault plane known as?

a. Footwall
b. Core
c. Flank
d. Hanging wall

7. Which isotope dating method is commonly used to determine the ages of detrital zircon grains in sandstone?

a. K-Ar
b. U-Pb
c. Rb-Sr
d. Sm-Nd

8. In general, which tectonic environment is most likely to include normal faults?

   a. Mid-ocean ridge
   b. Subduction zone
   c. Transform plate boundary
   d. Mantle hot spot

9. Which of the following up-section stratigraphic sequences is the clearest example of a marine transgression?

   a. Beach sand, open-shelf carbonate, shoreface deposits, fluvial sand
   b. Fluvial sand, beach sand, shoreface deposits, open-shelf carbonate
   c. Shoreface deposits, fluvial sand, open-shelf carbonate, beach sand
   d. Open-shelf carbonate, beach sand, fluvial sand, shoreface deposits

10. Which of the following minerals is NOT normally associated with hydrothermal alteration?

   a. Epidote
   b. Pyrite
   c. Hematite
   d. Olivine

11. What is a sandstone with >90% detrital quartz called?

   a. Feldspathic arenite
   b. Lithic arenite
   c. Quartz arenite
   d. Volcaniclastic

12. In which of the following tectonic environments is continental crust created?

   a. Subduction zone
   b. Mid-ocean ridge
   c. Back-arc basin
   d. Transform plate boundary

13. What type of acid is characteristic of "acid mine drainage"?

   a. Carbonic
   b. Hydrofluoric
   c. Sulphuric
   d. Nitric

14. Which type of fault usually has the steepest dip?

   a. Normal
   b. Reverse
   c. Thrust
   d. Strike-slip

15. Which of the following is the correct order of crystallization according to Bowen's reaction series?

a. Quartz, olivine, biotite, amphibole, pyroxene
b. Olivine, pyroxene, amphibole, biotite, quartz
c. Quartz, biotite, olivine, pyroxene, amphibole
d. Olivine, quartz, pyroxene, amphibole, biotite

16. A soil with high liquid limit and low plastic limit

a. has plastic behavior over a small range of water content.
b. has a high plasticity index.
c. has a soil description of "nonplastic."
d. has a low plasticity index.

17. Which of the following minerals is highest on the Mohs hardness scale?

a. Gypsum
b. Talc
c. Calcite
d. Corundum

18. In what type of tectonic environment are metamorphic core complexes normally located?

a. Subduction zones
b. Back-arcs
c. Transform plate boundaries
d. Hot spot

19. At an unfaulted outcrop, an ash bed depositionally overlies Mississippian limestone and is, in turn, depositionally overlain by Jurassic sandstone. Which of the following is a possible age of the ash bed?

a. Cretaceous
b. Archean
c. Permian
d. Quaternary

20. Which of the following lists minerals in order of least to most susceptible to weathering?

a. Olivine, amphibole, quartz, muscovite
b. Amphibole, olivine, muscovite, quartz
c. Quartz, muscovite, amphibole, olivine
d. Muscovite, olivine, quartz, amphibole

21. What is the total amount of gold in a 500,000 tonne ore deposit if the gold grade is 1.4 parts per million?

a. 700 kg
b. 357,000 tonnes
c. 357 kg
d. 700 tonnes

122

22. **Which type of sand dune commonly forms in areas with multiple wind directions?**

    a. Barchan
    b. Longitudinal
    c. Transverse
    d. Star

23. **In a 100 m interval of core through granitic bedrock, the total length of core pieces with individual lengths >100 mm is 31 m. In terms of rock quality designation, what is the rock mass quality of the cored interval?**

    a. Hard
    b. Fresh
    c. Weathered
    d. Intact

24. **Which of the following is a correct name for a contact between Triassic granite and Devonian limestone**

    a. Angular unconformity
    b. Disconformity
    c. Nonconformity
    d. Intrusive

25. **A paleoseismology trench is dug across an active fault at the site of a planned development. Mapping of the walls of the trench reveals evidence for six earthquakes along the fault over the last 2,400 years. What is the average earthquake recurrence interval of the fault at this location?**

    a. 400 years
    b. 14,400 years
    c. 144 years
    d. 40 years

26. **The vadose zone is a region of the subsurface that separates**

    a. the water table from bedrock.
    b. the ground surface from the water table.
    c. the ground surface from bedrock.
    d. the capillary fringe from the saturated zone.

27. **Which type of geophysical survey is most useful for locating a buried steel pipeline?**

    a. Gravity
    b. Refraction seismic
    c. Magnetics
    d. Reflection seismic

28. **A sample of granite from an outcrop produces a zircon U-Pb age of 1,000 Ma, a muscovite $^{40}Ar/^{39}Ar$ age of 500 Ma, and an apatite (U-Th/He age of 495 Ma). When was this granite exhumed to near the surface?**

    a. Mesoproterozoic
    b. Neoproterozoic
    c. Archean
    d. Cambrian

29. What type of drainage pattern is most likely to develop around the flanks of a modern stratovolcano?

    a. Rectangular
    b. Radial
    c. Trellis
    d. Dendritic

30. Which of the following is NOT a typical response of a coal seam on a geophysical wireline log?

    a. Low resistivity
    b. Low gamma
    c. Low velocity
    d. Low density

31. During an investigation, you need to collect data from along the high wall of an open pit mine. What is the best practice?

    a. Complete the task quickly before heavy equipment operators notice you are in the area.
    b. Approach the base of the high wall, but do not climb up it.
    c. Contact mine personnel to determine appropriate procedures.
    d. Collect data from other parts of the mine instead.

32. A copper orebody with a volume of 1 cubic kilometer contains 10 Mt of copper. The average density of the orebody is 3 g/cm³. What is the approximate average copper grade of the orebody?

    a. 33%
    b. 3.3%
    c. 0.33%
    d. 0.033%

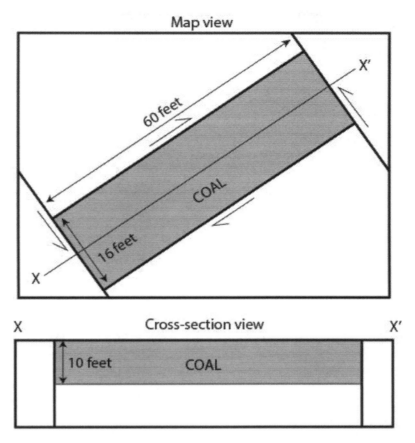

Figure 2

33. What is the approximate volume of coal available to mine from the area shown in Figure 2?

  a. 4 cubic yards
  b. 36 cubic yards
  c. 86 cubic yards
  d. 356 cubic yards

34. You are studying an unconfined aquifer that covers 10,000 square miles. Removing 5 x 10^{11} cubic feet of water from the aquifer lowers the water table by 10 feet. What is the approximate specific yield of the aquifer?

  a. 2%
  b. 6%
  c. 18%
  d. 42%

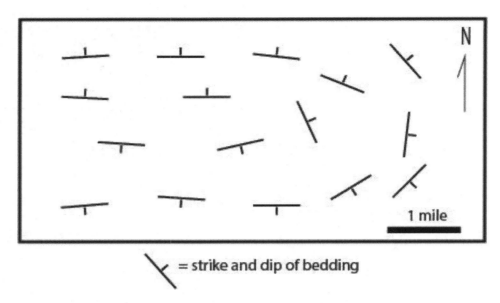

= strike and dip of bedding

Figure 3

35. What type of geologic structure is revealed by the structural measurements shown in Figure 3?

    a. East-dipping thrust fault
    b. East-plunging antiform
    c. West-dipping normal fault
    d. West-plunging synform

36. Petrographic analysis of a sandstone reveals that it has the following composition: 50% quartz grains, 30% andesite clasts, 15% feldspar grains, and 5% detrital mica. Which of the following is the MOST likely candidate for the provenance of the sandstone?

    a. Volcanic arc
    b. Carbonate shelf
    c. Oceanic plateau
    d. Passive margin sequence

37. Which of the following factors is LEAST important in determining the risk of a rockfall from a roadcut?

    a. Tsunami potential
    b. Orientation of joints
    c. Climate
    d. Angle of the slope

38. Which of the following is the most suitable for describing the stratigraphy of a region?

    a. A thrust fault
    b. A homocline
    c. A granitic intrusion
    d. A polydeformed terrane

126

39. You find trilobite fossils in a limestone. Which of the following is a possible age of the limestone?

    a. Ordovician
    b. Quaternary
    c. Cretaceous
    d. Proterozoic

40. Which elements are responsible for "hard water?"

    a. Si and O
    b. Ca and Mg
    c. Fe and Ni
    d. U and Th

41. Which of the following spatial data sets would be MOST helpful in determining slope stability of an area?

    a. Aeromagnetic data
    b. Satellite false-color imagery
    c. Radiometric data
    d. High-resolution digital terrain model

42. Which of the following is NOT a factor in determining the relative age of a soil?

    a. Thickness
    b. Grain size
    c. Number of soil horizons
    d. Contrast between adjacent horizons

43. What type of remotely sensed data would be LEAST useful in mapping gravel terraces as part of a neotectonics investigation?

    a. Airborne radiometrics
    b. Lidar data
    c. Air photos
    d. Synthetic-aperture radar imagery

44. On a stereonet, what is the orientation of the pole to a plane represented by?

    a. A point
    b. A straight line
    c. A curve
    d. A circle

45. Which of the following rock types contains the greatest weight percent SiO_2?

    a. Gabbro
    b. Rhyolite
    c. Basalt
    d. Andesite

46. Which type of faults have produced the largest earthquakes in recorded history?
- a. Right-lateral strike slip faults
- b. Normal faults
- c. Left-lateral strike slip faults
- d. Thrust faults

47. Which of the following are NOT contaminants covered by the Environmental Protection Agency National Primary Drinking Water Regulations?
- a. Organic chemicals
- b. Electromagnetics
- c. Radionuclides
- d. Microorganisms

48. Collection of which of the following geophysical data sets must be accompanied by base station measurements?
- a. Gravity
- b. Radiometric
- c. Magnetics
- d. Induced polarization

49. A granular soil specimen of 25 cm in length and 10 cm in diameter is placed under a constant hydraulic head of 35 cm. After 60 s, 400 cubic cm water have passed through the soil. What is the hydraulic conductivity of the soil specimen?
- a. 60 cm/s
- b. 6 cm/s
- c. 0.6 cm/s
- d. 0.06 cm/s

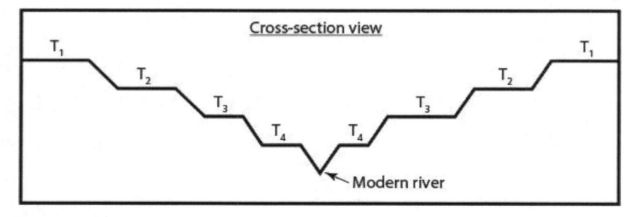

Figure 4

50. In Figure 4, what is the correct order, from oldest to youngest, of the formation of the river terraces?
- a. T_1, T_2, T_3, T_4
- b. T_4, T_3, T_2, T_1
- c. T_4, T_3, T_1, T_2
- d. T_4, T_2, T_1, T_3

51. Which of the following could produce an intersection lineation in a deformed rock?

   a. Cleavage and a stretching lineation
   b. An intersection lineation and a stretching lineation
   c. Bedding and cleavage
   d. Bedding and an intersection lineation

52. A water well is pumped at a rate of 10 gallons/minute. After 60 minutes, the drawdown is 100 feet. What is the specific capacity of the well?

   a. 6 gal/min/ft
   b. 1.67 gal/min/ft
   c. 0.167 gal/min/ft
   d. 0.1 gal/min/ft

53. A plutonic rock contains 50 wt% SiO_2, 3 wt% Na_2O, and 1 wt% K_2O. Based on these data, what is the rock classified as?

   a. Basalt
   b. Granite
   c. Gabbro
   d. Andesite

54. A potential client has contacted you about conducting an investigation of a property they are considering purchasing. You know the current owner of the property on a personal basis. What should you do in this case?

   a. Inform the current owner of potential interest in a purchase.
   b. Recuse yourself from the investigation due to a conflict of interest.
   c. Tell neither the potential client nor the current owner about the potential conflict of interest.
   d. Inform the potential client of your relationship with the current owner.

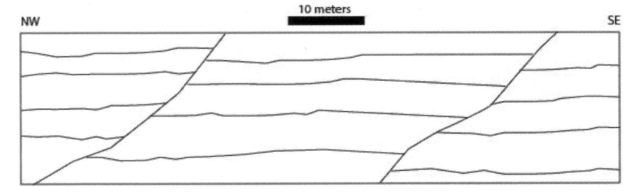

Figure 5

55. Figure 5 shows a sketched cross section of a large highway roadcut in an area of subhorizontal bedding. What are the main structural features evident from the sketch?

   a. NE-dipping reverse faults
   b. NW-dipping reverse faults
   c. SE-dipping normal faults
   d. NE-dipping normal faults

56. Which of the following lists detrital sediments in general order from most proximal to most distal?

    a.   Limestone, siltstone, conglomerate
    b.   Conglomerate, sandstone, siltstone
    c.   Sandstone, siltstone, conglomerate
    d.   Conglomerate, limestone, sandstone

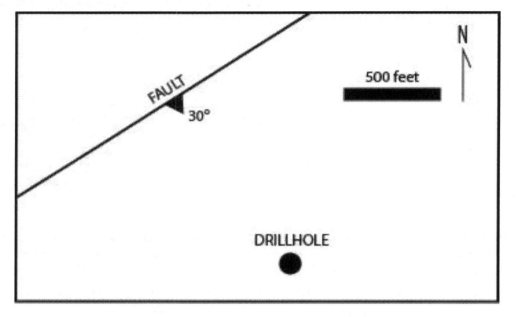

Figure 6

57. Figure 6 shows the area around a planned drillhole. To the NW of the drillhole is a fault that dips 30° to the SE. Which of the following is a reasonable prediction for the depth at which the drillhole will intersect the fault, assuming no other structural complications?

    a.   575 feet
    b.   1,000 feet
    c.   1,125 feet
    d.   2,600 feet

58. A sandstone bed contains a volcanic ash layer that has been dated at 100 Ma. Which of the following is the clearest chronostratigraphic correlation with the sandstone bed?

    a.   Devonian sandstone
    b.   Paleozoic rhyolite
    c.   Quaternary siltstone
    d.   Cretaceous limestone

59. You are compiling borehole records for a planned development. These records suggest that the site is underlain by 10 meters of unconsolidated sediment with numerous large boulders. Which of the following is NOT a likely environment for the formation of this sediment?

    a. A glacial moraine
    b. An alluvial fan
    c. An outwash plain
    d. A landslide deposit

60. In general, which of the following types of geophysical data is most useful in oil and gas exploration?

    a. Reflection seismic
    b. Refraction seismic
    c. Magnetotellurics
    d. Aeromagnetics

61. Which sedimentary structure is frequently associated with eolian deposits?

    a. Flaser bedding
    b. Cross-stratification
    c. Bouma sequences
    d. Reverse grading

62. Which of the following minerals is most commonly associated with hydrothermal deposits?

    a. Diamond
    b. Chalcopyrite
    c. Olivine
    d. Dunite

63. Axial planar cleavage is directly related to which of the following?

    a. Folding
    b. Normal faulting
    c. Strike-slip faulting
    d. Magmatism

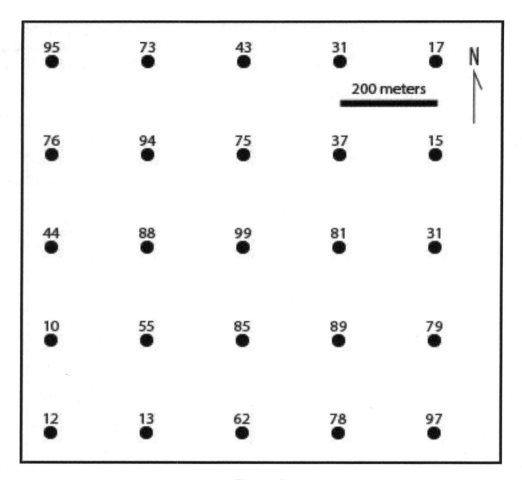

Figure 7

64. The map in Figure 7 shows a soil sampling grid in an area of copper exploration. Numbers refer to Cu concentrations (in parts per million) from a soil sample at that location. What are these results most compatible with?

    a.   A NW trending Cu deposit
    b.   A NE trending Cu deposit
    c.   A N-S trending Cu deposit
    d.   An E-W trending Cu deposit

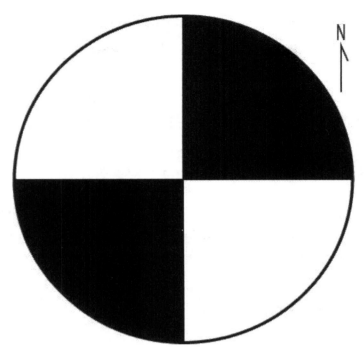

Figure 8

65. Figure 8 shows an earthquake focal mechanism. Which of the following types of faults is compatible with the focal mechanism?

    a. An E-W striking right-lateral fault
    b. An E-W striking left-lateral fault
    c. A N-S striking thrust fault
    d. A N-S striking normal fault

66. Which of the following band ratios from satellite visible infrared imagery is most useful for identifying iron-stained surficial rocks?

    a. Ratio of red to blue
    b. Ratio of green to blue
    c. Ratio of red to green
    d. Ratio of blue to green

67. Which of the following would be LEAST useful in a preliminary mineral exploration program?

    a. Soil sampling
    b. Vegetation sampling
    c. Groundwater sampling
    d. Stream sediment sampling

68. What distance does 1 cm represent on a map that has a scale of 1:100,000?

    a. 0.1 km
    b. 1 km
    c. 10 km
    d. 100 km

69. Rocks from which of the following geological periods are MOST likely to produce fossils?

    a.   Archean
    b.   Paleoproterozoic
    c.   Mesoproterozoic
    d.   Neoproterozoic

70. Which of the following geologic materials typically has the highest hydraulic conductivity?

    a.   Gravel
    b.   Unfractured granite
    c.   Silt
    d.   Clay

71. Your company is installing a series of new deep-water wells. What is the most significant environmental risk posed by drilling and installing the new wells?

    a.   Air contamination
    b.   Soil contamination
    c.   Groundwater contamination
    d.   Surface water contamination

72. Which of the following minerals is most soluble in water at neutral pH?

    a. Fe_2O_3
    b.   NaCl
    c. FeS_2
    d.   PbS

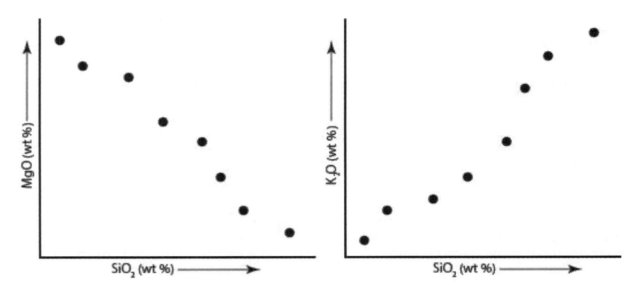

Figure 9

73. Whole rock geochemical data from a suite of volcanic rocks are shown in Figure 9. Arrows show the direction in which values are increasing on each axis. What is the relationship between K₂O and MgO for these rocks?

    a. K_2O and MgO are positively correlated.
    b. K_2O and MgO are negatively correlated.
    c. K_2O and MgO are identical.
    d. K_2O and MgO are uncorrelated.

74. What parameter is NOT in Darcy's Law?

    a.   Hydraulic conductivity
    b.   Discharge
    c.   Difference in hydraulic head
    d.   Specific capacity

75. Which of the following types of information would be most useful in investigating the structural geology of an area that is prospective for oil and gas?

    a.   Geochemical data from igneous rocks
    b.   Strikes and dips of bedding
    c.   Orientations of metamorphic lineation
    d.   Heat flow measurements

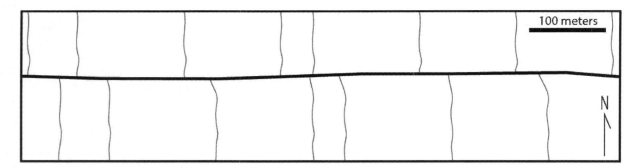

Figure 10

76. The map in Figure 10 shows an active fault cutting a number of stream beds. What is the sense of displacement along this fault?

    a. Right lateral
    b. Left lateral
    c. Dextral
    d. Vertical

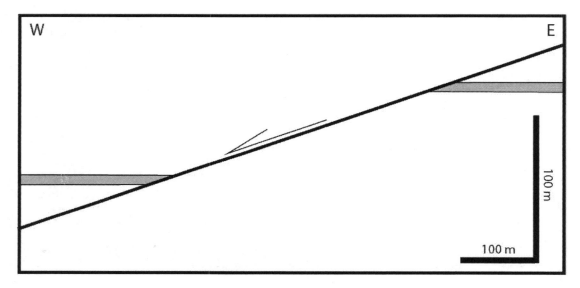

Figure 11

77. The cross section shown in Figure 11 has a vertical exaggeration of 2:1. What is the actual dip of the fault shown on the cross section?

    a. 10°
    b. 30°
    c. 45°
    d. 60°

78. Which of the following minerals is characterized by hexagonal symmetry?

    a. Corundum
    b. Halite
    c. Pyrite
    d. Andesite

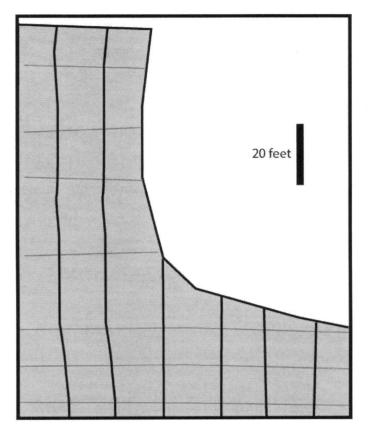

Figure 12

79. Figure 12 shows a cross-section view of a cliff that has subhorizontal bedding and subvertical jointing. What is the likely mode of failure for this outcrop?

    a. Lateral spreading
    b. Rock topple
    c. Lateral rotation
    d. Rock spreading

80. A submarine landslide is referred to as which of the following?

    a. Delta
    b. Lahar
    c. Olistostrome
    d. Alluvial fan

137

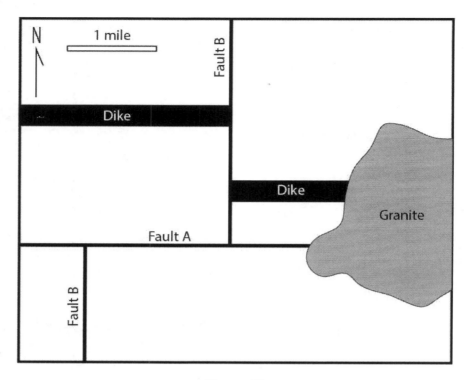

Figure 13

81. What is the correct order (from oldest to youngest) of geological events in the area shown in Figure 13?

a. Movement on Fault B, emplacement of dike, movement on Fault A, emplacement of granite
b. Emplacement of dike, movement on Fault B, emplacement of granite, movement on Fault A
c. Emplacement of dike, emplacement of granite, movement on Fault A, movement on Fault B
d. Emplacement of dike, movement on Fault B, movement on Fault A, emplacement of granite

82. In which environment are turbidites formed?

a. Deep marine
b. Shallow marine
c. Fluvial
d. Eolian

83. What is the difference between Quality Assurance (QA) and Quality Control (QC)?

a. Quality assurance is focused on outcomes, and quality control is focused on inputs.
b. Quality assurance is qualitative, and quality control is quantitative.
c. Quality assurance is focused on process, and quality control is focused on products.
d. Quality assurance can be measured, and quality control is descriptive.

84. Which of the following is NOT a characteristic of Bouma sequences?

a. Graded bedding
b. Traction bedding
c. Lamination
d. Massive bedding

85. What is the correct order of a Wilson cycle?

a. Continental collision, ocean basin formation, continental rifting, subduction
b. Continental rifting, ocean basin formation, subduction, continental collision
c. Continental collision, subduction, ocean basin formation, continental rifting
d. Continental rifting, subduction, ocean basin formation, continental collision

86. Which of the following correctly describes the grain size of a typical glacial moraine?

a. Poorly sorted
b. Poorly bedded
c. Fine grained
d. Coarse grained

87. A water well is drilled into an aquifer, and water flows out of the well with no pumping. Which of the following describes the aquifer?

a. Unconfined
b. Artesian
c. Low porosity
d. Low permeability

88. Geochemical analysis of a rock sample from an orebody reveals that it contains 0.2 grams/tonne of gold. What is the gold grade of the sample expressed in parts per million (ppm)?

a. 0.02
b. 0.2
c. 2.0
d. 20.0

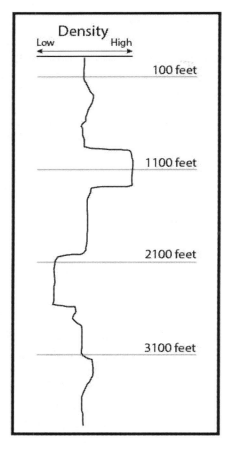

Figure 14

89. The geophysical log shown in Figure 14 is from a well drilled into a large basin. Given that most of the basin contains sedimentary rocks, which of the following depths is most likely to be associated with a sequence of basalt flows?

    a. 100 feet
    b. 1,100 feet
    c. 2,100 feet
    d. 3,100 feet

90. Which of the following types of coal is the highest rank?

    a. Lignite
    b. Bituminous
    c. Anthracite
    d. Subbituminous

91. Which mineral is the principal source of iron ore?

    a. Biotite
    b. Hematite
    c. Fayalite
    d. Pyrite

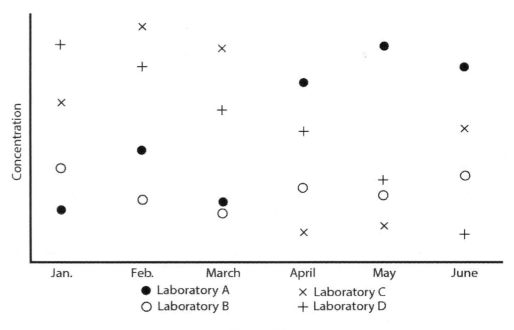

Figure 15

92. Figure 15 shows geochemical results of repeated measurements of a standard by four different laboratories. Based on these data, which laboratory produced the most reproducible results over the entire six-month period?

a. Laboratory A
b. Laboratory B
c. Laboratory C
d. Laboratory D

93. Which of the following correctly lists plutonic rocks in order from most mafic to most felsic?

a. Gabbro, granite, diorite
b. Gabbro, diorite, granite
c. Diorite, granite, gabbro
d. Granite, gabbro, diorite

94. What is an interface between layers of contrasting seismic properties referred to as?

a. Reflector
b. Refractor
c. Retractor
d. Respector

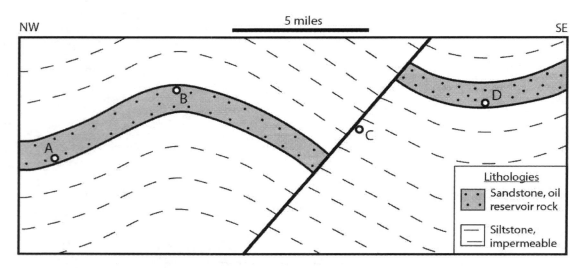

Figure 16

95. On the cross section shown in Figure 16, which of the following points is most clearly within a hydrocarbon structural trap?

    a. A
    b. B
    c. C
    d. D

96. In what type of environment do stromatolites form?

    a. Volcanic
    b. Eolian
    c. Deep marine
    d. Shallow marine

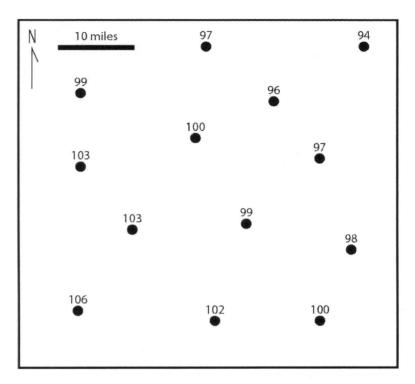

Figure 17

97. The map in Figure 17 shows depth (in feet) to the water table, as measured in a number of water wells in a low relief area. Depths are measured from a common horizontal datum. In what direction would you expect a groundwater contaminant plume to migrate in this area?

a. To the southwest
b. To the northeast
c. To the northwest
d. To the southeast

98. Which of the following is a key property of landfill caps?

a. High porosity
b. High permeability
c. Low permeability
d. Large grain size

99. Which of the following is NOT a potential cause of earthquakes?

a. Stresses at tectonic plate boundaries
b. Movement of magma below the surface
c. Groundwater withdrawal
d. Injection wells

143

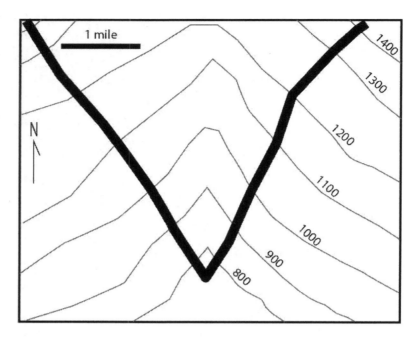

Figure 18

100. On the geologic map shown in Figure 18, numbers next to topographic contours are elevations in feet. The thick, black line is an outcrop of basalt. Based on this map, what direction is the basalt dipping?

    a.   To the south
    b.   To the north
    c.   To the east
    d.   To the west

101. Which of the following minerals is commonly associated with lead-zinc deposits?

    a.   Tremolite
    b.   Sphalerite
    c.   Anthracite
    d.   Biotite

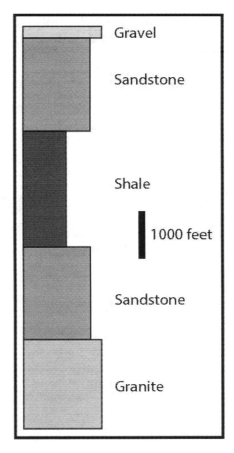

Figure 19

102. On the stratigraphic column shown in Figure 19, which of the following lithologies is the best candidate as a hydrocarbon source rock?

    a. Shale
    b. Granite
    c. Sandstone
    d. Rhyolite

103. Which of the following lithologies is LEAST likely to make a good aquifer?

    a. Sandstone
    b. Shale
    c. Gravel
    d. Fractured granite

104. Which of the following rock types is MOST likely to be associated with a copper porphyry deposit?

    a. Quartz monzonite
    b. Komatiite
    c. Basalt
    d. Banded iron formation (BIF)

105. A sandstone contains detrital zircons that are 300 million years old. Which of the following is NOT a possible depositional age of the sandstone?

    a. Miocene
    b. Cretaceous
    c. Triassic
    d. Cambrian

106. A hand sample of granite contains numerous crystals of a black, flaky mineral. This mineral is MOST likely

    a. quartz.
    b. biotite.
    c. K-feldspar.
    d. magnetite.

107. Which remotely sensed data set would be LEAST useful in identifying areas of dense vegetation?

    a. Black-and-white aerial photographs
    b. False-color Landsat imagery
    c. Airborne radiometrics
    d. Synthetic aperture radar

108. What is a layer of completely impermeable rocks referred to as?

    a. Aquifer
    b. Aquitard
    c. Aquiclude
    d. Aquicel

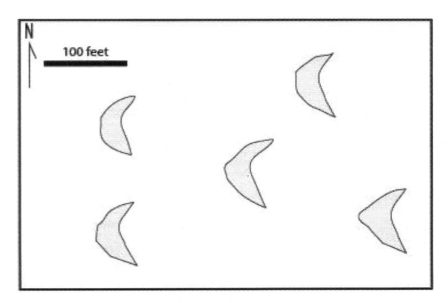

Figure 20

109. Figure 20 is a map of sand dunes. What is the prevailing wind direction of the area, based on the map?

    a. East to west
    b. West to east
    c. North to south
    d. South to north

110. Which of the following sedimentary features is NOT an indicator of shallow water deposition?

    a. Turbidites
    b. Mud cracks
    c. Evaporite beds
    d. Fossil reefs

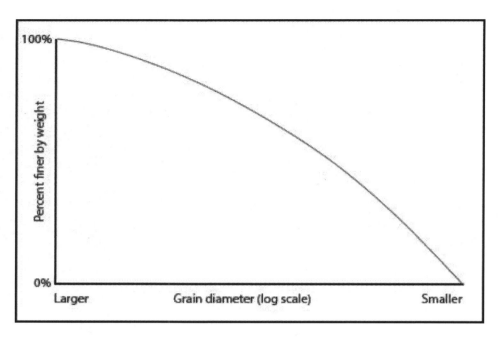

Figure 21

111. Figure 21 shows a grain-size distribution of a soil. Which of the following accurately describes this soil?

    a.   Well graded
    b.   Well bedded
    c.   Poorly bedded
    d.   Well sorted

112. What type of information is most useful in determining the boundaries of a watershed?

    a.   Reflectivity data
    b.   Paleontology records
    c.   Topographic information
    d.   Rainfall data

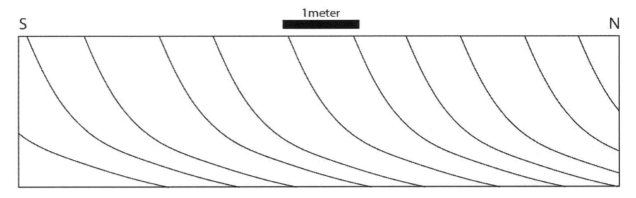

Figure 22

113. Figure 22 shows cross-stratification in an eolian sandstone. What is the current direction suggested by cross-stratification?

a. East to west
b. West to east
c. North to south
d. South to north

114. Which of the following factors is LEAST important in the design of a new landfill?

a. Water management system
b. Gas management system
c. Rock management system
d. Liner system

115. Which of the following does NOT apply to a water sample with high turbidity?

a. Contains a relatively large amount of total dissolved solids
b. Allows a relatively small amount of light to pass through
c. Allows a relatively large amount of light to pass through
d. May pose a risk to human health

116. As part of a site investigation, you compile a number of maps of the area that show soil type, locations of wells, and vegetation cover. Which of the following additional data sets would be most useful in assessing the risk of soil contamination of the site?

a. Gravimetric data
b. Soil chemistry data
c. Seismic data
d. Ground penetrating radar data

149

West   1meter   East

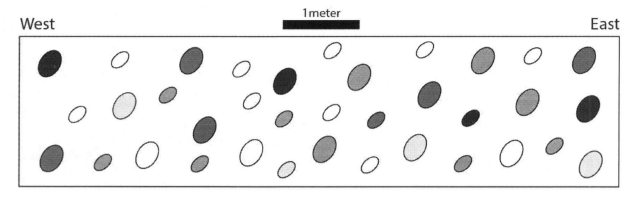

Figure 23

117. Figure 23 shows imbricated clasts in a stream cut through a riverbed. What is the current direction suggested by these clasts?

    a. North to south
    b. South to north
    c. East to west
    d. West to east

118. While making a geological map of a well-exposed area, you identify a regional-scale fold that has Permian sandstone in its core and Cretaceous limestone on the outer limbs. What is this fold?

    a. An anticline
    b. A syncline
    c. A homocline
    d. A monocline

119. A geological investigation of a region suggests that it is part of a Precambrian volcanic arc. Which of the following energy and mineral resources is the area MOST prospective for?

    a. Coal
    b. Mississippi Valley type Pb-Zn deposits
    c. Cu porphyries
    d. Volcanogenic massive sulphide deposits

120. Which of the following is NOT a standard part of personal protection equipment on an environmental cleanup site?

    a. Steel-toed boots
    b. Hard hat
    c. Respirator
    d. Gloves

121. What is the unit used to describe groundwater discharge?

    a. Density/time
    b. Time/volume
    c. Volume/time
    d. Time/mass

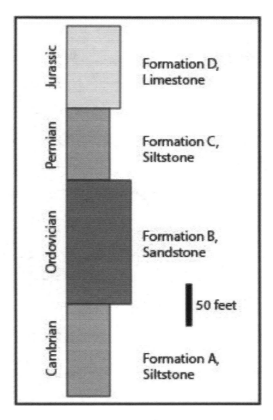

Figure 24

122. Figure 24 is a lithologic column that summarizes the stratigraphy of a basin. What type of contact separates Formation B from Formation C?

 a. Intrusive
 b. Fault
 c. Conformity
 d. Unconformity

123. You are logging drillcore from a basin to establish regional-scale stratigraphic correlations. Which of the following is NOT a meaningful parameter on which to base your correlations?

 a. Grain size
 b. Color
 c. Lithology
 d. Fossil assemblages

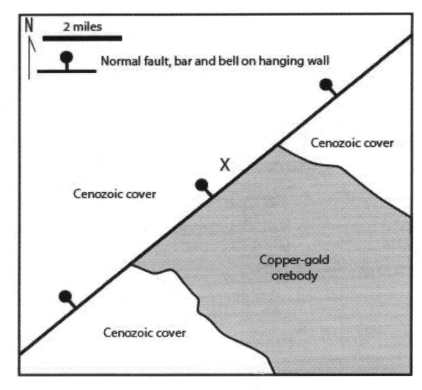

Figure 25

124. Figure 25 is a map that shows an outcropping ore deposit that is cut by a fault. Slickenlines on the fault surface plunge N45W. In what direction from the X would you explore to find the other part of the ore deposit?

    a.   To the NE
    b.   To the SE
    c.   To the SW
    d.   To the NW

125. Which of the following is recommended to have the lowest concentration in a sample of drinking water?

    a.   Chloride
    b.   Total dissolved solids
    c.   Sulfate
    d.   Copper

126. Survey data for two wells indicates that they have coordinates of (1,300N, 1,000E) and (1,000N, 1,400E), where the numbers refer to meters. What is the distance between the two wells?

    a.   300 m
    b.   400 m
    c.   500 m
    d.   600 m

127. Which of the following terms describes wind-blown dust?

a. Lahar
b. Lignite
c. Limonite
d. Loess

128. Which of the following values for Reynolds number applies to a turbulent flow?

a. 3,000
b. 300
c. 30
d. 3

129. You are collecting and preparing soil samples to be sent to a laboratory for chemical analysis. What is the purpose of including a chain-of-custody form with the samples?

a. To ensure that samples arrive at the proper address
b. To provide a list of sample numbers
c. To describe the proper analysis techniques
d. To maintain a record of sample handling

130. What are soils that deflect or "pump" during compaction a sign of?

a. Excess gravel content
b. Excess water content
c. Insufficient organic content
d. Insufficient water content

131. Which of the following is NOT a record of past earthquakes?

a. Offset rock layers
b. Volcanic ash beds
c. Tsunami deposits
d. Boulder displacement

132. Which of the following drilling techniques is most appropriate to obtain geotechnical soil samples during planning for construction of a new bridge?

a. Diamond drillcore
b. Auger
c. Hydraulic-rotary drilling
d. Direct-push drilling

133. Which type of river is MOST likely to develop in an area of low relief?

a. Meandering
b. Braided
c. Straight
d. Trellis

134. Blueschist-facies metamorphism implies which of the following combinations?

a. High pressure-high temperature
b. High pressure-low temperature
c. Low pressure-low temperature
d. Low pressure-high temperature

135. Which of the following rock types has the greatest density?

a. Granite
b. Sandstone
c. Limestone
d. Basalt

136. During a field investigation you find an outcrop of poorly consolidated gravel that is dipping 70°. Which of the following processes is MOST likely to be responsible for the outcrop?

a. Active folding
b. Deposition on a steep lake bottom
c. Deposition on a steep mountainside
d. Deposition from a steep river

137. Which of the following materials has the greatest specific yield?

a. Silt
b. Fine sand
c. Medium sand
d. Coarse sand

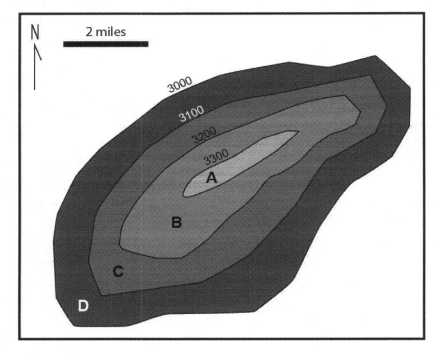

Figure 26

138. Figure 26 shows a geologic map of an area with upright stratigraphy. Contour labels are in feet above sea level. What is the correct stratigraphic order, listed from oldest to youngest?

a. Formation A, Formation B, Formation C, Formation D
b. Formation A, Formation D, Formation C, Formation D
c. Formation D, Formation C, Formation A, Formation B
d. Formation D, Formation C, Formation B, Formation A

139. Which of the following is LEAST likely to produce a linear feature ("lineament") on an air photo?

a. Fault
b. Sinkhole
c. Roadway
d. Bedding

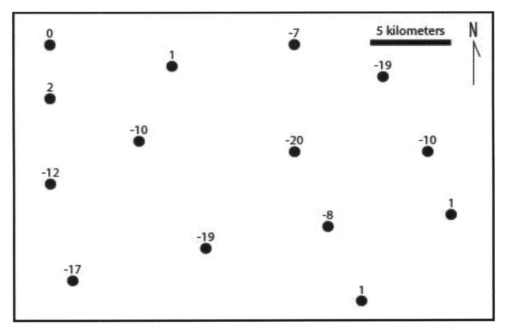

Figure 27

140. Figure 27 is a map showing changes in elevation at a number of survey points in an area of high groundwater withdrawal. Numbers refer to changes in elevation (in millimeters) over a five-year period. Positive numbers indicate increases in elevation, and negative numbers indicate elevation decreases. What pattern do these data suggest?

a. NW-SE subsidence
b. NE-SW subsidence
c. NW-SE inflation
d. NE-SW inflation

155

Answer Key and Explanations

1. D: The question is answered based on the principle of cross-cutting relationships, which states that a geologic feature that cuts another is the younger of the two. Fault B cuts Dike 2; therefore, Dike 2 must be older than Fault B. Fault A cuts Fault B, so Fault A is younger than Fault B. Dike 1 cuts Fault A, so Dike 1 is younger than Fault A.

2. C: Arkose is a type of detrital sedimentary rock that contains at least 25% feldspar. The answer cannot be A or D because neither basalt nor carbonate are detrital sedimentary rocks. The answer cannot be B because a detrital sedimentary rock containing >90% olivine could not also contain ≥25% feldspar.

3. B: The map scale is a ratio of distance on a map to the actual distance on the ground. A scale of 1:24,000 means that 1 inch on the map represents a distance of 24,000 inches (2,000 feet).

4. A: Bowl-shaped portions of valleys carved by glacial erosion are called cirques. The other choices are glacial features, but they are all hills or ridges, as opposed to depressions.

5. A: A fat clay is one with a high liquid limit. Under the United Soil Classification System, the letter C denotes clay, and H denotes a high liquid limit. The other choices are other types of fine-grained soils: OH is an organic-rich soil with a high liquid limit, CL is a clay with a low liquid limit ("lean clay"), and ML is silt with a low liquid limit.

6. D: For a dip-slip fault, the hanging wall lies above the fault plane. The footwall is below the fault plane. For reverse and thrust faults, the hanging wall moves up relative to the footwall, and for normal faults the hanging wall moves down relative to the footwall.

7. B: U-Pb geochronology is the most commonly used method for dating zircon grains. The other methods are not appropriate for dating zircon because of the low abundances of the parent isotopes (i.e., K) in zircon.

8. A: Mid-ocean ridges are plate boundaries where oceanic plates diverge from each other, so they are regions of normal faulting. Subduction zones are dominantly regions of thrust faulting, and transform plate boundaries are characterized by strike-slip faults. Mantle hot spots are not necessarily regions of regional-scale faulting.

9. B: Marine transgressions are represented by stratigraphic sequences that reflect an up-section change to deeper water conditions. Fluvial sands may be deposited above sea level, beach sands are deposited at sea level, shoreface deposits occur immediately off shore, and open-shelf carbonate is deposited in the shallow sea. Thus, answer B represents a continuous up-section change to a deeper water environment.

10. D: Olivine is not typically formed through hydrothermal alteration but rather through magmatic processes.

11. C: Quartz arenite is a sandstone with >90% detrital quartz. Feldspathic arenite contains <90% quartz, and lithic arenite contains a significant proportion of lithic fragments. A volcaniclastic rock is simply a clastic rock that contains volcanic fragments.

12. A: New continental crust is generated in continental arcs along subduction zones. Both mid-ocean ridges and back-arc basins are environments where new oceanic crust is created. Transform plate boundaries are not typically where new crust is formed.

13. C: Sulphuric acid is characteristic of acid mine drainage and is related to the presence of sulphide minerals within ore deposits.

14. D: Strike-slip faults commonly have near-vertical dips. By definition, thrust faults have shallower dips than reverse faults. Normal faults can have a range of dips but are usually in the range of approximately 10 to 60°.

15. B: Bowen's reaction series describes the order in which minerals crystallize from a cooling magma. The order progresses from Fe- and Mg-rich minerals such as olivine to silica-rich minerals such as quartz.

16. B: Plasticity index (PI) = liquid limit (LL) – plastic limit (PL), so a soil with high LL and low PL will have high PI. Such a soil has plastic behavior over a wide range of water content and would be described as plastic.

17. D: Corundum is the second-highest mineral on the Mohs hardness scale (only diamond is greater). The other options are the three lowest minerals on the Mohs hardness scale.

18. B: Metamorphic core complexes form in regions of large-magnitude crustal extension. They are most commonly located in extensional back-arc basins.

19. C: Because the outcrop is unfaulted, the ash bed must be Mississippian or younger as well as Jurassic or older. Of the options given, Permian is the only viable answer.

20. C: The minerals least susceptible to weathering at the Earth's surface are those that crystallized at the lowest temperature and vice versa. The order from least to most susceptible to weathering is the reverse of Bowen's reaction series.

21. A: The amount 1.4 parts per million (ppm) is equivalent to 1.4 grams/tonne, so a 500,000 tonne ore deposit would contain 700,000 grams of gold, or 700 kg.

22. D: Star dunes form their characteristic shapes due to multiple wind directions.

23. C: The rock quality designation (RQD) is the total length of individual core pieces >100 mm, divided by the length of the cored interval. RQD is low for weathered rocks and high for fresh rocks. In this case the RQD is 31%, which corresponds with a rock mass quality of "weathered."

24. D: An intrusive contact is one between an intrusive rock (e.g., granite or gabbro) and another rock type that is older than the intrusive rock.

25. A: The recurrence interval is the average duration between events, in this case earthquakes. If there were six earthquakes along the fault over a span of 2,400 years, then the average amount of time between earthquakes is 400 years.

26. B: The vadose zone is that area between the ground surface and the water table. Below the water table is the zone of saturation.

27. C: A magnetics survey would be most useful in this case. The other techniques are unlikely to achieve the spatial resolution necessary to locate a relatively small object such as a pipe.

157

28. D: Based on this information, the granite most likely crystallized 1,000 Ma (the Mesoproterozoic/Neoproterozoic boundary) but did not cool through the muscovite $^{40}Ar/^{39}Ar$ and apatite (U-Th)/He closure temperatures until 500–495 Ma, which is during the late Cambrian.

29. B: Radial drainage patterns frequently form around conical topographic features such as stratovolcanoes. Rectangular drainage patterns are often associated with bedrock that has a strong orthogonal jointing pattern, and trellis drainage often forms in regions with alternating more- and less-resistant bedrock units. Dendritic drainage patterns tend to form in areas where the bedrock is roughly uniformly resistant to erosion.

30. A: Coal seams are normally characterized by high resistivity relative to the rocks above and below them. Coal is also marked by low gamma, low velocity, and low density.

31. C: Mine high walls are frequently areas of restricted access due to safety concerns. The best practice on any mine site is to consult with mine personnel before conducting any activity.

32. C: The average copper grade is the mass of copper in the orebody divided by the total mass of the orebody. The mass of the orebody is determined by multiplying the average density by the volume. In this question, the mass of the orebody = 3 g/cm³ x 1 km³ = 3,000 Mt. The average copper grade is therefore 10 Mt/3,000 Mt = 0.0033 = 0.33%.

33. D: The coal resource in this example is a rectangular block, so its volume is simply length x width x height. In this question, volume = 60 ft x 16 ft x 10 ft = 9,600 ft³ = 356 yards³.

34. C: Specific yield is the ratio of the volume of water removed from an unconfined aquifer to the volume of the aquifer from which it was removed. This latter volume is the drop in the water table multiplied by the surface area of the aquifer. In this question, the volume of the aquifer from which water was removed = $10,000 \text{ mi}^2 \times \frac{27,878,400 \text{ ft}^2}{1 \text{ mi}^2} \times 10 \text{ ft} = 2.8 \times 10^{12} \text{ ft}^3$. The specific yield is therefore (5 x 10¹¹ ft³)/(2.8 x 10¹² ft³) = 0.18 = 18%.

35. B: The pattern of strike and dip measurements is indicative of an antiform that is plunging to the east.

36. A: Andesitic volcanoes are a characteristic of volcanic arcs, so a sandstone that contains 30% andesite clasts is likely to have been sourced from a volcanic arc. The other geologic settings are not typically associated with andesitic volcanoes.

37. A: Tsunami potential has little bearing on the assessment of rockfall risk, but the other factors are all important.

38. B: A homocline is a relatively uncomplicated area where all beds are dipping in the same direction. They are well suited for stratigraphic studies due to their lack of structural complications.

39. A: Trilobites appeared during the Cambrian and went extinct during the Permian. They thus spanned all of the Paleozoic Era.

40. B: Hard water frequently occurs in regions with limestone and dolostone bedrock. It occurs due to the abundance of Ca and Mg in calcite and dolomite.

41. D: A high-resolution digital terrain model is the only one of the options from which slope information can be derived directly.

42. B: Grain size is not a reliable indicator of the age of a soil, but the other soil factors all vary with age.

43. A: Mapping gravel terraces would involve identifying landforms. Air photos, Lidar, and synthetic-aperture radar data could all be useful for mapping landforms, but airborne radiometrics data would provide little relevant information.

44. A: The pole to a plane is a line in physical space, and lines are represented by points on a stereonet.

45. B: Rhyolite is a volcanic rock that is particularly rich in SiO_2. Andesite contains less, and basalt is a SiO_2-poor volcanic rock. Gabbro is the intrusive equivalent of basalt.

46. D: Most of the largest recorded earthquakes in Earth history have occurred along thrust faults in subduction zone settings.

47. B: The Environmental Protection Agency National Primary Drinking Water Regulations do not pertain to "electromagnetics" but do include guidelines for the other parameters.

48. A: Gravity surveys must be accompanied by repeated base station measurements during the survey due to natural drift of gravimeter readings.

49. D: Hydraulic conductivity is the rate at which water can move through a porous medium for a given hydraulic head.

50. A: River terraces become younger with decreasing elevation. They essentially track the downcutting of a river.

51. C: Intersection lineations are produced by the intersection of two planes. C is the only choice that includes two planar features. The intersection of bedding and cleavage is one of the most common types of intersection lineation.

52. D: Specific capacity has units of volume/time/length. It is the pumping rate divided by the amount of drawdown. In this question, specific capacity = 10 g/m / 100 ft = 0.1 g/m/ft.

53. C: Gabbro and basalt are types of igneous rocks that contain <53 wt% SiO2. The question specifies that it is a plutonic rock, so the correct answer is gabbro.

54. D: The most appropriate choice in this case is to notify the potential client about your relationship with the current owner. Simply knowing the current owner may not necessarily constitute a conflict of interest.

55. B: Offset of bedding suggests reverse movement along faults that are dipping to the NW.

56. B: In general, detrital sediments become finer grained with distance from their source. More proximal sediments are therefore relatively coarse grained, and distal sediments are fine grained. Limestone is a chemical sediment, not a detrital sediment.

57. A: The drillhole is roughly 1,000 feet from the fault, and the fault is dipping toward the drillhole at an angle of 30°, so the approximate depth at which the drillhole will intersect the fault is ~1,000 ft x tan(30°), which is ~575 feet.

58. D: If the sandstone contains a 100 Ma ash bed, then it must be Cretaceous. In terms of chronostratigraphy, the best correlation is with Cretaceous limestone.

59. C: Outwash plain sediments are typically fine grained. The other options are all the types of environment that could produce large boulders.

60. A: Reflection seismic data is commonly used in oil and gas exploration do determine the geometry of stratigraphic layers.

61. B: Large-scale cross-stratification is a classic sedimentary structure associated with eolian (i.e., wind-blown) deposits.

62. B: Chalcopyrite ($CuFeS_2$) is a common mineral in many hydrothermal ore deposits. Diamond and olivine are associated with mafic magmatism but not necessarily hydrothermal activity. Dunite is a type of rock, not a mineral.

63. A: Axial planar cleavage is a type of cleavage that forms parallel to the axial plane of a fold.

64. A: The data suggest an elongate soil Cu anomaly that extends from the NW corner of the map to the SE corner.

65. A: The diagram is compatible with either an E-W striking right-lateral fault or a N-S striking left-lateral fault. Answer A is the only possible correct answer.

66. A: Iron-stained rocks are various shades of red, so the most useful band ratio would be that of red to blue.

67. C: Because groundwater can be far traveled, samples of metal concentrations from water wells may not accurately reflect metal concentrations in the immediately underlying bedrock. Soil, vegetation, and stream sediment sampling are common tools in mineral exploration.

68. B: A distance of 1 cm on a map with a scale of 1:100,000 represents 100,000 cm, which is 1,000 m, or 1 km.

69. D: The earliest fossils appear in the fossil record during the Neoproterozoic Era. The other options are all older than Neoproterozoic and are therefore unlikely to contain fossils.

70. A: Hydraulic conductivity (units of length/time, i.e., velocity) is essentially the velocity of groundwater movement in a medium. In general, coarse-grained soils have greater hydraulic conductivity than fine-grained soils.

71. C: Particularly with deep wells, there is a risk of establishing a connection between shallow aquifers (which may be contaminated) with deeper aquifers that may serve as a drinking water supply. Screened intervals should be carefully planned to mitigate this risk.

72. B: NaCl (halite, or table salt) has a much greater solubility in water than Fe_2O_3 (hematite), FeS_2 (pyrite), or galena (PbS).

73. B: "Negative" correlation means that when one variable increases, the other decreases. Based on the data, MgO decreases and K_2O increases as SiO_2 increases. MgO and K_2O are therefore negatively correlated.

74. D: Darcy's Law is the relationship between discharge (one side of the equation) and hydraulic conductivity and difference in hydraulic head (other side of the equation).

75. B: Strikes and dips of bedding could be useful in identifying structural traps. The other types of information are not particularly relevant to oil and gas exploration.

76. B: Each stream bed is offset in a left-lateral sense across the fault.

77. A: Vertical exaggeration has the effect of making the dip of the fault appear to be steeper than it actually is. It appears to be dipping at ~30°, so the actual dip must be less than that.

78. A: Corundum has hexagonal symmetry.

79. B: Rock topple is usually associated with steep bedrock slopes. Topples involve the forward rotation of a rock mass out of the slope.

80. C: Olistostromes are submarine landslides. "Olistoliths" are the large clasts within an olistostrome.

81. D: The dike is cross-cut by Fault B, so the dike must be older than Fault B. Fault B is cross-cut by Fault A, so Fault B must be older than Fault A. Fault A is cross-cut by the granite (which also cross-cuts the dike), so Fault A must be older than the granite.

82. A: Turbidites are deposited from turbidity currents, which are most common in deep marine settings.

83. C: Quality assurance refers to processes designed to ensure quality, whereas quality control refers to measures taken to ensure that final products meet appropriate standards.

84. B: Traction bedding is not a feature of the Bouma sequence, but rather of riverbed deposits.

85. B: A Wilson cycle describes the important stages in the breakup of continents, subsequent formation of ocean basins, later development of subduction zones, and eventual continental collision.

86. A: Glacial moraines typically do not involve processes that sort material by grain size, so they are commonly poorly sorted.

87. B: An artesian well is one that flows to the surface without pumping.

88. B: A tonne equals 1,000 kg or 1 million grams. Grams/tonne and parts per million (ppm) are therefore equivalent ratios.

89. B: Basalt flows are higher density than sedimentary rocks, so the high density part of the log at ~1,100 feet of depth is the most likely the depth of buried basalt flows.

90. C: In order of increasing rank, the ranks of coal are lignite, subbituminous, bituminous, and anthracite.

91. B: Hematite (Fe_2O_3) is the principal mineral at many of the world's largest iron mines.

92. B: The results from Laboratory B have the least variation from month to month; therefore, they appear to be the most reproducible results.

93. B: Gabbro is the most mafic type of plutonic rock, diorite is intermediate, and granite is the most felsic.

94. A: On a seismic image, reflectors are interfaces (contacts) between layers that have different seismic properties.

95. B: A structural trap is a region where upward-migrating hydrocarbons collect due to a permeability boundary. The crests of anticlines are classic structural traps.

96. D: Stromatolites form in shallow water conditions where sunlight is plentiful. There are examples of both marine and lacustrine stromatolites.

97. A: The water table is shallowest in the NE part of the map and deepest in the SW. Groundwater flow direction is therefore probably from NE to SW.

98. C: One of the main purposes of a landfill cap is to prevent surface water from seeping into the landfill. Caps should therefore have low permeability.

99. C: Groundwater withdrawal is not a known cause of earthquakes, but all of the other options are.

100. A: This question is an example of a "three-point problem" or the "Rule of Vs." The strike-and-dip direction of the basalt can be determined by how it interacts with topography. The strike of the basalt is E-W because the points at which it intersects the same topographic contour fall along E-W lines. The basalt is decreasing in elevation to the south, so it is dipping to the south.

101. B: Sphalerite (Zn, Fe)S is an ore of zinc and is commonly found along with galena (PbS) in lead-zinc deposits.

102. A: Hydrocarbon source rocks are commonly organic-rick shales. The other choices are not particularly organic rich.

103. B: Permeability is a key attribute of a good aquifer. Of the options presented, shale has the lowest permeability and is therefore the least likely to make a good aquifer.

104. A: Quartz monzonite is a common rock type to form part of a porphyritic stock.

105. D: A sandstone containing 300 million-year-old detrital minerals must be 300 million years old or younger. The Cambrian Period spans from 541 to 485 million years, so the sandstone cannot be Cambrian in age.

106. B: Biotite is a black, flaky mineral that is commonly found in granite. Magnetite is also black, but it is not flaky.

107. C: Airborne radiometric data are most commonly used to detect radioactive elements such as K, U, and Th in the Earth's crust. This type of data would not be particularly useful in mapping vegetation.

108. C: An aquiclude is a layer of rocks that is completely impermeable. Aquicludes are types of aquitards.

109. B: The map shows barchan dunes. The tips of barchan dunes point in the wind's direction, in this case from west to east.

110. A: Turbidites are one of the key types of deep marine sediments. The other choices are all characteristic of shallow water deposition.

111. A: Well-graded soils have a wide range of grain size. Well graded is equivalent to poorly sorted and vice versa.

112. C: Watershed boundaries are defined by drainage divides. Topographic information is therefore useful for defining watershed boundaries.

113. D: The concave sides of foresets indicate the current direction. In this case, the concave sides are on the north, indicating south-to-north current direction.

114. C: Successful landfill designs include systems for liners, water management, and gas management.

115. C: Turbidity refers to the amount of light that will not pass through a water sample, so water with high turbidity allows a relatively small amount of light to pass.

116. B: Soil chemistry data would be most pertinent to the issue of soil contamination.

117. D: Water currents align clasts so that their long dimensions are pointing in, and tilted toward, the direction in which the current flows. In this example, imbrication suggests flow from west to east.

118. A: By definition, anticlines are folds that have old rocks in their cores and younger rocks on their outer limbs.

119. C: Cu porphyries are normally associated with volcanic arcs.

120. C: Although respirators may be required for some activities, they are a specialized type of equipment. The other choices are all standard personal protection equipment (PPE) on many job sites.

121. C: Groundwater discharge has units of volume/time, for example, gallons/minute.

122. D: The contact between Formation B and Formation C represents missing time because there are no Carboniferous, Devonian, or Silurian rocks. The contact is therefore an unconformity.

123. B: Color is not a reliable basis for stratigraphic correlations because a single stratigraphic unit may be different colors in different parts of a basin and different stratigraphic units may have the same color.

124. D: The fault is a normal fault, so the missing part of the ore deposit is likely in the hanging wall. Based on slickenline measurements the transport direction was to the NW (i.e., little strike-slip component), so the missing part is probably to the NW.

125. D: Chloride, total dissolved solids (TDS), and sulfate are all relatively common constituents of drinking water, so their recommended concentrations are relatively high. Recommended levels of copper in drinking water are much lower.

126. C: The two points are 300 m different in northing and 400 m different in easting. They are thus separated by 500 m (3-4-5 right triangle).

127. D: Loess is wind-blown dust.

128. A: Reynolds number describes the flow of fluids. A low Reynolds number describes laminar flow, and at values greater than approximately 2,600, flows become turbulent.

129. D: The purpose of a chain-of-custody form is to maintain a record of those who were in possession of samples from the time they were collected until the time they were analyzed.

130. B: "Pumping" soils are commonly caused by excess water content.

131. B: Volcanic ash beds are a record of past volcanic eruptions, but they are not necessarily records of past earthquakes.

132. D: Direct-push drilling is commonly used to collect soil samples for geotechnical investigations.

133. A: Meandering rivers are characteristic of low-relief areas.

134. B: Bluescist-facies metamorphic rocks form in environments of high pressure but low temperature. They are commonly associated with subduction zones.

135. D: Basalt has a density of roughly 3 g/cm^3. Granite, sandstone, and limestone generally have lower densities of approximately 2.6–2.7 g/cm^3. In general, specific yield is positively correlated with porosity.

136. A: Very few, if any, processes will deposit beds that dip 70°. Most stratified rocks are deposited in layers that are close to horizontal. The most likely cause of a bed dipping 70°is deformation of an originally horizontal layer.

137. D: According to Loheide II et al., 2005, coarse sand has the highest specific yield of the listed soil textures: 0.38. The same study gives values of 0.36 for medium sand, 0.33 for fine sand, and 0.026 for silt.

138. D: Because the beds are upright, the formation at lowest elevation is the oldest, and ages become progressively younger with increasing elevation.

139. B: Lineaments are simply linear features on air photos, including both natural and man-made features. Because sinkholes are typically roughly circular in map view, they are the least likely option to produce a lineament.

140. B: The data suggest a pattern of NE-SW subsidence.

Image Credits

How to Overcome Test Anxiety

Just the thought of taking a test is enough to make most people a little nervous. A test is an important event that can have a long-term impact on your future, so it's important to take it seriously and it's natural to feel anxious about performing well. But just because anxiety is normal, that doesn't mean that it's helpful in test taking, or that you should simply accept it as part of your life. Anxiety can have a variety of effects. These effects can be mild, like making you feel slightly nervous, or severe, like blocking your ability to focus or remember even a simple detail.

If you experience test anxiety—whether severe or mild—it's important to know how to beat it. To discover this, first you need to understand what causes test anxiety.

Causes of Test Anxiety

While we often think of anxiety as an uncontrollable emotional state, it can actually be caused by simple, practical things. One of the most common causes of test anxiety is that a person does not feel adequately prepared for their test. This feeling can be the result of many different issues such as poor study habits or lack of organization, but the most common culprit is time management. Starting to study too late, failing to organize your study time to cover all of the material, or being distracted while you study will mean that you're not well prepared for the test. This may lead to cramming the night before, which will cause you to be physically and mentally exhausted for the test. Poor time management also contributes to feelings of stress, fear, and hopelessness as you realize you are not well prepared but don't know what to do about it.

Other times, test anxiety is not related to your preparation for the test but comes from unresolved fear. This may be a past failure on a test, or poor performance on tests in general. It may come from comparing yourself to others who seem to be performing better or from the stress of living up to expectations. Anxiety may be driven by fears of the future—how failure on this test would affect your educational and career goals. These fears are often completely irrational, but they can still negatively impact your test performance.

> **Review Video: 3 Reasons You Have Test Anxiety**
> Visit mometrix.com/academy and enter code: 428468

Elements of Test Anxiety

As mentioned earlier, test anxiety is considered to be an emotional state, but it has physical and mental components as well. Sometimes you may not even realize that you are suffering from test anxiety until you notice the physical symptoms. These can include trembling hands, rapid heartbeat, sweating, nausea, and tense muscles. Extreme anxiety may lead to fainting or vomiting. Obviously, any of these symptoms can have a negative impact on testing. It is important to recognize them as soon as they begin to occur so that you can address the problem before it damages your performance.

> **Review Video: 3 Ways to Tell You Have Test Anxiety**
> Visit mometrix.com/academy and enter code: 927847

The mental components of test anxiety include trouble focusing and inability to remember learned information. During a test, your mind is on high alert, which can help you recall information and stay focused for an extended period of time. However, anxiety interferes with your mind's natural processes, causing you to blank out, even on the questions you know well. The strain of testing during anxiety makes it difficult to stay focused, especially on a test that may take several hours. Extreme anxiety can take a huge mental toll, making it difficult not only to recall test information but even to understand the test questions or pull your thoughts together.

> **Review Video: How Test Anxiety Affects Memory**
> Visit mometrix.com/academy and enter code: 609003

Effects of Test Anxiety

Test anxiety is like a disease—if left untreated, it will get progressively worse. Anxiety leads to poor performance, and this reinforces the feelings of fear and failure, which in turn lead to poor performances on subsequent tests. It can grow from a mild nervousness to a crippling condition. If allowed to progress, test anxiety can have a big impact on your schooling, and consequently on your future.

Test anxiety can spread to other parts of your life. Anxiety on tests can become anxiety in any stressful situation, and blanking on a test can turn into panicking in a job situation. But fortunately, you don't have to let anxiety rule your testing and determine your grades. There are a number of relatively simple steps you can take to move past anxiety and function normally on a test and in the rest of life.

> **Review Video: How Test Anxiety Impacts Your Grades**
> Visit mometrix.com/academy and enter code: 939819

Physical Steps for Beating Test Anxiety

While test anxiety is a serious problem, the good news is that it can be overcome. It doesn't have to control your ability to think and remember information. While it may take time, you can begin taking steps today to beat anxiety.

Just as your first hint that you may be struggling with anxiety comes from the physical symptoms, the first step to treating it is also physical. Rest is crucial for having a clear, strong mind. If you are tired, it is much easier to give in to anxiety. But if you establish good sleep habits, your body and mind will be ready to perform optimally, without the strain of exhaustion. Additionally, sleeping well helps you to retain information better, so you're more likely to recall the answers when you see the test questions.

Getting good sleep means more than going to bed on time. It's important to allow your brain time to relax. Take study breaks from time to time so it doesn't get overworked, and don't study right before bed. Take time to rest your mind before trying to rest your body, or you may find it difficult to fall asleep.

> **Review Video: The Importance of Sleep for Your Brain**
> Visit mometrix.com/academy and enter code: 319338

Along with sleep, other aspects of physical health are important in preparing for a test. Good nutrition is vital for good brain function. Sugary foods and drinks may give a burst of energy but this burst is followed by a crash, both physically and emotionally. Instead, fuel your body with protein and vitamin-rich foods.

Also, drink plenty of water. Dehydration can lead to headaches and exhaustion, especially if your brain is already under stress from the rigors of the test. Particularly if your test is a long one, drink water during the breaks. And if possible, take an energy-boosting snack to eat between sections.

> **Review Video: How Diet Can Affect your Mood**
> Visit mometrix.com/academy and enter code: 624317

Along with sleep and diet, a third important part of physical health is exercise. Maintaining a steady workout schedule is helpful, but even taking 5-minute study breaks to walk can help get your blood pumping faster and clear your head. Exercise also releases endorphins, which contribute to a positive feeling and can help combat test anxiety.

When you nurture your physical health, you are also contributing to your mental health. If your body is healthy, your mind is much more likely to be healthy as well. So take time to rest, nourish your body with healthy food and water, and get moving as much as possible. Taking these physical steps will make you stronger and more able to take the mental steps necessary to overcome test anxiety.

Mental Steps for Beating Test Anxiety

Working on the mental side of test anxiety can be more challenging, but as with the physical side, there are clear steps you can take to overcome it. As mentioned earlier, test anxiety often stems from lack of preparation, so the obvious solution is to prepare for the test. Effective studying may be the most important weapon you have for beating test anxiety, but you can and should employ several other mental tools to combat fear.

First, boost your confidence by reminding yourself of past success—tests or projects that you aced. If you're putting as much effort into preparing for this test as you did for those, there's no reason you should expect to fail here. Work hard to prepare; then trust your preparation.

Second, surround yourself with encouraging people. It can be helpful to find a study group, but be sure that the people you're around will encourage a positive attitude. If you spend time with others who are anxious or cynical, this will only contribute to your own anxiety. Look for others who are motivated to study hard from a desire to succeed, not from a fear of failure.

Third, reward yourself. A test is physically and mentally tiring, even without anxiety, and it can be helpful to have something to look forward to. Plan an activity following the test, regardless of the outcome, such as going to a movie or getting ice cream.

When you are taking the test, if you find yourself beginning to feel anxious, remind yourself that you know the material. Visualize successfully completing the test. Then take a few deep, relaxing breaths and return to it. Work through the questions carefully but with confidence, knowing that you are capable of succeeding.

Developing a healthy mental approach to test taking will also aid in other areas of life. Test anxiety affects more than just the actual test—it can be damaging to your mental health and even contribute to depression. It's important to beat test anxiety before it becomes a problem for more than testing.

> **Review Video: Test Anxiety and Depression**
> Visit mometrix.com/academy and enter code: 904704

Study Strategy

Being prepared for the test is necessary to combat anxiety, but what does being prepared look like? You may study for hours on end and still not feel prepared. What you need is a strategy for test prep. The next few pages outline our recommended steps to help you plan out and conquer the challenge of preparation.

STEP 1: SCOPE OUT THE TEST

Learn everything you can about the format (multiple choice, essay, etc.) and what will be on the test. Gather any study materials, course outlines, or sample exams that may be available. Not only will this help you to prepare, but knowing what to expect can help to alleviate test anxiety.

STEP 2: MAP OUT THE MATERIAL

Look through the textbook or study guide and make note of how many chapters or sections it has. Then divide these over the time you have. For example, if a book has 15 chapters and you have five days to study, you need to cover three chapters each day. Even better, if you have the time, leave an extra day at the end for overall review after you have gone through the material in depth.

If time is limited, you may need to prioritize the material. Look through it and make note of which sections you think you already have a good grasp on, and which need review. While you are studying, skim quickly through the familiar sections and take more time on the challenging parts. Write out your plan so you don't get lost as you go. Having a written plan also helps you feel more in control of the study, so anxiety is less likely to arise from feeling overwhelmed at the amount to cover.

STEP 3: GATHER YOUR TOOLS

Decide what study method works best for you. Do you prefer to highlight in the book as you study and then go back over the highlighted portions? Or do you type out notes of the important information? Or is it helpful to make flashcards that you can carry with you? Assemble the pens, index cards, highlighters, post-it notes, and any other materials you may need so you won't be distracted by getting up to find things while you study.

If you're having a hard time retaining the information or organizing your notes, experiment with different methods. For example, try color-coding by subject with colored pens, highlighters, or post-it notes. If you learn better by hearing, try recording yourself reading your notes so you can listen while in the car, working out, or simply sitting at your desk. Ask a friend to quiz you from your flashcards, or try teaching someone the material to solidify it in your mind.

STEP 4: CREATE YOUR ENVIRONMENT

It's important to avoid distractions while you study. This includes both the obvious distractions like visitors and the subtle distractions like an uncomfortable chair (or a too-comfortable couch that makes you want to fall asleep). Set up the best study environment possible: good lighting and a comfortable work area. If background music helps you focus, you may want to turn it on, but otherwise keep the room quiet. If you are using a computer to take notes, be sure you don't have any other windows open, especially applications like social media, games, or anything else that could distract you. Silence your phone and turn off notifications. Be sure to keep water close by so you stay hydrated while you study (but avoid unhealthy drinks and snacks).

Also, take into account the best time of day to study. Are you freshest first thing in the morning? Try to set aside some time then to work through the material. Is your mind clearer in the afternoon or evening? Schedule your study session then. Another method is to study at the same time of day that you will take the test, so that your brain gets used to working on the material at that time and will be ready to focus at test time.

STEP 5: STUDY!

Once you have done all the study preparation, it's time to settle into the actual studying. Sit down, take a few moments to settle your mind so you can focus, and begin to follow your study plan. Don't give in to distractions or let yourself procrastinate. This is your time to prepare so you'll be ready to fearlessly approach the test. Make the most of the time and stay focused.

Of course, you don't want to burn out. If you study too long you may find that you're not retaining the information very well. Take regular study breaks. For example, taking five minutes out of every hour to walk briskly, breathing deeply and swinging your arms, can help your mind stay fresh.

As you get to the end of each chapter or section, it's a good idea to do a quick review. Remind yourself of what you learned and work on any difficult parts. When you feel that you've mastered the material, move on to the next part. At the end of your study session, briefly skim through your notes again.

But while review is helpful, cramming last minute is NOT. If at all possible, work ahead so that you won't need to fit all your study into the last day. Cramming overloads your brain with more information than it can process and retain, and your tired mind may struggle to recall even previously learned information when it is overwhelmed with last-minute study. Also, the urgent nature of cramming and the stress placed on your brain contribute to anxiety. You'll be more likely to go to the test feeling unprepared and having trouble thinking clearly.

So don't cram, and don't stay up late before the test, even just to review your notes at a leisurely pace. Your brain needs rest more than it needs to go over the information again. In fact, plan to finish your studies by noon or early afternoon the day before the test. Give your brain the rest of the day to relax or focus on other things, and get a good night's sleep. Then you will be fresh for the test and better able to recall what you've studied.

STEP 6: TAKE A PRACTICE TEST

Many courses offer sample tests, either online or in the study materials. This is an excellent resource to check whether you have mastered the material, as well as to prepare for the test format and environment.

Check the test format ahead of time: the number of questions, the type (multiple choice, free response, etc.), and the time limit. Then create a plan for working through them. For example, if you have 30 minutes to take a 60-question test, your limit is 30 seconds per question. Spend less time on the questions you know well so that you can take more time on the difficult ones.

If you have time to take several practice tests, take the first one open book, with no time limit. Work through the questions at your own pace and make sure you fully understand them. Gradually work up to taking a test under test conditions: sit at a desk with all study materials put away and set a timer. Pace yourself to make sure you finish the test with time to spare and go back to check your answers if you have time.

After each test, check your answers. On the questions you missed, be sure you understand why you missed them. Did you misread the question (tests can use tricky wording)? Did you forget the information? Or was it something you hadn't learned? Go back and study any shaky areas that the practice tests reveal.

Taking these tests not only helps with your grade, but also aids in combating test anxiety. If you're already used to the test conditions, you're less likely to worry about it, and working through tests until you're scoring well gives you a confidence boost. Go through the practice tests until you feel comfortable, and then you can go into the test knowing that you're ready for it.

Test Tips

On test day, you should be confident, knowing that you've prepared well and are ready to answer the questions. But aside from preparation, there are several test day strategies you can employ to maximize your performance.

First, as stated before, get a good night's sleep the night before the test (and for several nights before that, if possible). Go into the test with a fresh, alert mind rather than staying up late to study.

Try not to change too much about your normal routine on the day of the test. It's important to eat a nutritious breakfast, but if you normally don't eat breakfast at all, consider eating just a protein bar. If you're a coffee drinker, go ahead and have your normal coffee. Just make sure you time it so that the caffeine doesn't wear off right in the middle of your test. Avoid sugary beverages, and drink enough water to stay hydrated but not so much that you need a restroom break 10 minutes into the test. If your test isn't first thing in the morning, consider going for a walk or doing a light workout before the test to get your blood flowing.

Allow yourself enough time to get ready, and leave for the test with plenty of time to spare so you won't have the anxiety of scrambling to arrive in time. Another reason to be early is to select a good seat. It's helpful to sit away from doors and windows, which can be distracting. Find a good seat, get out your supplies, and settle your mind before the test begins.

When the test begins, start by going over the instructions carefully, even if you already know what to expect. Make sure you avoid any careless mistakes by following the directions.

Then begin working through the questions, pacing yourself as you've practiced. If you're not sure on an answer, don't spend too much time on it, and don't let it shake your confidence. Either skip it and come back later, or eliminate as many wrong answers as possible and guess among the remaining ones. Don't dwell on these questions as you continue—put them out of your mind and focus on what lies ahead.

Be sure to read all of the answer choices, even if you're sure the first one is the right answer. Sometimes you'll find a better one if you keep reading. But don't second-guess yourself if you do immediately know the answer. Your gut instinct is usually right. Don't let test anxiety rob you of the information you know.

If you have time at the end of the test (and if the test format allows), go back and review your answers. Be cautious about changing any, since your first instinct tends to be correct, but make sure you didn't misread any of the questions or accidentally mark the wrong answer choice. Look over any you skipped and make an educated guess.

At the end, leave the test feeling confident. You've done your best, so don't waste time worrying about your performance or wishing you could change anything. Instead, celebrate the successful completion of this test. And finally, use this test to learn how to deal with anxiety even better next time.

Review Video: 5 Tips to Beat Test Anxiety
Visit mometrix.com/academy and enter code: 570656

Important Qualification

Not all anxiety is created equal. If your test anxiety is causing major issues in your life beyond the classroom or testing center, or if you are experiencing troubling physical symptoms related to your anxiety, it may be a sign of a serious physiological or psychological condition. If this sounds like your situation, we strongly encourage you to seek professional help.

Thank You

We at Mometrix would like to extend our heartfelt thanks to you, our friend and patron, for allowing us to play a part in your journey. It is a privilege to serve people from all walks of life who are unified in their commitment to building the best future they can for themselves.

The preparation you devote to these important testing milestones may be the most valuable educational opportunity you have for making a real difference in your life. We encourage you to put your heart into it—that feeling of succeeding, overcoming, and yes, conquering will be well worth the hours you've invested.

We want to hear your story, your struggles and your successes, and if you see any opportunities for us to improve our materials so we can help others even more effectively in the future, please share that with us as well. **The team at Mometrix would be absolutely thrilled to hear from you!** So please, send us an email (support@mometrix.com) and let's stay in touch.

> **If you'd like some additional help, check out these other resources we offer for your exam:**
> **http://MometrixFlashcards.com/ASBOG**

Additional Bonus Material

Due to our efforts to try to keep this book to a manageable length, we've created a link that will give you access to all of your additional bonus material:

mometrix.com/bonus948/asbog